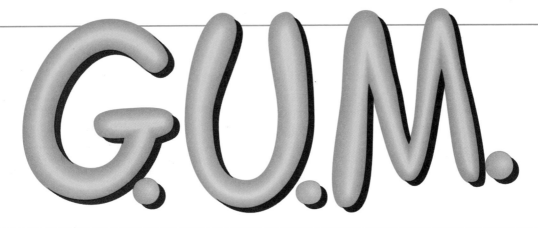

G.U.M.

Instruction and Practice for
Grammar, Usage, and Mechanics

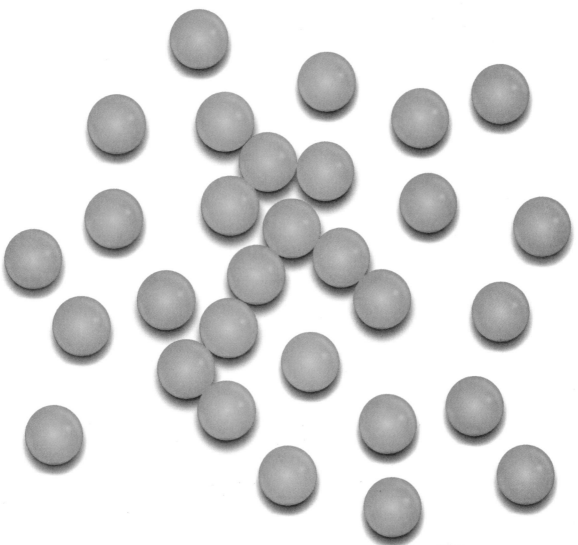

Zaner-Bloser, Inc.
Columbus, Ohio

W9-AWF-805

Grade Level Consultants

S. Elaine Boysworth
Lincolnton, North Carolina

Linda Crawford
Calhoun, Georgia

Martha Swan Novy
Florissant, Missouri

Heather Stanton
Colorado Springs, Colorado

Jaqueline Xavier
Cleveland, Ohio

Developed by Straight Line Editorial Development, Inc., and Zaner-Bloser, Inc.

Cover: Digital Photography by BLT Productions

Book Design and Production: Dominion Design

Illustration: Tom Kennedy

ISBN: 0-88085-881-8

Copyright © Zaner-Bloser, Inc.

Zaner-Bloser, Inc., P.O. Box 16764, Columbus, Ohio 43216-6764 (1-800-421-3018)

Printed in the United States of America

03 04 05 06 07 PO 9 8 7 6

Table of Contents

Unit 1 Sentence Structure

Looking Back **Innovations That Changed History**

Unit 2 Sentence Structure

Beasts & Critters **Sea Creatures**

Unit 3 Parts of Speech: Nouns, Pronouns, and Adjectives

Unforgettable Folks People Who Overcame Challenges

Unit 4 Parts of Speech: Verbs, Adverbs, Prepositions, and Conjunctions

The World Outside Cycles in Nature

Unit 5 Usage

Grab Bag — Celebrations of Many Cultures

Unit 6 Grammar

Timeless Tales — Folktale Characters

Unit 7 Mechanics

Great Getaways **Islands and Near-Islands**

Extra Practice

Unit Tests

Language Handbook

G.U.M. Indexes

Read and Discover

The development of agriculture / changed human society forever.
  a.   b.

Which part (a. or b.) of this sentence tells whom or what the sentence is about? ____

Which part (a. or b.) tells what happened? ____

Every sentence has a subject and a predicate. The **complete subject** is made up of a noun or pronoun and words that tell about it. The subject tells whom or what the sentence is about. The **complete predicate** is made up of a verb and words that tell what the subject is, has, or does.

See Handbook Sections 11, 12

Part 1

Underline the complete subject in each sentence once. Underline each complete predicate twice.

1. Prehistoric humans were hunter-gatherers for millions of years.

2. Small groups of people traveled around to the areas with the most plentiful plants and animals.

3. Earth's climate changed suddenly about eleven thousand years ago.

4. The familiar foods were often not available.

5. Some people experimented with agriculture in the Middle East, Asia, and Mexico.

6. People in these areas grew plants from wild seeds.

7. Nutritious grains were grown by these farmers.

8. They kept animals for their milk, wool, and meat.

9. The new farmers built permanent dwellings near their fields.

10. Some of these farmers lived in an area called the Fertile Crescent.

11. Humans considered land their property for the first time.

12. Some of the arid regions in Egypt and Sumeria had fertile soil.

13. Farmers developed complex irrigation, or watering, systems there.

14. Irrigation required the labor and cooperation of many people.

15. Extra food was produced as a result of irrigation.

16. Food production no longer required every person's effort.

17. Some people became craftspeople, soldiers, or merchants instead of farmers.

18. The abundant food supply enabled more people to live in villages.

19. These developments led to the establishment of the first civilizations.

Croplands in ancient Egypt were irrigated with water from the Nile River.

Part 2

Add a subject or a predicate to each phrase to make a sentence. Underline the complete subject in each sentence you write. Circle the complete predicate in each sentence.

20. hunted bison and mammoths _____

_____

21. agriculture _____

_____

22. grew barley and wheat _____

_____

23. the world's earliest civilizations _____

_____

24. flocks of sheep _____

_____

Part 3

> Complete subjects and predicates may be very short (*Dogs / bark.*) or very long. Short sentences can make a passage seem spare and direct. They tend to focus the reader's attention on actions and events. Long sentences can create a smooth flow that carries the reader along from idea to idea while providing clear descriptive or explanatory information.

Notice the differences between these two passages by famous authors. Draw a slash (/) between the complete subject and the complete predicate in each sentence.

> His face was sweaty and dirty. The sun shone on his face. The day was very hot.
>
> —Ernest Hemingway, from *In Our Time*

> The curious things about her were her hands, strange terminations to the flabby white arms splattered with pale tan spots—long, quivering hands with deep and convex nails.
>
> —Dorothy Parker, from "Big Blonde"

Write a paragraph of your own about meeting an unusual or interesting person. Try making the subjects and predicates in your sentences very short. Then rewrite your paragraph, adding words and phrases to make the subjects and predicates long. Now compare the two paragraphs. Which version do you prefer?

_____

_____

_____

_____

_____

Name _____

Looking Back

Read and Discover

a. **Oral stories of gods and heroes** carried the beliefs of a culture from one generation to the next.

b. Tell us the story of Gilgamesh.

The complete subject of sentence a. is in boldfaced type. Circle the most important word in the complete subject. Underline the verb that tells what the subject did.

Can you find a subject at the beginning of sentence b.? _____
Circle the word below that fits as the subject of sentence b.

Gilgamesh   You   Tell   Story

The **simple subject** is the most important word or words in the complete subject. It is a noun or pronoun and tells whom or what the sentence is about. The subject of a request or command (an imperative sentence) is usually not named. The person being spoken to, *you*, is the **understood subject**. The **simple predicate** is the most important word or words in the predicate. It is a verb. The simple predicate tells what the subject did or what was done to the subject. The simple predicate may also be a form of the verb *be*.

See Handbook Sections 11, 12

Part 1

Circle the simple subject in each sentence. If the understood subject is *you*, write *you* on the line. Underline the simple predicate.

1. The people of Sumeria developed a writing system more than 5,000 years ago. _____

2. Find the Euphrates River on a map. _____

3. Ancient Sumeria included the fertile lands near this river. _____

4. Some Sumerians owned large quantities of goods. _____   3000 B.C.

5. A record of these goods was often necessary for business purposes. _____

6. Sumerians drew marks or *symbols* on wet clay tablets for their records. _____

7. Some people became experts at the use of symbols. _____   2000 B.C.

8. These *scribes* could draw symbols for objects easily. _____

9. Ideas presented the scribes with a much greater challenge. _____   700 B.C.

10. Draw a symbol for "life" or "freedom." _____

11. Your drawing must be understandable to other people. _____   500 B.C.

12. Guess the Sumerian scribes' solution to this problem. _____

13. *Ti* meant both "arrow" and "life" in the Sumerian spoken language. _____   **The early symbol for *fish* changed over time.**

14. Clever scribes used a picture of an arrow as the symbol for both words. _____

15. Symbols eventually represented sounds such as *ti* instead of objects such as *arrow*. _____

16. People could then write any word in the Sumerian language. _____

Looking Back

G.U.M.

Part 2

Write five sentences about the invention of writing. You may use nouns and verbs from the word bank as simple subjects or simple predicates. Use the understood subject *you* in one of your sentences.

symbols recorded	scribe imagine	invention represented	draw Sumerians	wrote picture	arrow ideas

17. _____

_____

18. _____

_____

19. _____

_____

20. _____

_____

21. _____

_____

Part 3

A symbol that stands for a sound in a puzzle is called a *rebus*. For instance, a picture of an eye can stand for "I" in a rebus. Solve the rebus puzzles below to find the simple subject of each sentence. The first one has been done for you.

22. The [sun] + [key] pulled a wagon full of vegetables. ___donkey___

23. My favorite C + [sun] is winter. _____

24. The [cap] + 10 of the ship commanded the crew to raise anchor. _____

25. One [pen] + [knee] will buy you a gumball. _____

Name _____

Looking Back

Read and Discover

___ Clocks and calendars are very important in modern life.

___ They wake us up, measure our working hours, and inform us of holidays.

Write *S* next to the sentence with two or more simple subjects. Write *P* next to the sentence with two or more simple predicates.

> A **compound subject** is two or more subjects joined by a conjunction (*and, or*).
> A **compound predicate** is two or more verbs joined by a conjunction.
>
> See Handbook Sections 11, 12

Part 1

Each sentence below has either a compound subject or a compound predicate. If a sentence has a compound subject, circle the two or more nouns that are the simple subjects. If a sentence has a compound predicate, underline the two or more verbs that are the simple predicates.

1. The concept of time fascinates and perplexes humans. ✓
2. Prehistoric men and women probably saw time as a circle. ✓
3. These early people observed and noted regular changes in the sky. ✓
4. The sun rose and set every day. ✓
5. Spring, summer, fall, and winter occurred in the same sequence over and over. ✓
6. People in several regions studied and recorded these yearly cycles. ✓
7. The Sumerians, Mayas, and Chinese invented calendars independently. ✓
8. Calendar-makers carved marks in stone or tied knots in string. ✓
9. These early calendars predicted the times for harvests and indicated the days for festivals. ✓
10. The sun and stars change their position in the sky over the course of a year. ✓
11. The moon moves across the sky and seems to change shape. ✓
12. Ancient peoples observed and celebrated these celestial events. ✓
13. Many ancient temples and monuments face the dawn or the North Star.
14. The sun's yearly cycle and the cycle of the moon are out ✓ of step with each other.
15. This confused most ancient astronomers and caused ✓ inaccuracies in some calendars.
16. Modern astronomers and physicists occasionally add ✓ *leap seconds* to a year for greater accuracy.

This calendar stone shows the days of the Aztec month.

Part 2

Combine each pair of sentences to form one sentence that has either a compound subject or a compound predicate.

17. The world's first mechanical clock was made in China. The world's first mechanical clock showed changes in the phases of the moon. *The world's first mechanical clock was made in China and showed changes in the phases of the moon*

18. The Buddhist monk I-Hsing designed a mechanical clock. Then he built this clock. *The Buddhist monk I-Hsing designed and built this clock*

19. Gears controlled the clock's movements. Shafts controlled the clock's movements, too. *Gears and shafts controlled*

20. Water in a stream turned a water wheel. This water made the clock function. _____

21. A bell announced the time. A drum announced the time. _____

Part 3

> It is possible to have both a compound subject and a compound predicate in the same sentence. (*The boys and girls splashed and swam together.*) However, both parts of the compound subject must be performing both actions of the compound predicate. Avoid sentences like this one: *The wolves and frogs howled and croaked.* This sentence might make the reader think that the frogs howled and the wolves croaked.

On the lines below, rewrite the incorrect sentence as two separate sentences. Write *C* beside the sentence that uses compound subjects and predicates correctly.

22. The sun and moon light up the day and shine at night. ___

_____

23. Ice and snow come in winter and make travel difficult. ___

_____

Name _____

Looking Back

Read  and Discover

    a. Early peoples made crude tools and weapons out of stone, wood, and bone.

    b. The invention of bronze brought great changes to the ancient world.

Circle the nouns in sentence a. that tell what early peoples made. Circle the noun in sentence b. that tells what the invention of bronze brought.

The **direct object** is the noun or pronoun that receives the action of the verb. Only action verbs can take a direct object. A **compound direct object** occurs when more than one noun or pronoun receives the action of the verb. To find the direct object, say the verb and then ask "What?" or "Whom?" For example, to find the direct object of sentence b., ask "The invention of bronze brought what? Answer: It brought *changes*."

See Handbook Section 21

Part 1

Circle the direct object in each sentence. If there is a compound direct object, circle each part of the direct object.

1. Craftspeople first produced bronze in about 3800 B.C., in Sumeria.

2. These craftspeople melted copper in a kind of furnace.

3. They accidentally mixed arsenic and other minerals with the copper.

4. This combination produced a stronger metal.

5. Eventually, metalworkers combined copper and tin into bronze.

6. Sumerian metalworkers could form this new metal into almost any shape.

7. Craftspeople in Egypt and other nearby areas soon learned the secret of bronze production.

8. People made durable tools, weapons, and statues out of bronze.

9. Farmers tilled fields with bronze-tipped plows.

10. They could cultivate larger areas with these efficient plows.

11. Soon Middle Eastern civilizations needed new sources of tin.

12. This stimulated trade with distant regions.

13. People from widespread cultures exchanged ideas as well as goods.

14. The expansion of trade also encouraged the expansion of empires.

15. Nations conquered other nations for their tin.

16. Over time, however, the Iron Age overcame the Bronze Age.

17. Iron replaced tin as the main metal.

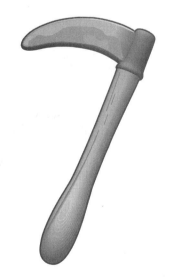

Tools like this bronze-tipped sickle made life a little easier for ancient farmers.

Looking Back

Part 2

Write a direct object from the word bank to complete each sentence. Draw an arrow from the verb to the direct object.

model	horse	trick	bronze	civilization	stories	Trojans

18. The Mycenaeans used _____ for weapons and sculptures during the Bronze Age in Greece.

19. In about 1200 B.C., some disastrous event destroyed their _____.

20. Greeks in later times told _____ about the heroic deeds and amazing palaces of their Bronze Age ancestors.

21. In one of these legends, the Greeks played a clever _____ on their enemies, the Trojans.

22. They built a huge wooden _____ of a horse, and some soldiers hid inside.

23. The Trojans brought the _____ inside their walled city.

24. In the middle of the night, the Greek soldiers climbed out of their hiding place and defeated the _____.

Part 3

An action verb that takes a direct object is a *transitive* verb. An action verb without a direct object is an *intransitive* verb. Many action verbs may be either transitive (*Mr. Garcia <u>runs</u> the store.*) or intransitive (*Mark <u>runs</u> fast.*), depending on whether they are used with a direct object. You will learn more about transitive and intransitive verbs in Lesson 32.

In the following sentences, write *transitive verb* on the line if there is a direct object. Write *intransitive verb* if there is no direct object.

25. Sculptors work very hard. _____

26. Sculptors work soft clay into figures. _____

27. They make molds from the clay figures. _____

28. Molten bronze pours easily. _____

29. The sculptor pours molten bronze into the mold. _____

30. This material hardens to make a permanent model of the sculpture. _____

Name _____

Looking Back

Read and Discover

In today's society, people give **clerks money** in exchange for food and other necessities.

Which boldfaced noun tells what people give? _____

Which boldfaced noun tells *to whom* they give it? _____

An **indirect object** is a person or thing to whom something is given, told, or taught. The indirect object is a noun or pronoun, and it comes before the direct object. To test whether a word is an indirect object, move it after the direct object and put the word *to* or *for* in front of it. Example: *People give money **to** clerks*.

See Handbook Section 21

Part 1

First underline the direct object in each sentence. Then circle the indirect object.

1. In ancient times, farmers traded others their crops in exchange for different foods or useful things.

2. For example, a farmer might have offered a neighbor some beans.

3. The neighbor might have offered the farmer some plums from her garden in exchange.

4. But what if a plum gave the farmer a stomachache?

5. The farmer might have traded a cousin the other plums for some cucumbers.

6. Then the farmer might have traded a friend some cucumbers in exchange for a chicken.

7. This complicated system caused people problems.

8. China probably gave the world its first monetary system.

9. Money provided people a convenient method of exchange.

10. People give money its value.

11. Merchants will trade you goods for money.

12. Paper money gives the public easy exchange.

13. Enough money will buy you almost any product.

14. History teaches us lessons about how the value of money can change.

15. In times of economic disaster, people have given merchants wheelbarrows full of paper money in exchange for a few days' food.

16. Many people today give cashiers a plastic card to complete a purchase.

The earliest coins were shaped like small tools.

Looking Back

Part 2

Rewrite each sentence, changing the underlined phrase into an indirect object.

17. Mary's grandfather showed his collection of old and rare money <u>to us</u>. _____

_____

_____

18. He told a story about the use of rice as money in seventeenth-century Japan <u>to Mary</u>. _____

_____

_____

19. He showed a playing card that was used as money in colonial Canada <u>to me</u>. _____

_____

_____

20. I made a thank-you card with drawings of coins on it <u>for him</u>. _____

_____

_____

Part 3

Write a word from the word bank to give each sentence an indirect object. Then use the numbered letters to form the mystery word.

coins	Mary	us	her	me	him

21. Mary's grandfather gave ___ ___ the idea of starting my own coin collection.
         4

22. I traded ___ ___ ___ a summer of yard work for some old coins.
         1

23. Mary's grandfather taught ___ ___ his methods for coin collecting.

24. He never gives the ___ ___ ___ ___ ___ a scrub or a polish.
         2   3

25. One year later I showed ___ ___ ___ ___ the coin collection her grandfather had inspired.
         5

Mystery word: ___ ___ ___ ___ ___
         1 2 3 4 5

Name _____

Looking Back

Read and Discover

Movable type is a **method** of printing with letter stamps.

Each letter is **separate**.

Circle the boldfaced noun that tells more about who or what the subject is. Underline the boldfaced adjective that tells what the subject is like.

A **predicate noun** follows a linking verb and tells more about who or what the subject is. A **predicate adjective** follows a linking verb and describes the subject.

See Handbook Section 12

Part 1

Draw a box around the linking verb in each sentence. Circle each boldfaced word that is a predicate noun. Underline each boldfaced word that is a predicate adjective.

1. First developed in 1045, movable type was a Chinese **invention**.
2. The inventor was **Bi Sheng**.
3. This type of printing was not **practical** in China at the time, however.
4. Chinese characters were too **numerous**.
5. Movable type was more **useful** in Europe.
6. Before the development of movable type, most European books were handmade **copies** of manuscripts.
7. Scribes were the experienced **writers** of these books.
8. Handwritten books were unique **works** of art.
9. The pages were **beautiful**, with elaborate decorations in the margins.
10. Unfortunately, these books were **expensive** and **scarce**.
11. The first European printer was **Johannes Gutenberg**.
12. 1456 was the **year** of his innovation.
13. The Roman alphabet is a **set** of 26 characters.
14. The model for Gutenberg's printing press was a **press** for grapes or cheese.
15. Its output was 300 **copies** per day.
16. Soon books and pamphlets were **available** to many more people.
17. New ideas became the **property** of everyone, not just the rich.

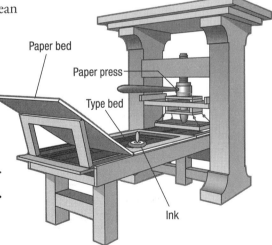

Paper bed

Paper press

Type bed

Ink

The printing press helped spread new ideas across the world.

Part 2

Write a predicate noun or a predicate adjective to **complete each sentence.**

18. My favorite book is _blue_ .

19. The main character in the book is _a boy_ .

20. This character's personality seems _strange_ .

21. The setting for that mystery book is _in a small town_ .

22. The mood of the story seems _puzzeling_ .

23. Even the illustrations appear _to be bizzare_ .

24. The villain changes in the story and becomes _animals_ .

25. Whenever I read this book, I feel _funny_ .

26. The author of this new adventure story has become _sick_ .

27. The most important problem in the novel's plot is _complete_ .

28. When I saw the cover of the book, I thought it looked _very plane_ .

29. Of all the books I've read, this one remains _the best_ .

Part 3

In the modern world, word processors help spread the written word. But sometimes words are mistyped. Circle the predicate noun in each sentence below. **Unscramble that word to find a word that makes sense.**

30. His best feature was his (slime) _s m i l e_

31. Manuela's tasty pies prove that she is a fine (brake) _b a k e r_

32. My favorite flowers are (sores) _r o s e s_

33. The distance 5,280 feet is a (lime) _m i l e_

34. Of all our field trips, my favorite place was the (diary) _d a i r y_

35. He ran as hard as he could, and his last jump was his greatest (pea) _l e a p_

Name _____

Looking Back

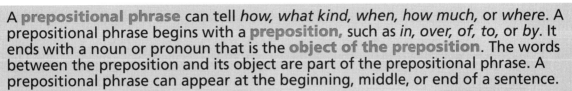

Read and Discover

Carracks once sailed throughout the world.
Where did these ships sail? ________________________

A **prepositional phrase** can tell *how, what kind, when, how much,* or *where.* A prepositional phrase begins with a **preposition,** such as *in, over, of, to,* or *by.* It ends with a noun or pronoun that is the **object of the preposition.** The words between the preposition and its object are part of the prepositional phrase. A prepositional phrase can appear at the beginning, middle, or end of a sentence.

See Handbook Section 20

Part 1

Underline each prepositional phrase. Circle the preposition that begins each phrase. Draw a box around the object of the preposition. There may be more than one prepositional phrase in each sentence.

1. In the fifteenth century, European shipbuilders built three-masted carracks with triangular sails.
2. The new design of these ships made long voyages easier.
3. The rudder and the compass, two inventions from China, helped sailors navigate and steer.
4. Europeans wanted silk and spices from Asia, and sailors began searching for better trade routes.
5. Seeking a new western route to Asia, Christopher Columbus landed on unfamiliar land.
6. Columbus thought the land was part of Asia, but others soon realized that this land to the west was an uncharted continent.
7. Soon sailors from many European countries were voyaging across the Atlantic.
8. In a few years, the invasion of the Americas had begun.
9. Corn, potatoes, and other nutritious crops from America were brought to Europe, and many European farm animals were brought to America.
10. People from different cultures exchanged ideas and customs.
11. The highly effective constitution of the Iroquois League would impress Benjamin Franklin and George Washington in later years.
12. This league comprised five Native American groups in the New York region.
13. The establishment of European colonies had terrible results for many Native Americans, however.
14. Thousands of Native Americans died in battle, and even more died from European diseases.
15. Africans were enslaved and brought to the American colonies in chains.
16. Many cultures and ways of life were lost to the world forever.

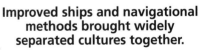

Improved ships and navigational methods brought widely separated cultures together.

Part 2

Rewrite each sentence. Add at least one prepositional phrase to make the sentence give more information. Use phrases from the word bank, or think of your own.

for the U.S. Constitution	from Native Americans	in their fields
of Native American nations	about new agricultural methods	of a democratic government
from European crops	in many regions	such as corn and potatoes

17. Native American groups developed innovative agricultural methods. _____

_____

_____

18. Their crops were different. _____

_____

19. Europeans learned. _____

_____

20. The Iroquois League provided an example. _____

_____

Part 3

What animal introduced to America by the Spanish became important to Native Americans? Underline each prepositional phrase. Then follow the directions through the maze to trace out the answer. **(21–36)**

Start at the square. Go to the star. Go through the fish to the heart. Go from the heart to the letter A. Loop twice around the flower. Stop at the tree. Go to the number 1. Follow a curved route to the triangle. Draw a line to the sun. Follow the path through the letter B and through the circle. Stop at the diamond. Loop to the number 2. Loop to the moon.

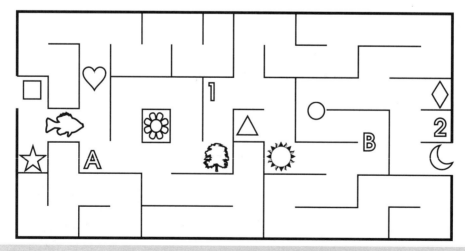

Name _____

Looking  Back

Read and Discover

Modern photography began **in the 1830s**.
Photographs gave people a new view **of the world**.

Which of the boldfaced prepositional phrases gives more information about a noun? _____

A prepositional phrase can modify, or tell more about, a noun or pronoun. Prepositional phrases that modify nouns or pronouns are called **adjectival prepositional phrases**. An adjectival prepositional phrase usually comes after the noun or pronoun it modifies.

See Handbook Section 20

Part 1

Underline each adjectival prepositional phrase. Circle the noun it tells about. A sentence may have more than one adjectival prepositional phrase. Be careful! Not all the prepositional phrases you find modify nouns or pronouns.

1. The man in the cloak holds a small box.

2. One side of the box has a hole in it.

3. He chooses an interesting scene near him and points the hole there.

4. Light rays enter the tiny hole in the dark box.

5. Inside the box the rays create a perfect miniature image of the scene.

6. This special dark box, a *camera obscura,* was an invention of the 1500s.

7. However, scientists in that era lacked knowledge of chemical processes.

8. Without that knowledge, film for the camera obscura could not be invented.

9. In the 1720s Johann Schulze, a scientist from Germany, made an important discovery.

10. Exposure to light turns some chemicals dark.

11. Schulze's discovery made the invention of photographic film possible.

12. The images inside the camera obscura could be captured and preserved.

13. Louis Daguerre, often called the inventor of photography, publicized his photographic process widely.

14. But William Henry Talbot's process became the model for modern photography.

15. Using Talbot's process, a photographer could create many copies of a single photograph.

16. By 1888, a Kodak camera from George Eastman made photography accessible to anyone.

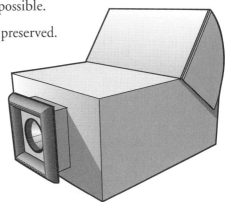

Artists often used images in a camera obscura to help them make sketches of large objects.

Looking Back

Part 2

Choose an adjectival prepositional phrase to complete each sentence. Write the phrase in the blank.

for close-up photography	with a telephoto lens	of José's photographs
of light	in his basement	near his home
as a photographer	of a baseball game	of his best picture
of a robin's nest		

17. José dreams of a career _____.

18. Last winter he bought a camera _____.

19. He borrowed a lens _____ from his uncle.

20. José experimented with different levels _____.

21. He took photographs _____ with high-speed film.

22. He climbed up a tree and took pictures _____.

23. José's uncle let him use the darkroom _____.

24. Some _____ turned out sharp and clear.

25. José made enlargements _____ and gave them to his mother and his uncle.

26. José plans to take a photography course at the community college _____.

Part 3

Read this short letter written by Abraham Lincoln during the Civil War. Note how he used prepositional phrases to convey his sympathy. List the eleven adjectival prepositional phrases in this letter.

Dear Madam, I have been shown in the files of the War Department a statement of the Adjutant-General of Massachusetts that you are the mother of five sons who have died gloriously on the field of battle. I feel how weak and fruitless must be any words of mine which should attempt to beguile you from the grief of a loss so overwhelming. But I cannot refrain from tendering to you the consolation that may be found in the thanks of the Republic they died to save. I pray that our heavenly Father may assuage the anguish of your bereavement, and leave you only the cherished memory of the loved and lost, and the solemn pride that must be yours to have laid so costly a sacrifice upon the altar of freedom.

—Abraham Lincoln, *Letter to Mrs. Bixby*

27. _____

28. _____

29. _____

30. _____

31. _____

32. _____

33. _____

34. _____

35. _____

36. _____

37. _____

Name _____

Looking Back

Read  and Discover

    In the 1940s, computer programmers could not create new programs efficiently. Each new program required a complete set **of machine instructions.** Grace Murray Hopper, a U.S. Navy computer expert, changed computer programming forever **with one brilliant invention.**

Which of the boldfaced prepositional phrases tells *when* about a verb?

_____

Which tells *how* about a verb? _____

Which does not modify a verb? _____

> A prepositional phrase can modify, or tell more about, a verb, an adverb, or an adjective. These prepositional phrases are called **adverbial prepositional phrases**. Many adverbial prepositional phrases tell *when, where, how,* or *how long* something was done.
>
> **See Handbook Section 20**

Part 1

Underline each adverbial prepositional phrase. Circle the verb or verb phrase it modifies. A sentence may have more than one adverbial prepositional phrase.

1. Rear Admiral Grace Hopper developed the first computer compiler in 1952.

2. Machine instructions were gathered within the compiler.

3. Programmers could now use the same routine in many different programs.

4. Hopper's bosses had not encouraged her in her efforts.

5. Automatic programming seemed impossible to them.

6. Hopper was irritated by such old-fashioned thinking.

7. In the computer industry, changes come fast.

8. Hopper contributed a great deal to computer science.

9. In the 1950s she developed COBOL, described as the first user-friendly computer programming language.

10. Businesses use COBOL for data processing.

Grace Murray Hopper

11. In 1964 Hopper received the Society of Women Engineers Achievement Award.

12. She was given the award because of her original computer programming systems.

13. Hopper first joined the United States Naval Reserve during World War II.

14. She retired in 1966, but she accepted a new assignment one year later.

15. In 1986, at age 80, Hopper retired again.

16. Throughout her long and brilliant career, Hopper made important contributions to computer science, business, and national security.

Looking Back

Part 2

Write an adverbial prepositional phrase to complete each sentence. Use your imagination. Be sure the phrase you write answers the question in parentheses.

17. My new computer will be delivered _____.

    (When?)

18. I will put my new computer _____. (Where?)

19. I will control the cursor on the screen _____.

    (How?)

20. I have been studying computer science _____.

    (For how long?)

Part 3

Poets commonly use adverbial prepositional phrases in descriptions. Underline the adverbial prepositional phrases in the excerpt below. Be careful not to mark phrases that begin with *to* and end with a verb. **(21–26)**

> She dwelt among the untrodden ways
>
>   Beside the springs of Dove;
>
> A maid whom there were none to praise,
>
>   And very few to love.
>
> A violet by a mossy stone
>
>   Half hidden from the eye!
>
> Fair as a star, when only one
>
>   Is shining in the sky.
>
>   —William Wordsworth, from "Lucy"

Now write a short poem of your own that includes at least two adverbial prepositional phrases. Circle these prepositional phrases.

_____

_____

_____

_____

_____

_____

Name _____

26

G.U.M.

Looking Back

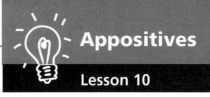
Read  and Discover

    a. The *spinning jenny* was a thread-making machine.
    b. The *spinning jenny*, a thread-making machine, helped bring about the Industrial Revolution.

Underline the phrase in sentence b. that tells who or what the spinning jenny was. What punctuation marks separate this phrase from the rest of the sentence? _____

An **appositive** is a phrase that identifies a noun. An appositive follows the noun it identifies and is usually separated from the rest of the sentence by commas.

See Handbook Section 24

Part 1

Underline the appositive in each sentence. Circle the noun it identifies.

1. The Industrial Revolution, a vast change in working methods, began in England in the 1750s.

2. Before 1750 most people lived in rural areas where they farmed or participated in *domestic industry*, work done in the home.

3. Clothing and other goods were either made at home or made by craftspeople, trained workers who crafted each item by hand.

4. The Industrial Revolution began in towns where textiles, woven cloths, were produced.

5. English colonies in America began producing large quantities of cotton, a cheap and useful alternative to wool.

6. Inventors created complex machines, the spinning jenny and others, which enabled spinners to make thread faster.

7. To keep up with the growing supply of cotton thread, inventors created power looms, machines for weaving thread into cloth quickly.

New machines changed the way people worked and lived in industrialized countries.

8. These new machines were housed in textile mills, cloth factories whose machines were powered by water or steam.

9. People moved from the hinterlands, the distant rural regions, into cities to work in factories.

10. Many people, children as well as adults, endured dangerous conditions in the factories.

11. Some people resisted these large changes; the Luddites, gangs of unhappy workers, smashed machines in the new factories.

12. New working methods, methods opposed by the Luddites, brought changes in politics and education.

13. Young unmarried women, the bulk of the workers in many textile factories, were able to have some financial independence for the first time.

14. The middle class, mainly merchants and professional people, grew and gained political power.

15. Education, once the privilege of the rich, became available to many more young people.

Part 2

Rewrite each pair of sentences as one sentence. Change the underlined sentence into an appositive.

16. <u>The steam engine was a very important invention.</u> The steam engine was first used mainly in factories. _____

    _____

17. <u>John Fitch was a silversmith and clockmaker.</u> John Fitch built a boat powered by steam in 1787.

    _____

    _____

18. <u>Fitch's creation was a small, smoky, uncomfortable boat.</u> Fitch's creation was never popular.

    _____

    _____

19. Two other inventors later built more successful steamboats. <u>Robert Fulton and Nicholas Roosevelt each built steamboats that were successful.</u> _____

    _____

    _____

20. Peter Cooper built the *Tom Thumb* in 1830. <u>The *Tom Thumb* was the earliest steam-powered railroad train.</u> _____

    _____

Part 3

All of the appositives covered so far have been separated from the rest of a sentence by commas. These appositives just give more information about the nouns they describe. But some appositives should **not** be set off by commas. If an appositive is vital to the meaning of the sentence, it should not be set off by commas.

Examples Sarah Joseph, <u>my friend from camp</u>, sent me a letter.
(The appositive *my friend from camp* is not essential to the sentence; it tells more about Sarah Joseph and should be set off by commas.)

My friend <u>Sarah Joseph</u> went to camp with me.
(The appositive *Sarah Joseph* is necessary to explain which friend is meant.)

Add commas if they are needed around the appositives in the following sentences. Write *C* if no commas are necessary.

21. My cousin Li is the oldest of all my cousins. ____

22. Li the oldest of all my cousins graduated from high school yesterday. ____

Name _____

Looking Back

A **sentence diagram** is a picture of a sentence that shows how the parts of a sentence fit together. Diagraming sentences can help you understand how the words in a sentence are related.

Diagraming Subjects and Verbs

A short sentence consisting of a simple subject and a simple predicate is diagramed this way:

Gold melts.   Gold | melts

Look at the structure of the diagram. Based on its structure, complete these sentences:

1. The simple subject and simple predicate go on a _____ line.
    horizontal/vertical

2. A _____ line divides the subject and predicate.
    horizontal/vertical

3. The subject goes to the _____ of the vertical line, and the predicate goes on the
    left/right
    _____ side.
    left/right

Use what you have learned to diagram these sentences. Include only the simple subject and the simple predicate. Ignore all the other words in the sentences.

4. The miners rested.

5. A storm approached.

6. Rain fell.

Diagraming Adjectives and Articles

An adjective (describing word) or an article (*a, an, the*) goes on a slanted line below the word it modifies. Look at the way this sentence has been diagramed.

The weary miners rested.   miners | rested
                            The weary

Now diagram these sentences.

7. A violent storm approached.

8. Torrential rains fell.

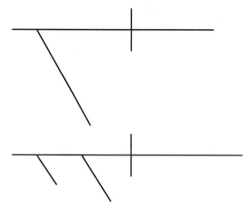

9. The wild rivers flooded.

Diagraming Direct Objects

A direct object (a noun that receives the action of the verb) is placed on a horizontal line to the right of the verb. Notice how the diagram changes when a direct object is added.

Few miners discovered gold.

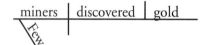

How is the vertical line that separates the direct object and the verb different from the vertical line that separates the subject and predicate?

_____

_____

Use what you have learned to diagram the simple subjects, simple predicates, adjectives, articles, and direct objects in these sentences.

10. One miner found a huge nugget.

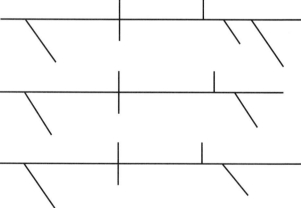

11. Warm rains melted the snow.

12. Icy water filled the reservoir.

Now diagram these sentences on another sheet of paper.

13. Heavy rains eroded the hillsides.

14. The floods uncovered more gold.

15. Surprised miners staked new claims.

16. The eager men led difficult lives.

17. Some miners left their families.

18. Many miners lost their lives.

19. A few miners found immense wealth.

20. The majority met great disappointment.

Name _____

Looking Back

Writing Sentences

These sentences need your help. Rewrite each one so it is clearer and makes better sense.

1. With triangular sails and three masts, European shipbuilders built large ocean-going ships. _____
   _____
   _____

2. Growing demand fueled an explosive growth of exploration and trade in Europe for treasures from
   distant lands. _____
   _____
   _____

3. Silk dresses and spices were comfortable to wear and made food taste better. _____
   _____
   _____

4. Soon, more people in Europe that only the extremely wealthy could previously afford began to
   acquire goods. _____
   _____
   _____

5. Brave captains sailed the tall ships to distant lands, and then these captains traded European goods
   for silks and spices. _____
   _____
   _____

All the sentences in a paragraph relate to a single topic. A paragraph should have a topic sentence, at least two supporting sentences, and a concluding sentence. Notice these kinds of sentences in this model paragraph.

topic sentence
(states the main idea you are making)

supporting sentences
(give details to support your main idea)

concluding sentence
(summarizes the paragraph or restates the topic sentence)

Electric roller skates would be a useful invention, and they would be fun to use, too. Electric skates, or "electroblades," would give people a cheaper, safer way to travel. Running on rechargeable batteries, electroblades would save energy and reduce air pollution. People using electroblades would save money because electroblades would cost a lot less than cars. Since fewer people would be driving cars, there would also be fewer auto accidents. **Because skating is fun, people would actually enjoy traveling to work or school!**

Writing a Paragraph

The sentences you repaired on page 31 can be reordered to make a paragraph. Decide which sentence is the topic sentence, which are the supporting sentences, and which is the concluding sentence. Reorder the sentences, and write the paragraph on the lines below.

_____

_____

_____

_____

_____

_____

_____

_____

Think of a new invention that would make your life easier, safer, or more comfortable. Write a paragraph explaining why you think this invention would be useful. Be sure to include a topic sentence, two or more supporting sentences, and a concluding sentence.

_____

_____

_____

_____

_____

_____

_____

_____

_____

Read your paragraph again. Use this checklist to make sure it is complete and correct.

- ❏ My paragraph has a topic sentence.

- ❏ My paragraph has at least two
  supporting sentences.

- ❏ All my sentences are clear and make sense.

- ❏ I have used prepositional phrases correctly.

- ❏ My paragraph has a concluding sentence.

Name _____

Looking Back

Proofreading Others' Writing

Read this passage about patents and find the mistakes. Use the proofreading marks to show how the mistakes should be fixed.

Proofreading Marks

Mark	Means	Example
ℒ	delete	This machine is is broken, too.
∧	add	This machine is broken too.
≡	make into a capital letter	this machine is broken, too.
/	make into a lowercase letter	This Machine is broken, too.
⊙	add a period	This machine is broken, too⊙
sp	fix spelling	This macheen is broken, too.

My Idea for a Great Invention

You have just put the finnishing touches on your marvelous new invention, electric in-line skates. Before you send your skates to the assembly line, however, consider this question: What's to prevent other people from stealing your design and copying your invention. The answer is that you can obtain leagle protection for you idea from the united states Patent and Trademark Office.

In simplest terms, a patent is an agreament between the inventor and the rest of the nation. When the government issues a patent, it grants an inventor all rights to manufacture and profit from his or her invention. Once you have a patent for your electric in-line skates. No one can copy your idea exactly. Obtaining a patent isn't complicated, but it does take time, usually more than two years

the Patenet and Trademark Office or PTO recieves about 100,000 patent applications every year. Each application is carfully evaluated by the staff at the PTO. First, officials must make sure that the invention hasn't already been patented by someone else. They must also decide weather the invention deserves a patent. It has to be entirely new, Not a variation of something that already exists. The invention must also be useful.

You don't need to put off production. While you are awaiting a response, however. Your skates can make their Debut in malls everywhere even if you haven't received your patent. Just make sure to put the notation *patent pending* somewhere on the product. These words arent a legal guarantee, but they our usually enough to discouradge other people from producing exact copies of your invention.

Proofreading Your Own Writing

You can use the checklist below to help you find and fix mistakes in your own writing. Write the titles of your own stories or reports in the blanks at the top of the chart. Then use the questions to check your work. Make a check mark (✓) in each box after you have checked that item.

Titles

Proofreading Checklist for Unit 1

Does each sentence have a subject and a predicate?				
Have I used appositives correctly?				
Have I used prepositional phrases to make my writing more precise?				
Have I varied the length and type of sentences to add variety to my writing?				
Do all my sentences state complete thoughts?				

Also Remember . . .

Does each sentence begin with a capital letter?				
Does each sentence end with the right end mark?				
Have I spelled each word correctly?				
Have I used commas correctly?				

Your Own List

Use this space to write your own list of things to check in your writing.

Name _____

Looking Back

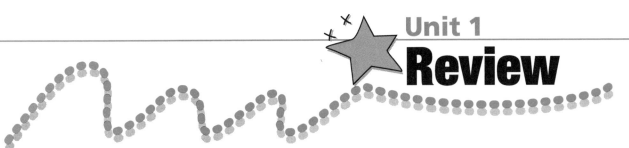
Subjects and Predicates

Underline the complete subject in each sentence. Circle the simple subject. If the understood subject is *you*, write *you* on the line.

1. Some inventions change almost everyone's life. _____

2. Imagine a world without telephones! _____

3. The hours after school would be long and quiet. _____

Underline the complete predicate in each sentence. Circle the simple predicate.

4. The United States needed a cheap replacement for rubber during World War II.

5. Engineer James Wright experimented with a substitute for rubber.

6. This substitute would be used in the production of jeep tires and military gear.

7. His strange substance was not useful.

8. The stretchy stuff bounced well.

9. Toy stores sell his compound as "Silly Putty."

Draw one line under each compound subject in these sentences. Draw two lines under each compound predicate.

10. Levi Strauss invented blue jeans and became world-famous.

11. Miners and cowboys needed durable clothes in the old West.

12. Strauss designed and made overalls out of denim, a heavy cloth.

13. Blue jeans were useful for work and became a fashion item by 1935.

Objects, Predicate Nouns, and Predicate Adjectives

Circle the term in parentheses that correctly describes the boldfaced word in each sentence.

14. The ice cream cone is an American **invention**. (predicate noun/direct object)

15. Two vendors at the 1904 St. Louis World's Fair created **it**. (predicate adjective/direct object)

16. People at the fair were **hungry** for snacks. (predicate noun/predicate adjective)

17. An ice cream vendor needed more **dishes**. (direct object/indirect object)

18. He was becoming **desperate**. (predicate adjective/direct object)

19. A nearby waffle vendor gave **him** some rolled waffles. (direct object/indirect object)

20. The ice cream vendor put **ice cream** on the waffle cones. (predicate noun/direct object)

21. He offered **customers** this portable treat. (direct object/indirect object)

22. The ice cream cone was an instant **hit**. (predicate noun/predicate adjective)

23. Ice cream cones are a common **sight** on warm summer evenings. (direct object/predicate noun)

Prepositional Phrases

Underline the prepositional phrase or phrases in each sentence. Circle the preposition. Draw a box around its object.

24. For many years, zippers and buttons were the main fasteners in the garment industry.

25. A mountain climber in Switzerland invented Velcro.

26. Prickly burrs clinging to his clothing gave him an idea.

27. Pairs of prickly cloth strips could substitute for zippers!

28. Some shoes, especially for children, are fastened with Velcro.

29. By the late 1950s, textile looms produced sixty million yards of Velcro.

Circle each adjectival prepositional phrase. Underline each adverbial prepositional phrase. Draw a box around the word each phrase modifies.

30. The invention of the Frisbee was a happy accident.

31. The creator of this toy was the Frisbie Pie Company.

32. The Frisbie Pie Company was located in Bridgeport, Connecticut.

33. Their pies were sold in round metal pans.

34. The family name was etched across the bottom of these pans.

35. Students at Yale University saved the pie pans.

36. They flipped these metal pans to one another.

37. The pans sailed gracefully through the air.

38. The students' name for this new game was "Frisbie."

39. Plastic Frisbees were soon sold throughout the country.

40. This game is still a popular activity among children and adults.

Appositives

Underline the appositive in each sentence.

41. H. Cecil Booth, an inventor of the late 1890s, lay on the floor and inhaled dust through a cloth as an experiment.

42. The secret, finding the right kind of filtering bag, would be his path to success.

43. His messy experiment resulted in a suction cleaning machine, the vacuum cleaner.

44. Regina and Hoover, early commercial vacuum cleaners, were known for their fine quality and reliability.

45. Some people today use a Rainbow sweeper, a water-filtered vacuum device.

Name _____

COMMUNITY LEARNING OPPORTUNITIES

In **Unit 1** of *G.U.M.*, students learned about **different types of sentences** and **sentence structures** and used what they learned to improve their own writing. The content of these lessons focuses on the theme **Innovations That Changed History**. As students completed the exercises, they learned the stories behind some of the most influential creations in history—and some of the strangest. These pages offer a variety of activities that reinforce skills and concepts presented in the unit. They also provide opportunities for the student to make connections between the historical material in the lessons and innovative, productive activities going on today in the community.

Innovation Next Door

Identify a factory or manufacturing company in or near your community that produces something interesting or especially useful. Then arrange to visit it during working hours to see for yourself how they produce their products. You might begin by contacting your Chamber of Commerce and asking for the names of some local factories or plants. Here are some questions you might try to answer about the place you select:

- What is the most interesting or important product manufactured here? What is innovative about it? What is its function?
- What raw materials are needed to produce the product? Where do these come from?
- What sequence of steps is involved in making the product? What is innovative about this process?
- Where is the finished product sold?
- Who are potential buyers of the product?
- How is the product transported?

Write answers to these questions in complete sentences. Check to make sure that each sentence has a subject and a predicate. Then use the questions and answers to prepare an oral or written report.

All-Star Inventors

Learn more about great inventors of the past and present by writing a business letter to the Inventors Hall of Fame. The Inventors Hall of Fame is housed at The Inventure Place in Akron, Ohio. It contains exhibits and displays about George Washington Carver, Thomas Edison, Alexander Graham Bell, and many other inventors. Here's the address:

> The Inventure Place
> 221 South Broadway
> Akron, Ohio 44308-1505
> (800) 968-4332
> e-mail: www.invent.org

Ask for information about one of these topics:

- inventors from your city or state
- the origins of one of your favorite products or devices
- the life and work of an inventor you admire

HINT: To review the format of a business letter, see *G.U.M.* Handbook Section 35.

Bright Ideas

Close your eyes and imagine an invention that would make life in your community easier, safer, or more fun. Draw a sketch of your invention. Then write a description of what it would do and how it would work. Use prepositional phrases to help readers understand where and when your invention would be used. Use appositives to give more information about your invention.

> **Example** My invention is a magnetic repulsion system, a device for preventing auto accidents. This system uses electromagnetism to deflect oncoming vehicles. It can be installed in any auto or truck. A car equipped with this system can sense when another vehicle is on a collision course with it. When the system senses that a collision may occur, it activates an extremely powerful electromagnet in the part of the car that may be hit. The magnetic force produced is so great that it deflects the other car and prevents a direct collision.

Patent Pending

Learn more about the process of obtaining a patent for an invention. Use this form to help you gather information and organize notes.

United States Patent and Trademark Office

Address: _____

Telephone Number: _____

Questions I Want to Ask: _____

_____

_____

My Findings

Types of Patents:

1. _____
2. _____
3. _____

Cost of Obtaining a Patent: _____

Process of Obtaining a Patent:

1. _____
2. _____
3. _____
4. _____
5. _____
6. _____

Name _____

Looking Back

Read  and Discover

Read these four kinds of sentences.

> Wow, that creature must be 40 feet long! Is it a whale?
> No, it's a whale shark, the world's largest fish.
> Tell me more.

Write the end mark that follows the command. ____

Write the end mark that follows the sentence that shows excitement. ____

Write the end mark that follows the question. ____

Write the end mark that follows the statement. ____

A **declarative sentence** makes a statement and ends with a period. An **interrogative sentence** asks a question and ends with a question mark. An **imperative sentence** gives a command and ends with a period or an exclamation point. An **exclamatory sentence** shows excitement and ends with an exclamation point. Begin every sentence with a capital letter.

See Handbook Section 10

Part 1

Add the correct punctuation mark to each sentence. Then label it *declarative, interrogative, imperative,* or *exclamatory.*

1. Listen to this _____

2. The mouth of a whale shark is big enough to swallow two people whole _____

3. What a big mouth _____

4. Are these fish dangerous to humans _____

5. No, whale sharks eat only very small fish and plankton _____

6. If a whale shark accidentally swallows something large, it turns its stomach inside out to get rid of it _____

7. Imagine getting swallowed and spat out again _____

8. How can such a huge creature live on tiny animals _____

9. Look at this picture of plankton _____

10. Wow, it looks like a big cloud in the water _____

11. Whale sharks swim with their mouths wide open through clouds of plankton, filtering out millions of creatures _____

12. Do some whales eat that way, too _____

13. Yes, baleen whales use the bony plates in their mouths as strainers to separate tiny creatures from seawater and eat them _____

14. May I borrow that book about whale sharks _____

15. Remember to return it to the library _____

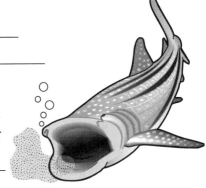

A whale shark weighs as much as an elephant.

Part 2

Rewrite each sentence so it is the type of sentence indicated in parentheses.

16. You should tell me about the differences between whale sharks and other sharks. (imperative)

_____

_____

17. Most sharks bear live young. (interrogative) _____

_____

18. Whale sharks lay eggs the size of footballs! (declarative) _____

_____

19. Whale sharks are amazing animals. (exclamatory) _____

_____

20. I don't understand why whale sharks aren't classified as whales. (interrogative) _____

_____

21. Aren't whales mammals and whale sharks fish? (declarative) _____

_____

22. Will you read this book to learn more about whale sharks? (imperative) _____

_____

Part 3

Authors often use a variety of sentence types to make their writing more interesting. Herman Melville's novel *Moby-Dick* begins with the famous imperative sentence, "Call me Ishmael." Notice the declarative, interrogative, imperative, and exclamatory sentences the author uses in this passage.

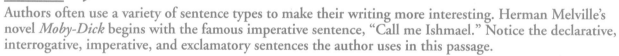

> Go from Corlears Hook to Coenties Slip, and from thence, by Whitehall, northward. What do you see?—Posted like silent sentinels all around the town, stand thousands upon thousands of mortal men fixed in ocean reveries....Are the green fields gone? What do they here?
> But look! Here come more crowds, pacing straight for the water, and seemingly bound for a dive. Strange! Nothing will content them but the extremest limit of the land…
>
> —Herman Melville, from *Moby-Dick*

Imagine you are a diver seeing a whale shark for the first time. Write three short sentences of different types giving your impressions.

23. _____

24. _____

25. _____

Name _____

Beasts & Critters

Read  and Discover

a. The seahorse has a horselike head **and** a curly tail.
b. The seahorse resembles a horse, **but** it is a true fish.

Cross out the boldfaced conjunction in each sentence.
Which sentence could be written as two separate sentences? _____

> A **simple sentence** is made up of a subject and a predicate and expresses only one complete thought. It is an *independent clause*. A **compound sentence** is made of two closely related independent clauses. The two clauses can be joined by a comma and a coordinating conjunction (*and*, *but*, or *or*) or by a semicolon (;).
>
> **See Handbook** Sections 8, 13, 22

Part 1

Write *S* next to each simple sentence. Write *CD* next to each compound sentence. Circle the comma and conjunction or the semicolon in each compound sentence.

1. Most seahorses are less than six inches long, but the Eastern Pacific seahorse can be fourteen inches long. _____

2. Seahorses are covered with knobby, bony armor; few predators will eat them. _____

3. Seahorses are not strong swimmers. _____

4. They live in warm, shallow water in the shelter of seagrass beds. _____

5. Like a monkey's tail, a seahorse's tail can grasp things; scientists call this kind of tail *prehensile*. _____

6. Seahorses must grasp stems of seagrass with their tails, or currents might sweep them away. _____

7. A seahorse sucks plankton through its tube-shaped mouth. _____

8. A seahorse's eyes swivel independently; it can spot prey in any direction. _____

9. Seahorses change color in response to their surroundings. _____

10. The seahorse looks strange, but its appearance is not its most unusual feature. _____

11. Virtually unique in the animal kingdom, the male seahorse can become pregnant. _____

12. At the full moon, the female seahorse lays eggs in the male seahorse's *brood pouch*. _____

13. The brood pouch is like a kangaroo's pouch, and the male seahorse nurtures the eggs inside it. _____

14. Seahorses are *monogamous;* they remain with the same mate throughout the breeding season. _____

15. After about two weeks, tiny seahorses emerge from the pouch. _____

Some seahorses can have as many as 300 babies at a time!

Part 2

Rewrite each pair of simple sentences as one compound sentence.

16. Sea dragons are related to seahorses. They look even stranger. _____

_____

17. They live among leafy seaweed. Their bodies have developed leaflike appendages. _____

_____

18. Sea dragons are perfectly camouflaged. Most predators wouldn't eat this bony creature anyway.

_____

_____

19. Male seahorses bear young. So do male sea dragons. _____

_____

20. Male sea dragons have no brood pouch. They are still able to nurture eggs. _____

_____

Part 3

Use clues from Parts 1 and 2 to complete the puzzle.

Across
2. Ocean vegetation
4. Remaining with one mate
5. A tail capable of grasping
6. Any animal that hunts other animals for food

Down
1. Tiny ocean life
2. A fish that resembles a horse
3. Water that moves in a pattern

Now use two of the words in the puzzle to write a compound sentence.

21. _____

_____

Name _____

Beasts & Critters

Read and Discover

Although California sea otters are mammals, <u>they usually spend their entire lives in the water</u>.

Look at the two parts of this sentence. Which part makes sense by itself?

_____

a. the boldfaced part   **b.** the underlined part

An **independent clause** is a group of words with a subject and a predicate that makes sense by itself. A **dependent clause** has a subject and a predicate, but it does not express a complete thought by itself. It needs—or is dependent on—an independent clause. Often a dependent clause begins with a subordinating conjunction such as *although, because, if, as,* or *when.* When a dependent clause begins a sentence, it is separated from the independent clause with a comma.

See Handbook Sections 8, 13

Part 1

Draw one line under each independent clause. Draw two lines under each dependent clause. Circle the subordinating conjunction that begins each dependent clause.

1. When sea otters sleep, they roll themselves in a floating blanket of kelp.

2. A sea otter usually dives to the bottom if it becomes hungry.

3. When it has found a clam or a sea urchin and a flat rock, it brings them back to the surface.

4. The otter floats on its back while it prepares its lunch.

5. As the otter holds the rock on its chest, it bangs the clam or sea urchin against the rock.

6. After the shell breaks open, the otter has a tasty meal.

7. Otters smile as they eat.

8. Because shells often have sharp edges, an otter carefully holds its lips away from its teeth in a grin.

9. Whales, walruses, sea lions, and dolphins can thrive in icy ocean water because they have a thick layer of insulating blubber under their skin.

Sea otters use rocks as tools to break open shells.

10. Although sea otters have no blubber, their dense, luxurious fur keeps them warm.

11. As an otter grooms its fur, tiny insulating air bubbles are trapped among the hairs.

12. An otter would freeze to death if it did not groom itself regularly.

13. People once hunted sea otters because their fur is so warm and soft.

14. When a 1911 treaty finally put an end to the slaughter, sea otters had almost become extinct.

15. Although they have been an endangered species for many years, sea otters are making a comeback.

Part 2

Draw a line to match each dependent clause with an independent clause. Then write the new sentences you have created on the lines. Be sure to add punctuation.

Dependent Clauses

although otters are no longer threatened by hunting

if there was a major oil spill

since otters eat fish

when storms hit the California coast

when human volunteers teach orphaned pups how to live in the ocean

Independent Clauses

orphaned baby sea otters are sometimes washed ashore

more otters survive in the wild

they face other threats

hundreds of California sea otters might die in the muck

fisheries see them as competitors

16. _____

_____

17. _____

_____

18. _____

_____

19. _____

_____

20. _____

_____

Part 3

On the lines below, write three funny or unusual dependent clauses. (Example: "After the octopus waved goodbye,") Trade papers with a partner. Complete your partner's sentences by writing an independent clause to go with each dependent clause. Take your own paper back and read the independent clauses your partner wrote.

21. _____

_____

22. _____

_____

23. _____

_____

Name _____

Beasts & Critters

Read  and Discover

    a. Although octopuses once had a reputation as horrible monsters, most of these shy animals are not dangerous to humans.

    b. Octopuses are the smartest invertebrates; they are as intelligent as house cats.

Cross out the comma in sentence a. and the semicolon in sentence b. Which sentence begins with a clause that would *not* be a sentence if a period were added to it? _____
Which sentence could become two separate sentences? _____

A dependent clause must be joined with an independent clause to make sense. A sentence made up of an independent clause and a dependent clause is a **complex sentence**. A dependent clause often begins with a subordinating conjunction such as *although, because, if, as,* or *when.*

See Handbook Sections 8, 13, 22

Part 1

Write *CX* next to each complex sentence. Write *CD* next to each compound sentence. Then circle each dependent clause and draw a box around each independent clause.

1. Because octopuses have no backbone, scientists call them invertebrates. _____

2. Octopuses are good hunters; they have a hard, beaklike mouth and eight legs with suckers. _____

3. Although octopuses have eight legs, they do not use them for swimming. _____

4. Octopuses take in water and squirt streams of it from their saclike bodies, and this propels them through the ocean. _____

5. If an octopus loses a leg, it can grow another. _____

6. An octopus might grab its prey with its legs, or it might drop down on top of its prey like a net. _____

Because octopuses are flexible, they can squeeze through crevices.

7. Though the octopus is a hunter, it is hunted by other creatures as well. _____

8. Seals, dolphins, and humans hunt octopuses; some people eat octopus meat raw in sushi. _____

9. Although octopuses are not related to seahorses, both animals change color for camouflage. _____

10. When an octopus is threatened, it squirts out a spray of black ink. _____

11. Because the cloud of ink is shaped like the octopus itself, it confuses the attacker. _____

12. Female octopuses lay as many as 80,000 eggs, and they tend them in underwater nests for six months or more. _____

13. The female octopus usually starves to death while she watches over her eggs. _____

14. Scientists call octopuses, squid, and nautiluses *cephalopods;* this word means "head-footed." _____

15. Scientists chose this name because the legs of these animals seem to grow from their heads. _____

Part 2

Combine each pair of simple sentences to create a complex sentence. Include the subordinating conjunction given in parentheses.

16. (because) The nautilus has two hundred tentacles and a spiral shell. It is not easily recognized as a relative of the octopus. _____

_____

17. (when) Dinosaurs roamed the earth. Thousands of shelled creatures like the nautilus filled the seas.

_____

_____

18. (because) Its hard shell protects it from water pressure. The nautilus can survive at extreme depths.

_____

_____

19. (although) There are many chambers in a nautilus shell. The animal lives only in the outermost one.

_____

_____

20. (as) The nautilus pumps liquid in or out of the inner chambers of its shell. It lowers or raises itself in the water. _____

_____

Part 3

A complex sentence is made up of two clauses and shows the relationship between the clauses. It can make a narrative flow more smoothly. A *compound-complex* sentence goes even further. It joins three or more clauses together with subordinating and coordinating conjunctions. A compound-complex sentence includes both dependent and independent clauses. Authors can pack a huge amount of information into one compound-complex sentence.

Read the passage below and underline the compound-complex sentence. How many independent clauses does this sentence contain? _____ How many dependent clauses does it contain? _____

 As the boat bounced from the top of each wave the wind tore through the hair of the hatless men, and as the craft plopped her stern down again the spray slashed past them. The crest of each of these waves was a hill, from the top of which the men surveyed for a moment a broad tumultuous expanse, shining and wind-riven.

          —Stephen Crane, from "The Open Boat"

Now find your own examples of compound-complex sentences in a story or textbook chapter you are currently reading. List at least three on another sheet of paper. Circle each independent clause and underline each dependent clause in these sentences.

Name _____

Beasts & Critters

Read and Discover

Scientists have developed submarines that can explore the deepest reaches of the ocean.
Underline the dependent clause that tells what kind of submarines have been developed. Could this part stand alone as a sentence? _____

An **adjective clause** is a dependent clause that describes a noun or a pronoun. An adjective clause always follows the word it describes and begins with a relative pronoun such as *who, whom, whose, which,* or *that.*

See Handbook Sections 8, 13, 17g

Part 1

Underline the adjective clause in each sentence. Circle the noun the clause describes. Draw a box around the relative pronoun.

1. Explorers who first descended to the sea's deep regions returned with tales of bizarre, unknown creatures.

2. These creatures, which have adapted to conditions in the dark water below 1,000 feet, are unlike any others.

3. Many have huge eyes and mouths as well as organs that glow in the inky darkness.

4. Some deep-sea creatures glow for reasons that are sinister.

5. The deep-sea angler has a glowing plume that dangles over its mouth.

6. The plume, which resembles a tiny organism, attracts would-be predators.

7. The angler eats any fish that comes close enough.

8. The umbrella mouth gulper eel has a mouth that expands for huge bites.

9. This two-foot-long creature can eat fish that are larger than itself.

10. It couldn't eat an oarfish, whose narrow body can grow up to thirty-five feet long.

11. Sailors whom oarfish frightened on occasional trips to the surface probably started the old legends of "sea serpents."

12. Imaginary animals could never be as strange as the real animals that inhabit the deep sea.

13. The giant squid, which lives in the depths, can grow up to sixty feet long.

14. Divers who have seen these rare creatures consider themselves fortunate.

15. Clear photographs of strange creatures that live deep in the ocean are quite valuable.

deep-sea angler

umbrella mouth gulper eel

oarfish

Beasts & Critters

Part 2

Rewrite each pair of sentences as one complex sentence; change the underlined sentence into an adjective clause beginning with *who*, *which*, or *that*.

16. Bizarre undersea "gardens" were discovered by scientists. <u>The scientists studied thermal springs on the ocean floor.</u> _____

_____

17. The scientists found ten-foot-long bright red worms. <u>These worms bloomed from the tops of white tubes.</u> _____

_____

18. Huge clumps of the worms grew around warm water. <u>The water streamed from volcanic rifts.</u>

_____

_____

19. The scientists also found foot-long clams with bright red meat. <u>The meat was colored by hemoglobin.</u>

_____

_____

Part 3

Find six words in the puzzle. Write them where they fit in the blanks.

A	A	E	Z	W	X	J	N	F	M	J
Q	N	D	X	H	A	S	M	P	N	P
W	G	E	C	R	B	K	Q	L	B	R
G	L	O	W	I	N	G	X	U	N	E
Z	E	M	V	X	F	L	W	M	V	D
R	R	H	B	Y	G	Z	R	E	C	A
T	Z	J	N	P	S	X	P	C	X	T
Y	A	T	T	R	A	C	T	S	Z	O
P	R	K	M	S	Z	V	S	H	L	R
S	X	L	Q	D	H	B	D	J	K	S

Across

— — —

— — — — — — —

— — — — — — —

Down

— — — — — —

— — — — — —

— — — — — — —

Use the words you found to make a complex sentence. Include an adjective clause that begins with *that*.

20. _____

_____

Read and Discover

An 8,000-pound elephant seal sleeps wherever it wants.
Underline the dependent clause that tells where an elephant seal sleeps.
Does this part of the sentence make sense by itself? _____

An **adverb clause** is a dependent clause that tells about a verb, an adjective, or an adverb. Adverb clauses tell *where, when, why,* or *how much*. They often begin with a subordinating conjunction such as *than, although, because, if, as, as if, while, when,* or *whenever*.

See Handbook Sections 8, 13, 22

Part 1

Underline the adverb clause in each sentence.

1. Before they adapted to life in the sea, seals were land animals similar to dogs and bears.

2. When seals' ancestors moved to the water, their bodies slowly changed over a long period of time.

3. Now flippers paddle where paws once stepped.

4. Although seals still have all the bones for four legs, only the ankle and foot bones protrude from their barrel-shaped bodies.

5. A seal's shape improves its speed in the water because currents flow smoothly past its streamlined body.

6. As seals developed their swimming ability, they gave up most of their agility on land.

7. However, eared seals, or sea lions, move more quickly on land than true seals do.

8. While eared seals can walk on their flippers, true seals must wriggle on land with a caterpillarlike motion.

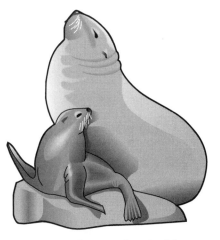

Fur seals were hunted for their coats, but now they are protected.

9. If they must find food or evade a predator, some seals can dive down to 2,900 feet below the surface.

10. Seals need sharp vision because there is little light in the ocean's depths.

11. Although they spend most of their time in the water, seals come to beaches for the breeding season.

12. Seals often breed where they were born.

13. Mother seals nurse their pups while males compete for beach territory.

14. Male elephant seals on breeding beaches look as if they are immense slugs.

15. After the new pups have been weaned, the seals return to the sea.

Part 2

Rewrite each pair of simple sentences as one complex sentence. Use the word in parentheses to change the underlined sentence into an adverb clause.

16. (because) <u>Seals' eyes look much like human eyes.</u> The Scottish have made up legends about seal-people, or *selkies.* _____

_____

17. (although) <u>Selkies wear seal skins.</u> They look like humans underneath. _____

_____

18. (since) <u>Selkies can't swim in their natural form.</u> They must wear a fish or seal skin. _____

_____

19. (whenever) <u>The moon is full.</u> Selkies shed their skins and dance on the beach in human form.

_____

_____

20. (If) <u>A human steals a selkie's skin.</u> The selkie will be in that human's power. _____

_____

21. (When) <u>The selkie gets its skin back.</u> It will return to the sea. _____

_____

Part 3

In this activity, you will distinguish among adverbs, adverb phrases, and adverb clauses. Draw a line from each sentence to the correct description of the boldfaced word or words.

22. The selkie danced **when the moon was full.**   adverb (one word)

23. The selkie danced **gracefully.**   adverb phrase (no verb)

24. The selkie danced **after midnight.**   adverb clause (has a verb)

25. Their flippers paddle **through the water.**   adverb (one word)

26. Their flippers paddle **where paws once stepped.**   adverb phrase (no verb)

27. Their flippers paddle **agilely.**   adverb clause (has a verb)

Name _____

Beasts & Critters

Read and Discover

a. Crabs use their claws **to defend themselves.**
b. Crabs belong **to the crustacean family.**

Look at each boldfaced phrase. In which phrase is *to* followed by a verb? _____

In which phrase is *to* followed by an article, an adjective, and a noun? _____

An **infinitive** is a phrase made up of *to* followed by the present form of a verb (*to defend*). Infinitives may act as adjectives, adverbs, or nouns. An **infinitive phrase** is made up of an infinitive and any other words that complete its meaning. In sentence a. above, *to defend themselves* is an infinitive phrase.

See Handbook Section 25

Part 1

Underline each infinitive phrase.

1. Scientists use the term *exoskeleton* to talk about a crab's shell.

2. Most crabs *molt,* or shed their rigid shells, in order to grow larger.

3. Just after molting, without a hard shell to protect them, crabs are very vulnerable.

4. The hermit crab finds an abandoned spiral shell to make its home.

5. When a hermit crab grows too large for its shell, it searches for another shell to occupy.

6. If a crab loses a leg, it is able to *regenerate,* or grow another.

7. Eyes perched high on stalks allow a ghost crab to watch for prey while the rest of its body is buried in sand.

8. The pea crab is tiny enough to live inside the shell of a live oyster.

9. On the other hand, you might need a twelve-foot-long ruler to measure an adult giant spider crab.

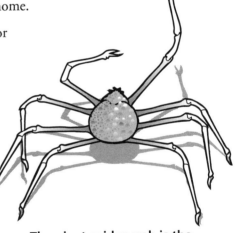

The giant spider crab is the world's largest crustacean.

10. Because the giant spider crab normally lives at depths of around 1,200 feet, divers are rarely able to observe this amazing creature.

11. You might be surprised to find that some "crabs" are not crabs at all.

12. Many people assume horseshoe crabs to be crustaceans, but they are actually relatives of spiders and scorpions.

13. These creatures appear to have changed little since prehistoric times.

14. They were already ancient animals when dinosaurs began to prowl the earth.

15. Scientists hope the horseshoe crab will be able to survive for another 360 million years.

Part 2

Write an infinitive from the word bank to complete each sentence.

to lay	to grasp	to describe	to molt	to wait

16. People use the phrase "shaking hands" _____ the mating ritual of the Alaskan king crab.

17. A male king crab looks for a female who is preparing _____, or shed her skin.

18. He uses his powerful claws _____ her front legs tightly until molting occurs.

19. Only after molting is the female crab able _____ eggs.

20. The male crab may have as long as two weeks _____, but he hangs on nonetheless.

Part 3

Many *aphorisms,* or sayings, use infinitives to name actions. Underline the infinitive phrases in the following well-known aphorisms. Note that the last aphorism contains an understood infinitive, indicated in brackets.

"It is better to give than to receive."
—Anonymous

"'Tis better to have loved and lost than never to have loved at all."
—Alfred, Lord Tennyson

"To err is human, to forgive divine."
—Alexander Pope

"It is better to know some of the questions than [to know] all of the answers."
—James Thurber

Write an aphorism of your own, using an infinitive, to give your reader advice.

21. _____

_____

_____

_____

Name _____

Read and Discover

Armed with a deadly weapon, the scorpionfish swims calmly through tropical waters.

Circle the two verbs in the sentence above. Which verb has a subject just before it? _____

Which verb is part of a phrase with no subject? _____

Sometimes a verb does not act as the simple predicate of a sentence. A **verbal** is a word formed from a verb that plays another role in the sentence. One type of verbal is a **participle**. A participle may be a present participle (usually the present form + -ing: *eating*) or a past participle. Regular verbs form the past participle by adding -ed (*armed*). Irregular verbs change their spelling in the past participle (*eaten, brought*). A **participial phrase** is made of a participle and other words that complete its meaning. A participial phrase can act as an adjective. In the sentence above, *Armed with a deadly weapon* is a participial phrase describing a scorpionfish.

See Handbook Sections 18d, 25

Part 1

Underline each participial phrase. Then circle the participle.

1. Even a very hungry predator will avoid a fish covered with venomous spines.

2. Fearing the effects of the poison, divers stay well away from this colorful fish.

3. The fish displaying colorful, feathery fins with stripes is a turkeyfish, one variety of scorpionfish.

4. Children visiting aquariums often watch this beautiful fish for many minutes.

5. The type of scorpionfish known as the lionfish is also admired for its beauty.

6. A scorpionfish displaying its stripes and colors is giving a warning to other creatures.

7. Not all scorpionfish have colors or stripes decorating their bodies.

8. A type of scorpionfish called the stonefish has no distinctive markings.

9. Resembling a rock, the stonefish attracts no attention.

10. Lying motionless on the ocean floor, it waits for a slow-moving fish.

11. Seeing only a gray lump, other fish swim into this creature's reach.

12. Divers exploring the ocean floor may mistake a stonefish for a rock.

A scorpionfish can be extremely dangerous.

13. Needle-sharp spines hidden beneath the stonefish's skin deliver a painful, dangerous sting.

14. Venom injected by the stonefish quickly circulates through the diver's body.

15. Fortunately, an antidote to stonefish venom is available in a number of cities near parts of the ocean inhabited by stonefish.

16. A sting victim taken quickly to a hospital has a good chance for survival.

Beasts & Critters

Part 2

A participial phrase must be placed near the noun or pronoun it modifies or it can create confusion for the reader. The participial phrase in each sentence below is misplaced. Rewrite each sentence so that it makes sense.

17. Known throughout the world for its teeming sea life, Alex and Shanna couldn't wait to dive at the Great Barrier Reef. _____

_____

18. Hardened skeletons of dead water animals make up the coral in this reef called *polyps*. _____

_____

19. Alex and Shanna hired an instructor not knowing how to scuba dive. _____

_____

20. They gazed through their face masks at the astonishing creatures around them enjoying their new experience. _____

_____

_____

21. Covered with waving tentacles, Alex stared at a flowerlike sea anemone. _____

_____

22. Shanna pricked her finger on a spiky spine trying to pick up a sea urchin. _____

_____

Part 3

Read the excerpt below. By repeating participial phrases, the poet has created a feeling of excitement that carries the reader through the poem. Underline the participial phrases that help create this feeling.

Screaming the night away
With his great wing feathers
Swooping the darkness up;
I hear the Eagle bird
Pulling the blanket back
Off from the eastern sky.
    —Anonymous, "Iroquois Invitation Song"

What noun do these participial phrases describe?

23. _____

Name _____

Beasts & Critters

Read and Discover

a. **Building a coral reef** takes many centuries.
b. Tiny animals create the reef by **depositing calcium carbonate**.

Circle the simple predicate in each sentence. Draw a box around each verb form ending in *-ing*. Is either *-ing* form part of a simple predicate? _____
Is the boldfaced phrase in sentence a. the subject of the sentence, the direct object, or an object of a preposition? _____
Is the boldfaced phrase in sentence b. the subject of the sentence, the direct object, or the object of a preposition? _____

> A **gerund** is a verbal that acts as a noun. All gerunds are verb forms that end with *-ing*. A **gerund phrase** is made up of a gerund and the other words that complete its meaning. In the sentences above, *Building a coral reef* and *depositing calcium carbonate* are gerund phrases.
>
> **See Handbook Section 25**

Part 1

Underline each gerund phrase. Draw a box around the gerund itself.

1. Swimming near coral reefs will acquaint you with many colorful fish.

2. The long blue teeth of the harlequin tusk fish are ideal for crushing the hard shells of clams.

3. Living among an anemone's poisonous tentacles might seem impossible.

4. The striped clownfish can do this because it is not harmed by the stinging of the anemone.

5. The beaklike mouth of the parrotfish is effective in grinding coral into sand.

6. This fine sand seems perfect for building sandcastles.

7. Spindly little spider crabs protect themselves by establishing homes inside hollow tube sponges.

8. A tiny cleaner shrimp attracts a reef fish by waving its long antennae.

9. Cleaner shrimp help reef fish by eating parasites off their skin.

10. Seeing the bright blue fringe on the four-foot-wide mouth of a giant clam is an unforgettable experience.

11. Diving around reefs is made dangerous by scorpionfish and other fish with venomous spines.

12. Swimming in the ocean with an open wound is a dangerous thing to do.

13. Sharks sometimes find prey by following the smell of blood.

14. Protecting live coral is a difficult task.

15. People harm coral by taking pieces as souvenirs.

16. Crown-of-thorns starfish have destroyed entire colonies of coral by devouring those tiny creatures.

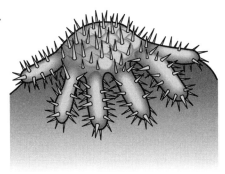

The crown-of-thorns starfish preys on living coral.

Part 2

Imagine you and your family are taking a vacation to an island in the South Pacific. Describe what you will do on this vacation by writing a gerund phrase to complete each sentence. The gerunds in the word bank may give you some ideas.

visiting catching	swimming painting	diving protecting	photographing helping	eating avoiding	watching seeing

17. I would enjoy _____.

18. _____ would be a new experience for me.

19. I would start each day by _____.

20. After breakfast I might try _____.

21. _____ would be fun for everyone in the family.

22. I would learn about coral reefs by _____.

23. Since I saw a documentary film on the tide-water pools I think _____ _____ would be fun.

24. _____ is something that swimmers and divers should try to do.

25. _____ would be a great activity toward the end of the day.

Part 3

Authors, poets, and filmmakers frequently use gerund phrases as titles of works. "Crossing the Bar" is one of Alfred, Lord Tennyson's best-known poems, and "Stopping by Woods on a Snowy Evening" is one of Robert Frost's most famous works. *Living Free* is a popular movie about African lions.

Look in a library and in the entertainment section of a newspaper to find five other works that have gerund phrases as titles. List these titles on the lines below.

26. _____

27. _____

28. _____

29. _____

30. _____

Name _____

Read and Discover

Rays are related to sharks, both have skeletons made of cartilage. Although rays look very different. Differences in appearance or the way animals look to the observer are not always significantly important to the classification of those animals that may seem so different from each other. Circle the dependent clause that is missing an independent clause. Underline the sentence that is written incorrectly because it is made up of two independent clauses without a conjunction. Write *X* at the beginning of the sentence that uses a lot of words to say very little.

A **fragment** does not tell a complete thought. A **run-on sentence** is a compound sentence that is missing a comma and a conjunction. A **comma splice** is a run-on sentence that has a comma but is missing a conjunction. A **ramble-on** sentence is correct grammatically but contains extra words and phrases that don't add to its meaning. Avoid fragments, run-ons, comma splices, and ramble-ons in the final versions of your written work.

See Handbook Sections 8, 14, 22

Part 1

Write *F* after each fragment. Write *RO* after each run-on. Write *CS* after each comma splice. Write *RA* after each ramble-on sentence.

1. Rays have wide, flat bodies and narrow tails, they are shaped almost like kites. _____

2. Rays flap their fins like a bird's wings they fly through the water. _____

3. Although their eyes are on the tops of their heads. _____

4. Mouths on the underside. _____

5. Rays cannot see their food, they must sense it with smell, touch, and electrosensors. _____

6. The low placement of the ray's mouth on the underside or bottom of its head makes the ray very well-suited for bottom feeding, or eating food off the sea floor, because its mouth is on the bottom near its food which is also there as well. _____

7. If a ray senses prey on the ocean floor. _____

8. The ray's flat body drapes over the prey its mouth sucks the animal up. _____

9. Poisonous spines at the base of a stingray's tail. _____

10. Huge manta rays grow up to 20 feet across, these harmless animals eat only plankton. _____

11. A manta can jump six feet above the surface of the water it glides on its immense winglike fins. _____

12. Another fish in the ray family is the guitarfish, which was probably named in this way because it resembles that popular musical instrument known as the guitar, which has a shape somewhat similar to the shape of this fish. _____

Electric rays can attack with electric shocks of up to 200 volts.

Part 2

Rewrite the sentences from Part 1 that are listed below. Correct any fragments, run-ons, and comma splices. Shorten the ramble-ons. There is more than one way to correct each sentence. **(13–19)**

Sentence #2 _____

_____

Sentence #3 _____

_____

Sentence #5 _____

_____

Sentence #8 _____

_____

Sentence #9 _____

_____

Sentence #10 _____

_____

Sentence #12 _____

_____

_____

Part 3

This monster ramble-on sentence contains more than 50 words. Cross out unnecessary words, phrases, and clauses to make the sentence as short as possible. Write your revised sentence below.

Like sharks, most fish of the ray variety, including the manta ray, the stingray, and most other rays, are covered all over their bodies with toothlike scales, that resemble tiny teeth but are really scales, and which make the skin of these sharklike fish feel rough if you touch it with your hand.

20. _____

_____

Now try writing a monster sentence of your own. Start with a simple sentence, such as *The ray was swimming.* Add words, phrases, and clauses that add too much information for one good sentence. Then trade papers with a partner and trim each other's monster sentence.

21. _____

_____

_____

Name _____

Beasts & Critters

Diagraming Compound Subjects

A sentence with a compound subject is diagramed this way:

Whales and dolphins swim.

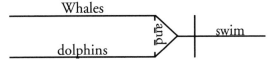

Diagram these sentences on the lines provided. (Refer to page 29 if you need help.)

1. Kevin and I saw two dolphins.

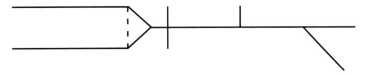

2. Roger and Ana spotted a whale.

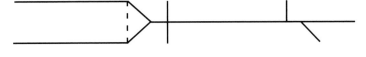

3. The passengers and crew shouted.

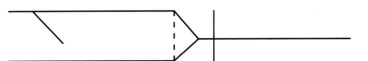

Diagraming Compound Predicates

A sentence with a compound predicate is diagramed this way:

The whales leap and dive.

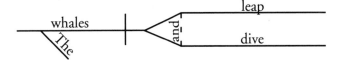

Try diagraming these sentences.

4. The dolphins chattered and whistled.

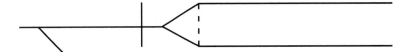

5. Onlookers pointed and yelled.

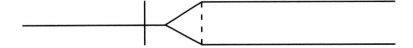

6. One child laughed and clapped.

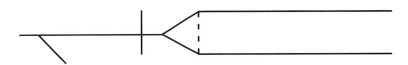

Diagraming Compound Sentences

A compound sentence is diagramed this way:

One whale leaped and another dove.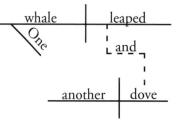

Try diagraming these compound sentences.

7. I carried binoculars, but they broke.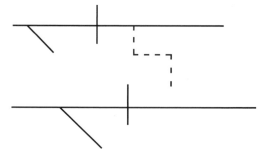

8. Ana had an extra pair, and I borrowed them.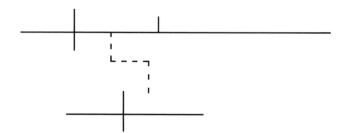

9. The ship lurched, and some passengers stumbled.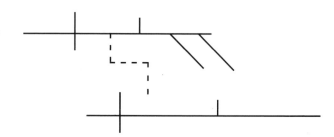

10. The stormy clouds parted, and the sun shone.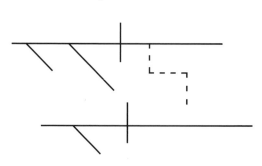

Name _____

Beasts & Critters

Writing Sentences

The writer of these sentences has tried to include too many ideas. Rewrite each sentence as two or three shorter, clearer sentences. Make sure each sentence you write is complete.

1. Due to the great energy they expend, otters eat tremendous amounts of food, so they spend most of their day diving for shellfish such as abalone and sea urchins, which they crack with the help of a rock which they lay on their stomachs and use as an anvil.

_____
_____
_____
_____
_____
_____
_____

2. Otters seem to smile as they eat the meat from the shellfish they have broken when they hold their lips away from their teeth because the broken shells often have sharp edges.

_____
_____
_____
_____
_____
_____

There are four kinds of sentences—a statement, a question, a command, and an exclamation. Any of these sentences may be simple, compound, or complex. Notice the different types of sentences in this model paragraph.

question — **Have you ever wondered what life is like at the bottom of the ocean?** Last month I had a chance to find out by studying it with my own eyes. I rode in a

statements — submersible to explore an oceanic trench off the Pacific

complex sentence — Coast. *Because the bottom of the trench is so deep, no sunlight reaches the creatures there.* Several fish that I saw glow through a process called *bioluminescence*. **Imagine**

command — **seeing an anglerfish use its glowing lure to attract**

exclamation — **prey.** *Wow, that was impressive!*

Writing a Paragraph

The sentences you repaired on page 61 can be used to make a paragraph. Decide what order the sentences should be in. Then revise at least two of the sentences so your paragraph has a variety of sentence types. Use the model on page 61 as a reference. Write the paragraph on the lines below.

_____

_____

_____

_____

_____

_____

_____

Imagine that you are an ocean diver. You have just returned from a dive during which you saw many unusual creatures. Write a paragraph about your experience. Vary the types of sentences you use, and include different types of phrases to add variety and interest to your paragraph.

_____

_____

_____

_____

_____

_____

_____

_____

_____

Read your paragraph again. Use this checklist to evaluate your writing.

- ❏ Does my paragraph have a topic sentence?
- ❏ Have I used at least two of the four kinds of sentences?
- ❏ Have I included at least one compound or one complex sentence?
- ❏ Do my sentences have correct punctuation?
- ❏ Does my paragraph have a concluding sentence?

Name _____

Beasts & Critters

Proofreading Others' Writing

Read this passage about sperm whales and find the mistakes. Use the proofreading marks below to show how each mistake should be fixed.

Proofreading Marks

Mark	Means	Example
ℒ	delete	Sperm whales eats squid, sharks, and other fish.
∧	add	Sperm whales eat squid, sharks, ^and^ other fish.
≡	make into a capital letter	sperm whales eat squid, sharks, and other fish.
⊙	add a period	Sperm whales eat squid, sharks, and other fish⊙
⌃	add a comma	Sperm whales eat squid⌃ sharks, and other fish.
(sp)	fix spelling	Sperm whales eat sqid, sharks, and other fish.
/	make into a lowercase letter	Sperm Whales eat squid, sharks, and other fish.

Sperm Whales

Sperm whales are the largest toothed Whales in the world. a fully grown sperm whale. Can meshure anywhere from 38 to 60 feet in lenth and can be identified by its massive head.

groups of whales consisting primarily of females and there young travel through warm tropical waters. These groups are called pods. The young whales are raised not only by their mothers but by the other adults in the pod as well?

Young males leave the group by the time they are six they migrate to colder waters. They travel alone or with samll groups of other males. It is thought that the males leave their famly units so that there is less competition for food, they eat enormous quantities of food to satisfy their huge appetites. Adult males, called bulls, can be nearly one-third biger than the females.

After many years, when they are ready to mate, Bulls return to the warmer waters in which they were raised. They usually swim with many groups of female whales. Before they find an appropriate mate.

People of various societies have created storys legends and works of art featuring whales. Perhaps the most famous whale in literature is the male sperm whale that is the focus of the action in Herman melville's novel *Moby-Dick*

Proofreading Your Own Writing

You can use the list below to help you find and fix mistakes in your own writing. Write the titles of your own stories or reports in the blanks at the top of the chart. Then use the questions to check your work. Make a check mark (✓) in each box after you have checked that item.

Titles

Proofreading Checklist for Unit 2

Have I used the correct punctuation at the end of each kind of sentence?				
Have I used a comma and coordinating conjunction or a semicolon to separate compound sentences?				
Have I avoided run-on sentences, comma splices, and sentence fragments?				
Is each sentence an independent clause or an independent clause and a dependent clause?				

Also Remember . . .

Does each sentence begin with a capital letter?				
Have I spelled each word correctly?				
Have I used commas correctly?				

Your Own List

Use this space to write your own list of things to check in your writing.

Name _____

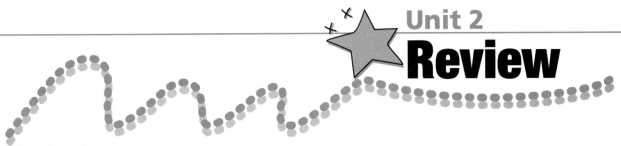
Kinds of Sentences

Draw three lines (≡) under each letter that should be capitalized. Add correct punctuation. Label each sentence *declarative, interrogative, imperative,* or *exclamatory.*

1. tell me about prehistoric sea creatures _____

2. giant sea scorpions once grew eight feet long _____

3. wow, that's amazing _____

4. what else lived in ancient seas _____

Simple Sentences, Compound Sentences, Complex Sentences

Write *S* next to each simple sentence. Write *CD* next to each compound sentence. Write *CX* next to each complex sentence.

5. Before anything lived on land, the seas were filled with creatures. _____

6. Trilobites were once the most numerous species on the earth, but they died out about 300 million years ago. _____

7. These small bottom-dwellers had armored shells and many simple legs. _____

8. Because huge fish dominated the world about 400 million years ago, scientists call that period the Age of Fishes. _____

9. Armor of heavy, bony plates protected these fish. _____

10. Although they did not have real teeth, these monsters bit with the sharp, exposed edges of their armor. _____

11. Sharks developed in this period, and modern sharks are very similar to these prehistoric sharks. _____

Dependent Clauses and Independent Clauses

Draw one line under the independent clause in each sentence. Draw two lines under the dependent clause.

12. When some fish with lungs emerged on land, they became the first amphibians.

13. Although most types of fishes with lungs died out millions of years ago, the modern lungfish still survives.

Adjective Clauses

Underline the adjective clause in each sentence. Then circle the noun it modifies.

14. Plesiosaurs, which grew up to 46 feet long, were whalelike dinosaurs.

15. Some had necks that were double the length of their bodies.

16. Scientists who study plesiosaurs say these dinosaurs flapped their flippers like wings.

Adverb Clauses

Underline the adverb clause in each sentence.

17. When the dinosaurs dominated Earth, some took to the sea.

18. Many of these animals developed fins or flippers where they once had legs.

19. Although ichthyosaurus resembled a modern porpoise, it was not a mammal but a reptile.

20. Scientists chose the name *ichthyosaurus* because it means "fishlike lizard."

Infinitive Phrases and Participial Phrases

Underline each infinitive phrase. Circle each participial phrase.

21. The large dinosaur swimming gracefully in this picture is a plesiosaur.

22. The plesiosaur's long neck helped it to hunt food.

23. Stretching its long neck, the plesiosaur looked for prey.

24. Using its tail as a rudder, the mosasaur swam effectively.

25. Miners in Holland in 1780 were the first people to find a mosasaur fossil.

26. Scientists hope to find more fossils of this ancient aquatic creature.

Gerund Phrases

Underline each gerund phrase.

27. Meeting a sea scorpion must have been an unpleasant experience for ancient sea creatures.

28. The sea scorpion's huge claws were ideal for grabbing prey.

29. The sea scorpion ended the struggles of its victims by stinging them with its venomous tail.

Avoiding Fragments, Run-ons, Comma Splices, and Ramble-ons

Identify each item as a fragment, a run-on, a comma splice, or a ramble-on by writing *F, RO, CS,* or *RA* next to each.

30. Ammonites were tentacled animals they lived in spiral shells. _____

31. Similar to the modern nautilus. _____

32. Ammonites changed through the ages, scientists use ammonite fossils to date rock layers. _____

33. Because the shells of the ammonites that lived in one period look very different from the shells of ammonites that lived in another period, scientists can look at the fossils of ammonites from each of these periods and notice the variations between them. _____

34. Another fish thought to be extinct is the coelacanth, one was caught near South Africa in the 1930s. _____

35. The coelacanth, related to the lungfish. _____

Name	

Beasts & Critters

COMMUNITY LEARNING ▾▾▾▾▾▾▾▾▾▾▾▾▾▾ OPPORTUNITIES ▾▾▾▾▾▾▾▾

In Unit 2 of *G.U.M.*, students learned more about **different types of sentences and sentence structures** and used what they learned to improve their own writing. The content of these lessons focuses on the theme **Sea Creatures**. As students completed the exercises, they learned about some of the most impressive and unusual inhabitants of the world's oceans. These pages offer a variety of activities that reinforce skills and concepts presented in the unit. They also provide opportunities for the student to make connections between the material in the lessons and the community at large.

Local Fishes

Find out where the nearest saltwater aquarium is located. If possible, arrange to visit the aquarium. You might consider taking a younger family member with you and sharing with that person some of the things you have learned about the ocean in Unit 2.

Laws of the Sea

Because of its limited supply of fish and the presence of valuable minerals on and under the ocean floor, the question of who owns the world's oceans has become increasingly important. Learn about laws that govern the ocean. You might begin by finding out what the Law of the Sea Treaty, drafted in 1982 by the United Nations, suggests as fair use of the world's oceans. Find out which nations signed the treaty, which did not, and why. Summarize the information in a report.

Saving Water

Although many places have plenty of water for people to use however they want, other places face a shortage of usable water. People there must follow strict conservation rules so everyone will have the water they need for daily living. Organize a campaign to raise public awareness of water conservation in your school or neighborhood. Call your local water department and ask for water-saving tips. Make posters showing some of these suggestions, and display them at school or in other places so people will be motivated to take part in your campaign.

Sea Dreams

Learn about job opportunities for people who love the ocean and the creatures that inhabit it. Such opportunities include careers in marine biology, marine geology, and underwater archaeology. Organizations that offer maritime careers include the Merchant Marines and the United States Coast Guard. Choose one occupation that interests you and learn more about it. Try to answer these questions:

- What skills are required to do this job?
- What preparation and training would I need for this job?
- Where is this training available?
- How long does it take to become proficient at this work?
- What is a typical working day like in this profession?

If possible, interview an adult you know who has a maritime job you might be interested in. Take notes during the interview, and share the results of the interview with your class. Use the planning guide on the next page to help you plan the interview and organize your notes.

Interview Planner

Person I am interviewing:

Name _____

Age _____

Occupation _____

Number of years employed in that field _____

Date of interview: _____

Questions to ask:

1. _____
   _____

2. _____
   _____

3. _____
   _____

4. _____
   _____

5. _____
   _____

6. _____
   _____

7. _____
   _____

8. _____
   _____

Notes:

_____

_____

_____

_____

_____

Name _____

Beasts & Critters

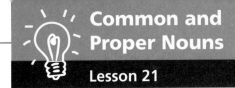
Read and Discover

Roger Williams overcame difficult **challenges** to found the colony of **Rhode Island**.

Circle the boldfaced words that name particular persons, places, things, or ideas.

A **common noun** names any person, place, thing, or idea. A **proper noun** names a particular person, place, thing, or idea. Proper nouns must be capitalized. A proper noun made of several words (*Harriet Tubman* or *East Greenwood School*) is considered one proper noun.

See Handbook Section 15

Part 1

Circle the proper nouns in the sentences below. Underline the common nouns.

1. Roger Williams was a minister who came to Boston with the Puritans in 1631.

2. The Puritans had come to America so they could worship freely.

3. They did not give that privilege to others in their colony, however.

4. They felt that their ideas were best, and they wrote laws saying everyone must hold the same beliefs they did.

5. Roger Williams disagreed.

6. He felt that all people should be allowed to worship as they wanted.

7. He also believed that the Native Americans owned the land and that the colonists had no claim to it unless they bought it fairly.

8. Williams's radical ideas about religious freedom and fairness to Native Americans got him into trouble, but he never went back on his convictions.

Roger Williams founded Rhode Island on the principle of religious freedom.

9. In October 1635, the government of Massachusetts banished Williams from the colony.

10. The government tried to send him back to England, but Williams fled through the woods to stay with the Narragansett.

11. The Narragansett welcomed Williams and helped him learn their language, Algonquian.

12. After a few months, Williams purchased land from these Native Americans.

13. The land was located at the head of the bay now known as Narragansett Bay.

14. On this site he founded a settlement he called Providence.

15. The settlement grew into the colony of Rhode Island, where religious freedom was the right of all people.

Part 2

Proper nouns specify whom and what you are talking about. Rewrite each sentence, and replace each common noun with a proper noun from the word bank. You may also need to change other words in your sentences.

| England | Narragansett | Roger Williams | Algonquian | *A Key into the Language of America* |

16. The minister became friendly with the local residents. _____

_____

17. He stayed with them and learned to speak their language. _____

_____

18. He later wrote a book. _____

_____

19. It was published in another country. _____

_____

Part 3

Use information from Parts 1 and 2 to complete the puzzle.
Then circle the proper nouns you wrote.

Across
6. Native American group
7. Roger Williams's occupation
8. Settlers

Down
1. Strong beliefs
2. Group that went to Boston in search of freedom
3. A European island country
4. A special right
5. Another word for *liberty*

Name _____

Unforgettable Folks

Read and Discover

The Iditarod sled dog **race** is one of the greatest **challenges** a **person** can face.

Circle the boldfaced nouns that name a single person, place, or thing.

A **singular noun** names one person, place, thing, or idea. A **plural noun** names more than one. Most nouns add *s* or *es* to form the plural. The spelling of some nouns changes when *es* is added to form the plural (*sky / skies; wolf / wolves*). A few nouns do not add *s* or *es* to form the plural; instead, they change spelling (*woman / women*). A few other nouns have the same form in the singular and plural (*deer / deer*).

See Handbook Sections 18f, 29

Part 1

Circle each singular noun. Underline each plural noun.

1. The Iditarod covers over 1,000 miles of Alaskan wilderness and lasts about 14 days.

2. Competitors, known as *mushers,* ride in sleds pulled by 12 to 16 dogs paired in harnesses.

3. Mushers must drive their sleds through blizzards and other perils.

4. Strong bonds form between the mushers and their dogs.

5. These animals spend much of their lives in harnesses.

6. A dog first pulls a sled when it is a puppy.

7. Veterinarians examine and treat the dogs during the race.

8. The dogs wear hand-sewn booties to protect their feet.

9. Mushers pick up boxes packed with supplies and food at stops along the trail.

10. A pilot equipped with a radio flies over the course and calls for help if a team is in trouble.

Susan Butcher is the only person ever to win the Iditarod three years in a row.

11. A musher must be a well-conditioned athlete and a skillful driver to achieve victory.

12. Some people think the dogs are the true heroes, however.

13. The first Iditarod was held on the hundredth anniversary of the purchase of Alaska by the United States from Russia.

14. Two Alaskans with a fondness for history, Joe Reddington and Dorothy Page, developed the idea of a long race on sleds.

15. The Iditarod honors the mushers and dogs who braved the elements to establish villages in the frozen wilderness.

Unforgettable Folks

Part 2

Write the plural form of each singular common noun you identified in Part 1.

16. _____
17. _____
18. _____
19. _____
20. _____
21. _____
22. _____
23. _____
24. _____
25. _____
26. _____
27. _____

28. _____
29. _____
30. _____
31. _____
32. _____
33. _____
34. _____
35. _____
36. _____
37. _____
38. _____
39. _____

Part 3

A collective noun names a group of people or things that act as one unit. *Class, flock,* and *orchestra* are collective nouns. Circle the words below that are collective nouns. Then use three of them in sentences.

| family | fleet | deer | team | mice |
| jury | sled dogs | committee | animals | audience |

40. _____

_____

_____

41. _____

_____

_____

42. _____

_____

_____

Name _____

Unforgettable Folks

Read  and Discover

Wilma **Rudolph's** triumph over a crippling disease made her a truly remarkable champion.

Circle the part of the boldfaced word that shows ownership.

> A **possessive noun** shows ownership. **Singular** nouns add an apostrophe and *s* to form the possessive (*worker / worker's*). Most **plural** nouns add an apostrophe after the *s* to form the possessive (*workers / workers'*). Plurals that don't end in *s* (*men / mice*) add an apostrophe and *s* (*men's / mice's*) to show possession.
>
> See Handbook Sections 7, 30

Part 1

Underline each singular possessive noun. Circle each plural possessive noun. There may be more than one possessive noun in each sentence.

1. Wilma Rudolph's early childhood was made painful by a series of illnesses.

2. She was stricken with pneumonia and scarlet fever, and soon afterward she contracted polio, that era's most dreaded childhood disease.

3. That illness's effects left her with one leg paralyzed.

4. Wilma's mother had a family of 19 children, but she found time to get expert treatment for her young daughter's condition.

5. Every week she and Wilma traveled 50 miles by bus from Clarksville, Tennessee, to a hospital in Nashville to obtain doctors' help.

6. The Rudolphs, an African American family, had to sit in the back of the bus; Wilma Rudolph never forgot segregation's injustice.

In 1961 Rudolph received the Sullivan Award, given each year to the top U.S. amateur athlete.

7. Thanks to the treatments and to her mother's encouragement, Wilma began to improve.

8. In time she was able to walk with a brace's support, but she was determined to walk without it.

9. By junior high, Wilma no longer needed the brace, and she joined the girls' basketball team.

10. Her legs' muscles were now strong, and she starred in basketball.

11. This brilliant athlete's greatest triumphs would come in the sport of track and field; she first qualified for the United States Olympic Team in 1956, at the age of 16.

12. At the 1960 Olympics, Rudolph became the first American woman to win three gold medals, gaining recognition as the world's greatest woman sprinter.

13. The champion's homecoming parade in Clarksville was the first integrated event in the town's history.

14. Rudolph set world records in the women's 100- and 200-meter races and the 4 x 100-meter relay.

15. Working with young people after her Olympic triumphs, Rudolph became many youths' inspiration.

Unforgettable Folks

Part 2

Rewrite each sentence, shortening the underlined section by using a possessive noun.

16. The biographies of many athletes include stories of their triumphs over physical problems. _____

_____

_____

17. Swimmer Tom Dolan was the first American gold medalist in the 1996 Olympics. _____

_____

18. An abnormally narrow windpipe provides Dolan with air at only 20 percent of the capacity of a

normal windpipe. _____

_____

19. The condition which Dolan has only makes him train harder. _____

_____

20. The persistence of this swimmer has brought him a world record and a gold medal in the men's

400-meter medley. _____

_____

Part 3

Circle six nouns hidden in the puzzle. Write each one in the column where it belongs. Then write the possessive form of each noun.

F	A	M	I	L	Y	C	D
Q	T	H	B	S	D	H	I
W	H	J	N	P	F	I	S
R	L	K	M	O	G	L	E
T	E	L	Q	R	H	D	A
Y	T	Z	W	T	J	R	S
P	E	X	R	S	K	E	E
S	S	C	T	S	L	N	B
D	M	V	W	O	M	E	N

Singular Nouns   **Possessive Forms**

21. _____   _____

22. _____   _____

Plural Nouns   **Possessive Forms**

23. _____   _____

24. _____   _____

25. _____   _____

26. _____   _____

Use one of the possessive forms you wrote in a sentence about Wilma Rudolph.

27. _____

_____

Name _____

Unforgettable Folks

Read and Discover

I have always admired Nelson Mandela.

Circle the word in the sentence that shows who is speaking.

A **pronoun** can take the place of a noun. **Personal pronouns** can be used to stand for the person speaking, the person spoken to, or the person spoken about. **First person** pronouns refer to the speaker (*I, me*) or include the speaker (*we, us*). **Second person** pronouns refer to the person being spoken to (*you*). **Third person** pronouns refer to the person, place, or thing being spoken about (*he, him, she, her, it, they, them*). **Remember to use this information when you speak, too.**

See Handbook Section 17a

Part 1

Circle each personal pronoun. Write *1* if it is a first person pronoun, *2* if it is second person, or *3* if it is third person.

1. Do you know who Nelson Mandela is? _____

2. In 1994 he became the first Black president of South Africa. _____

3. I am amazed by the obstacles Mandela overcame to reach the presidency. _____

4. From the 1940s through the 1980s, South Africa's laws took away most of Black South Africans' lands and prohibited them from voting. _____

5. We learned in history class that this system was known as *apartheid*. _____

6. Nelson Mandela joined the African National Congress, a group that denounced apartheid and acted to try to end it. _____

7. The South African government imprisoned him for taking action against apartheid. _____

8. Although Mandela was a prisoner for 27 years, he never lost hope. _____

9. Mandela secretly wrote a book and helped other prisoners as they waged a struggle for better prison conditions. _____

10. You may be glad to know that international outrage finally led to Mandela's release. _____

11. Mandela negotiated the end of apartheid with South African President F. W. De Klerk, and together they were awarded the Nobel Peace Prize. _____

12. Nelson Mandela is a hero to me. _____

13. This great leader's courage is an example for all of us. _____

14. He proved to the world that oppression can be ended without widespread bloodshed. _____

Nelson Mandela helped end *apartheid* in South Africa.

Unforgettable Folks

Part 2

Write four sentences about a hero of yours, using the types of personal pronouns indicated.

15. first person: _____

_____

16. second person: _____

_____

17. third person singular: _____

_____

18. third person plural: _____

_____

Part 3

The word *he* once was accepted as a universal pronoun that could refer to anyone, male or female, if a generalization about people was being made.

| Example | Early childhood experiences affect a person for **his** entire life. |

Now most writers try to avoid the use of universal *he*. Here are two ways the sentence above might be revised.

Solution #1:
Make the noun and the word it refers to plural.

Early childhood experiences affect people for their entire lives.

Solution #2:
Replace *his* with *his or her.*

Early childhood experiences affect a person for his or her entire life.

Try both of these solutions for replacing the universal *he* in these sentences.

The food a person eats affects his health.

19. _____

_____

20. _____

_____

Each student scheduled his choice of activity during gym class.

21. _____

_____

22. _____

_____

Name _____

Unforgettable Folks

Read and Discover

a. Keiran bought a book about the history of human flight.
b. Keiran bought himself a book about the history of human flight.
Circle the word in sentence b. that tells for whom the book was bought.

> A **compound personal pronoun** ends in *-self* or *-selves*. It usually shows that the subject of a sentence is doing something to itself. (*I dressed myself in blue.*) Sometimes it gives emphasis. (*He cooked the chicken himself. Carolyn herself made the arrangements.*) A compound personal pronoun refers back to the subject of the sentence. The noun that a pronoun replaces is its **antecedent**.
> 📢 **Remember to use this information when you speak, too.**
>
> See Handbook Section 17e

Part 1

Circle each compound personal pronoun in the paragraphs below. Draw a box around the antecedent of each pronoun you circle. (1–11)

Since ancient times, we humans have imagined ourselves flying. Until recently, however, airplane pilots have not been able to lift themselves off the ground without the help of an engine.

In the 1970s engineer Paul MacCready dedicated himself to the dream of achieving human-powered flight. MacCready's first successful plane, the *Gossamer Condor*, had a wingspan of almost 100 feet but was made of extremely light materials. By itself the plane weighed only 70 pounds. Bicyclist Bryan Allen pedaled hard in the cockpit to spin the plane's propeller and lift himself and the *Condor* into the air for a flight of over one mile.

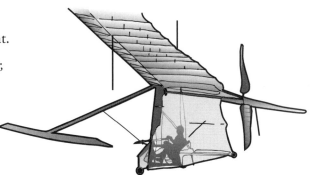

Paul MacCready and his team achieved the previously impossible goal of human-powered flight.

After the success of the *Gossamer Condor,* MacCready and his team set themselves another challenge. Their new plane, the *Gossamer Albatross,* was designed to carry a pilot across the 22.5-mile-wide English Channel. Bryan Allen volunteered himself again to be both pilot and power source. Can you imagine yourself fluttering a few feet above the waves, being held aloft only through frantic pedaling? Because air turbulence would almost certainly slow the plane to a standstill at some points, MacCready and his team resigned themselves to having to tow the plane now and then. But, in an amazing feat of endurance, Bryan Allen managed the crossing by himself and made history a second time.

The *Gossamer Condor* is on display at the National Air and Space Museum in Washington, D.C. I hope to see that historic plane myself someday.

Part 2

Rewrite each sentence, replacing the underlined word or words with a compound personal pronoun.

12. Jasmine bought <u>Jasmine</u> a model of the *Gossamer Condor*. _____

_____

13. We put it together <u>without help</u>. _____

_____

14. I gave <u>me</u> three tries to get the plane to fly. _____

_____

15. After a successful flight, the model plane settled <u>the plane</u> on a patch of soft grass. _____

_____

Part 3

Imagine that you piloted the *Gossamer Condor* on a short flight. Write an account of your experience. Use a compound personal pronoun in each sentence.

_____

_____

_____

_____

_____

_____

_____

_____

_____

_____

_____

_____

_____

_____

_____

_____

Name _____

Unforgettable Folks

Read and Discover

Isabel Allende **wrote** a **book** about **her** daughter, Paula.

Circle the boldfaced word that shows ownership or indicates a relationship. To whom does it refer? _____

Possessive pronouns show ownership. The possessive pronouns *her, his, its, their, my, our,* and *your* can replace possessive nouns. (*Nancy's house is blue.—Her house is blue.*) The possessive pronouns *hers, his, theirs, mine, ours,* and *yours* can replace both a possessive noun and the noun that is a possession. (*Nancy's house is the blue house.—Hers is the blue house.*)

See Handbook Section 17d

Part 1

Circle the possessive pronouns. There may be more than one in each sentence.

1. My favorite author is Isabel Allende.

2. Who is yours?

3. Allende was an investigative journalist in her native country, Chile.

4. Its government was overthrown in the 1970s.

5. At that time her uncle, Salvador Allende, was the president of that country.

6. Many people lost their lives, and Allende was forced to flee.

7. In exile in Venezuela, Allende heard that her grandfather was very ill in Chile.

8. She began writing him a long letter about the Allende family in which she recalled all their sad, happy, and wonderful stories.

Isabel Allende has lived in places on three continents.

9. This long letter grew into her first great novel, *The House of the Spirits.*

10. My favorite of Allende's books, *Paula,* also had its beginning as a letter.

11. Allende was taking care of her daughter, Paula, who lay in a coma for a year as the result of an illness.

12. She wrote Paula a letter, relating in great detail the story of Paula's life and hers.

13. Allende hoped Paula would read the letter when she recovered from her coma, but Paula never regained consciousness.

14. Greatly saddened by Paula's death, Allende almost gave up writing her marvelous stories.

15. But instead she decided to create for her daughter the best memorial she could.

16. People all over the world have read Allende's book *Paula* and as a result keep her memory alive.

Unforgettable Folks

Part 2

Rewrite each sentence, replacing each group of underlined words with a possessive pronoun.

17. I really like <u>James Herriot's</u> book *All Creatures Great and Small.* _____

_____

18. <u>The book's</u> subject is the life of a country veterinarian. _____

_____

19. <u>Trisha and Maria's</u> class went to see a movie based on it. _____

_____

20. That red book over there is <u>the one belonging to me.</u> _____

_____

21. <u>The one belonging to you</u> is on the table. _____

_____

Part 3

Circle the possessive pronouns in the riddles below. Then try to solve the riddles.
(Answers are given below.)

22. You can see mine, his, hers, and theirs, but you can never see yours.

23. Nobody wanted it. First it was hers, and then it was mine, and now it's yours.

24. The more you give yours, the more others give you theirs.

25. What is it, do you suppose? The more I take from mine, the bigger it grows.

Now write two of your own riddles using possessive pronouns, and give them to a friend to solve.

26. _____

_____

_____

27. _____

_____

_____

(answers: 22: your back; 23: a cold; 24: friendship; 25: a hole)

Name _____

Unforgettable Folks

Read and Discover

Who is Stephen Hawking? He is a brilliant physicist **who** has developed new theories about black holes.

Draw a box around the boldfaced word that asks a question. Circle the boldfaced word that refers to the noun just before it.

> When the pronouns *who, whom, whose, which,* and *that* are used to introduce an adjective clause, they are called **relative pronouns**. A relative pronoun always follows the noun the adjective clause is describing. When the pronouns *who, whom, whose, which,* and *what* are used to begin a question, they are called **interrogative pronouns**.
>
> **See Handbook** Sections 17g, 17h

Part 1

Circle each relative pronoun. Underline the noun the adjective clause is describing. Draw a box around each interrogative pronoun.

1. Stephen Hawking has a disease that has left him almost completely paralyzed and unable to speak.

2. He taps out messages on a special computer, which communicates the messages with its synthesized voice.

3. What effects has this disability had on Hawking's work?

4. Stephen Hawking's brilliant mind is the only tool that he needs for the study of black holes.

5. Who knows the meaning of the term *black hole*?

6. Dying stars whose masses are great enough may collapse in on themselves.

7. They then form black holes, areas that do not allow the escape of any matter or energy, not even rays of light.

8. There are many theories that attempt to describe black holes.

9. Which did Hawking think up?

Stephen Hawking studied physics and mathematics at Oxford and Cambridge in England.

10. He developed the widely accepted theory that describes *singularities*.

11. What is a singularity?

12. It is the infinitely dense point that scientists believe lies at the heart of a black hole.

13. Hawking has also envisioned shrinking black holes, whose final explosions would release huge bursts of energy.

14. There are several physicists who disagree with this theory, however.

15. Who do you believe is correct, Hawking or his critics?

Part 2

Complete each sentence by writing a relative pronoun or an interrogative pronoun.

16. Hawking has proposed many theories _____ cannot be proven.

17. _____ could prove that other universes exist next to ours?

18. Hawking has a theory _____ proposes the existence of *wormholes*.

19. _____ is a wormhole?

20. A wormhole is a tiny spot _____ connects one universe to another.

21. *A Brief History of Time,* _____ Hawking published in 1988,

    explains his ideas in relatively simple terms.

22. People _____ read this book may not understand all of Hawking's

    ideas, but they are likely to learn a great deal about the universe.

Part 3

As you revise your writing, keep in mind these tips about the correct usage of relative pronouns:
1. *Who* is used only to refer to people.
2. *That* and *which* refer to things.
3. *Which* is generally used to introduce nonrestrictive clauses. These clauses are set off by commas and provide information about the noun they describe.
4. *That* is used to introduce restrictive clauses. These clauses are not set off by commas. They give information about a noun that is essential to the meaning of the sentence.

Circle the relative pronoun that is used incorrectly in each sentence. Then rewrite each sentence with the appropriate relative pronoun.

23. My favorite chapter of *A Brief History of Time* is the one which tells about black holes. _____

    _____

24. In this section, Hawking describes what would happen to a person which flew a spaceship into a

    black hole. _____

    _____

25. The black hole's gravity, that is immensely powerful, creates forces that would compress and pull the

    spaceship out of shape. _____

    _____

26. People that watched the spaceship from a distance would see it fall more and more slowly into

    the hole. _____

    _____

Name _____

Unforgettable Folks

Read and Discover

Someone is coming across the ice!
Circle the word that refers to an unknown person.

Indefinite pronouns refer to persons or things that are not identified. Indefinite pronouns include *all, anybody, both, either, anything, nothing, everyone, few, most, one, no one, several, nobody,* and *someone.*

See Handbook **Section 17f**

Part 1

Circle each indefinite pronoun in these sentences.

1. Does anybody know about the explorations of Sir Ernest Shackleton?

2. This British captain was the first one to locate the South Magnetic Pole.

3. In 1914 he led an expedition to cross Antarctica, a challenge no one had ever attempted before.

4. He set out in the sailing ship *Endurance* with a crew of 27, but soon everything went wrong.

5. The *Endurance* became trapped in ice far from the Antarctic shore, and there was nothing the crew could do to free it.

6. Everyone loaded the ship's supplies into lifeboats and began walking across the frozen sea, dragging the boats.

7. Shackleton and his crew walked 250 miles before they saw anything besides water and ice.

8. Finally the men reached a tiny island, but they found nothing to eat there.

Siberian ponies pulled heavy loads on one Shackleton expedition.

9. Winter was coming and supplies were running out; Shackleton knew he had to do something to save his crew.

10. Someone had to seek help, so Shackleton and five crew members sailed away in a small lifeboat.

11. Everything was against these brave sailors: they faced huge waves and violent storms, and they had little water to drink.

12. After almost two weeks of sailing, somebody saw land!

13. Shackleton landed on the treacherous coast of South Georgia Island and climbed over a mountain before he found anyone able to rescue the rest of the crew.

14. Because of Shackleton's courage, everybody was saved.

15. Few could have done what Ernest Shackleton and his crew did.

Unforgettable Folks

Part 2

Complete each sentence by writing an indefinite pronoun.

16. It was more than forty years before _____ tried to cross Antarctica again.

17. A person who had been _____ of Shackleton's original team members backed a new expedition in 1957.

18. The new team traveled by dog sled and snowmobile; _____ were very useful.

19. _____ of the snowmobiles had to be connected together by cable.

20. That way, if _____ fell into a crevasse in the ice, the cable could be used for a rescue.

21. _____ went well on this expedition.

22. The team had several close calls, but _____ stopped them from traveling the 2,158 miles.

Part 3

Circle the indefinite pronoun in each sentence. Then write the answer to each clue. Each answer appears in this lesson.

23. Thanks to his bravery, everyone on the expedition survived.

    __ __ __ __ __ __ __ __ __
    10   12   2   7

24. Before Shackleton found it in 1908, no one had determined its location.

    __ __ __ __ __ __ __
             8 5

    __ __ __ __ __ __ __
       6   13   9

    __ __ __
    4   11

25. All should agree that this was a good name for Shackleton's ship.

    __ __ __ __ __ __ __ __ __
    3   14   1

Use the numbered letters to answer this question:

What was the name of the tiny island where most of Shackleton's crew awaited rescue?

__ __ __ __ __ __ __ __   __ __ __ __ __ __
1 2 3 4 5 6 7 8   9 10 11 12 13 14

Name _____

Unforgettable Folks

Read and Discover

The Two Fridas is a colorful, memorable painting.
Circle the two words that describe the painting. Draw a box around the short word that comes right before these words.

Adjectives describe nouns and pronouns. Some adjectives, like *colorful* and *memorable*, **describe** or tell **what kind**. Others, like *many* and *six,* tell **how many**. The **articles** *a, an,* and *the* are also adjectives.

See Handbook Section 16

Part 1

Circle each adjective that tells *what kind*. Underline each adjective that tells *how many*. Draw a box around each article. Finally, draw a star above the noun each adjective describes.

1. Frida Kahlo was an important modern painter.

2. As a young child in Mexico, much of her creative life was spent in bed; she was stricken with polio, which left her with a weak right leg.

3. As a teenager, while a passenger on a bus, Kahlo was in a dreadful accident.

4. The terrible injuries left her in continuous pain.

5. Several months after the accident, Kahlo began painting.

6. Her vivid paintings, mostly self-portraits that dealt with feminist issues, expressed her pain as well as her joy in life.

7. In 1929 she married the famous muralist Diego Rivera.

8. Under his guidance she became a skillful painter.

9. Kahlo painted many portraits of herself over the years.

10. In one self-portrait, twisted roots grow from her body.

11. Another self-portrait shows her head on the body of a wounded deer.

12. In addition to her self-portraits, Kahlo created precise, detailed images of individual events on canvas.

13. Kahlo's paintings can evoke strong emotions.

14. Over the course of her short career, Kahlo made about two hundred paintings that told the story of her life.

15. As Kahlo gained importance as a leading Mexican artist, her paintings were classified as national treasures by the government of Mexico.

Frida Kahlo used images from traditional Mexican art in many of her paintings.

Part 2

Complete these sentences with adjectives from the word bank, or use your own words.

memorable	straight	happy	imaginative	zany
curly	strange	flowing	bright	blue
green	beautiful	pleasant	angry	a
brown	curious	frizzy	pale	an

16. If I were painting a self-portrait, it would be ____ _____ painting.

17. I would use _____ colors.

18. In the painting, I would have _____ hair.

19. My eyes would be _____.

20   I would have ____ _____ expression.

21. The background would be _____.

Part 3

Circle four adjectives and four nouns in the puzzle. Then write each word in the correct group.

A	R	T	M	X	Z	T	P
A	P	U	U	T	L	E	R
Z	A	C	R	H	X	R	U
X	I	Z	A	E	H	R	S
B	N	E	L	X	Z	I	Z
G	T	I	I	Q	O	B	P
N	E	R	S	X	Z	L	K
T	R	Q	T	V	E	E	X
F	A	M	O	U	S	P	T
A	C	C	I	D	E	N	T
P	S	E	V	E	R	A	L

Adjectives

22. _____

23. _____

24. _____

25. _____

Nouns

26. _____

27. _____

28. _____

29. _____

Now choose at least one noun and one or more adjectives and write a sentence about Frida Kahlo.

30. _____

_____

_____

Name _____

Unforgettable Folks

Read and Discover

This is a picture of Mary Patten.
That ship is a replica of the one she commanded.

Circle the word that modifies the noun *ship* and tells *which one*. Underline the word that stands for the noun *picture*.

This, these, that, and *those* are **demonstratives**. Demonstrative adjectives describe nouns and tell which one. Demonstrative pronouns take the place of nouns. *This* and *these* refer to a thing or things close by. *That* and *those* refer to a thing or things farther away. **Remember to use this information when you speak, too.**

See Handbook Sections 16, 17i

Part 1

Circle each demonstrative adjective. Underline each demonstrative pronoun. Draw a box around each noun the demonstrative modifies or replaces.

1. This is an old map of San Francisco Bay.

2. Fast-sailing clipper ships from New York used to dock in that bay.

3. Those ships carried supplies to California during the Gold Rush, which began in 1849.

4. The sea route was 15,000 miles long, but clipper ships could cover that distance much faster than wagons could travel 3,000 miles overland to San Francisco.

5. In 1856 Captain Patten, of the clipper ship *Neptune's Car,* took his 18-year-old wife on this perilous journey.

6. That was not their first voyage together; she had traveled with him around the world and was an expert sailor.

7. Early in the trip, this brave young woman's husband became ill with tuberculosis.

8. That terrible disease was common in the nineteenth century.

9. The captain became too sick to command the ship, so a new commander had to be chosen from among those on board.

10. In that era, women were not expected to command ships, but no one on the ship besides Mary Patten knew how to navigate.

11. Soon after she took command, the ship entered the treacherous seas surrounding Cape Horn; this was the most dangerous part of the journey.

12. A series of terrible storms battered the ship; the crew had never seen gales like those before.

13. To avoid the storms, Mary Patten dared to sail into freezing Antarctic waters, and that risk paid off.

14. Patten guided the *Neptune's Car* to San Francisco, and the crew called her a hero for this achievement.

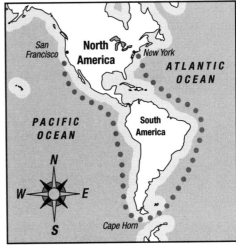

Mary Patten sailed a clipper ship around Cape Horn in the 1850s.

Unforgettable Folks

Part 2

Rewrite each sentence, replacing the underlined words with a demonstrative pronoun or with a demonstrative adjective and any other needed words.

15. <u>The model I'm pointing to</u> is a replica of another clipper ship. _____

_____

_____

16. <u>The three masts shown in the model</u> would have risen one hundred feet above the deck. _____

_____

_____

17. <u>The mast closest to the front of the ship</u> is called the foremast. _____

_____

_____

18. <u>The model across the room</u> is a replica of a five-masted ship from the late nineteenth century.

_____

_____

Part 3

Authors and speakers sometimes begin sentences with demonstrative pronouns for a dramatic or stirring effect. Circle the demonstrative pronouns in the famous quotations below.

This was their finest hour.
—Sir Winston Churchill (England, 1940)

These are the times that try men's souls.
—Thomas Paine (North America, 1776)

This is my own, my native land!
—Sir Walter Scott (Scotland, 1805)

Now research what the demonstrative pronoun refers to in each quotation. The place and time the quotation was said or written may give you a hint. Write your answers on the lines below.

19. _____

_____

20. _____

_____

21. _____

_____

Name _____

Unforgettable Folks

Diagraming Understood *You*

Imperative sentences (commands) usually contain the understood *you* as the subject. When the subject is understood, write *(you)* in the sentence diagram, like this:

Light the candle.

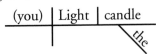

Try diagraming these sentences.

1. Set the table.

2. Light the fire.

3. Slice the cake.

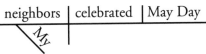

Diagraming Possessive Pronouns

Look at the way the possessive pronouns *my* and *their* are diagramed in these sentences.

My neighbors celebrated May Day.

We decorated their garden.

Now diagram these sentences.

4. My sister made a salad.

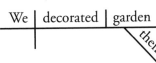

5. Alex brought his guitar.

6. Your lasagna and my chili fed everyone.

7. Our celebration pleased everybody.

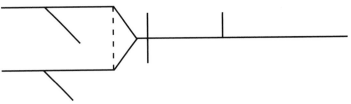

Unforgettable Folks

Diagraming Demonstrative Pronouns

You have learned that the demonstrative pronouns *this, that, these,* and *those* take the place of nouns. Look at how the demonstrative pronouns in these sentences are diagramed.

My grandfather carved **this**.

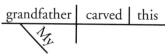

That demands courage.

8. Based on these diagrams, which sentence below tells where to place a demonstrative pronoun in a sentence diagram? _____

    a. Always place it where the subject belongs.   **b.** Always place it where the direct object belongs.

            c. Put it wherever the noun it replaces would go.

Now diagram these sentences.

9. These need repair.

10. We ate those.

11. This works better and costs less.

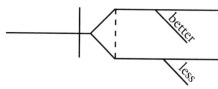

Diagraming Indefinite Pronouns

Indefinite pronouns include *anybody, somebody, both,* and *no one.*

12. Where do you think an indefinite pronoun belongs in a sentence diagram? _____

    a. where the subject goes   **b.** where the predicate goes

            c. wherever the noun it replaces would go

Try diagraming these sentences.

13. Everyone liked your song.

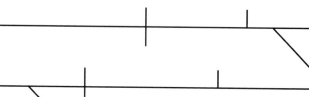

14. The music bothered no one.

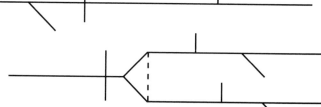

15. Somebody ate my sandwich and drank my juice.

Name _____

Writing Sentences

These sentences need help! Rewrite them so they give more information about Susan Butcher and her accomplishments. Refer to Lesson 22 if you need to.

1. Susan Butcher had some animals with her. _____
   _____
   _____

2. She was in a race. _____
   _____
   _____

3. She won three times. _____
   _____
   _____

4. She was the winner. _____
   _____
   _____

5. It wasn't an easy journey. _____
   _____
   _____

When you write a paragraph, always include a topic sentence, two or more supporting sentences that add details about your topic, and a concluding sentence. Your reader will enjoy your paragraph more if you include colorful adjectives and use pronouns and possessives appropriately. Notice how this model paragraph is written.

topic sentence

supporting sentences

colorful adjectives

pronouns and possessives

concluding sentence

> *My father is a hero to me because he was willing to risk everything to gain freedom.* After the Vietnam War ended in 1975, life became very difficult for many people in Vietnam. Late in 1976 *my* father decided to escape. Crowded together with twelve other people in a small wooden boat, *he* endured a dangerous journey across the stormy South China Sea. After being picked up by a fishing boat, *he* came to the United States to start a new life. Here *he* has built a successful business, publishing a newspaper in Vietnamese. *My* father says *he* is grateful for the freedom of speech allowed in the United States. *I* am also very glad to be living in the United States. *I will always be grateful to my father for having the courage to seek freedom.*

Writing a Paragraph

The sentences you revised on page 91 can be used to make a paragraph. Decide what order the sentences should be in. Write the paragraph on the lines below. Add other words, such as transition words, if necessary.

_____

_____

_____

_____

_____

_____

_____

Write a paragraph about one of your personal heroes. You might write about someone you learned about in Unit 3 or about another person. Refer to the model paragraph on page 91 if you need help. Be sure to include a variety of interesting adjectives. Use pronouns and possessives when appropriate.

_____

_____

_____

_____

_____

_____

_____

_____

_____

_____

Read your paragraph again. Use this checklist to evaluate your writing.

- ❏ Does my paragraph have a topic sentence?

- ❏ Have I included a variety of interesting descriptive words in my supporting sentences?

- ❏ Have I used pronouns and possessives appropriately?

- ❏ Do my sentences have correct punctuation?

- ❏ Does my paragraph have a concluding sentence?

Name _____

Unforgettable Folks

Proofreading Others' Writing

Read this passage about sea turtles' eggs and find the mistakes. Use the proofreading marks to show how the mistakes should be fixed.

Proofreading Marks

Mark	Means	Example
ℒ	delete	Sea turtles hidde their eggs in sand.
∧	add	Sea turtles hide their egg in sand.
≡	make into a capital letter	sea turtles hide their eggs in sand.
⌣	close up	Sea tur tles hide their eggs in sand.
sp	fix spelling	Sea tirtels hide their eggs in sand.
⊙	add a period	Sea turtles hide their eggs in sand⊙
/	make into a lowercase letter	Sea Turtles hide their eggs in sand.

Guardian of the Eggs

Georgias' Barrier Islands are among the few places in the united states where sea turtles can find open beach land to lay there eggs. these round eggs, about the size of table tennis balls, are wite and leathery. Its common on warm summer nights there to see a female turtle drag her self high onto the beach, dig a hole, deposit more than a 100 eggs, cover up the hole, and then slowly return to the ocean. These sea turtles that consistently brede along the southeastern koastline are called *loggerheads*.

By hiding her eggs. The mother turtle does all she can to protect her young. But without some extra help, many of the turtle eggs laid on them islandses wouldn't never hatch. Wild pigs and other animals dig up turtle eggs and eat them. Humans also dig up turtle nests It has taken speshel efforts by naturalists to protect the eggs.

Carol Ruckdeschel one of the turtle egg guardians on the Barrier Islands. each summer night for a number of years Ruckdeschel has patrolled the beachs, watching for turtles and driving off predators and human trespassers. Its not easy to stay awake ever nite for sevrel monthes, but Ruckdeschel believes that helping sea turtles excape extinction is worth missing sum sleep.

Proofreading Your Own Writing

You can use the checklist below to help you find and fix mistakes in your own writing. Write the titles of your own stories or reports in the blanks at the top of the chart. Then use the questions to check your work. Make a check mark (✓) in each box after you have checked that item.

Titles

Proofreading Checklist for Unit 3

Have I capitalized proper nouns?				
Have I written plural forms of nouns correctly?				
Have I written possessive forms of nouns correctly?				
Have I used correct forms of personal pronouns?				
Have I used possessive pronouns correctly?				
Have I used appropriate relative pronouns?				

Also Remember . . .

Does each sentence begin with a capital letter?				
Have I spelled each word correctly?				
Have I used commas correctly?				

Your Own List

Use this space to write your own list of things to check in your writing.

Name _____

Singular Nouns and Plural Nouns

Underline the correct plural form in parentheses.

1. Most people's (lifes/lives) involve some sort of challenge.

2. Challenges make our (victorys/victories) sweeter.

3. There are (touches/touchs) of greatness in all of us.

Common Nouns and Proper Nouns

Write whether the boldfaced word is a *common* noun or a *proper* noun.

4. In **Raden Kartini's** time, few Indonesian girls received an education. _____

5. Kartini rebelled against this restrictive **system**. _____

6. A **princess**, she insisted on going to school. _____

7. Kartini spent her life working for **girls'** education. _____

8. She founded a school for boys and girls in the town of **Japara**. _____

9. Many of **Indonesia's** women consider Kartini a hero. _____

Singular Possessive Nouns and Plural Possessive Nouns

Write the plural possessive noun from the sentences above.

10. _____

Write the singular possessive nouns from the sentences above.

11. _____   12. _____

Personal Pronouns

Circle each personal pronoun. Write *1* if it is a first person pronoun, *2* if it is second person, or *3* if it is third person.

13. I admire Raden Kartini. _____

14. Kartini wanted all women in Indonesia to have the same educational opportunities she had. _____

15. What would you have done in a similar situation? _____

Kinds of Pronouns

Circle the phrase that tells what kind of pronoun the boldfaced word is.

16. Mount Everest, **which** is more than 29,000 feet high, is the tallest mountain in the world.

   relative pronoun   indefinite pronoun   interrogative pronoun

17. **What** are the climbing conditions on Mount Everest?

   compound personal pronoun   interrogative pronoun   possessive pronoun

18. **Its** steepness and dangerous crevasses make this mountain extremely difficult to climb.

   relative pronoun   compound personal pronoun   possessive pronoun

19. The air **itself** is so thin that climbers take oxygen to breathe.

   indefinite pronoun   possessive pronoun   compound personal pronoun

20. **Who** are Sir Edmund Hillary and Tenzing Norgay?

   possessive pronoun   interrogative pronoun   relative pronoun

21. They are the climbers **who** first scaled Mount Everest successfully.

   compound personal pronoun   possessive pronoun   relative pronoun

22. **No one** else had reached the top and returned alive.

   indefinite pronoun   interrogative pronoun   compound personal pronoun

23. A team set up camps on the lower slopes, but Hillary and Norgay continued on by **themselves**.

   compound personal pronoun   relative pronoun   possessive pronoun

24. Hillary and Norgay made **their** final camp almost 28,000 feet up the mountainside.

   relative pronoun   possessive pronoun   interrogative pronoun

25. **Both** then began the climb to the top.

   interrogative pronoun   indefinite pronoun   compound personal pronoun

26. **Nothing** could have been more exciting than reaching Everest's peak.

   compound personal pronoun   relative pronoun   indefinite pronoun

27. Hillary wrote about **his** experiences in *High Adventure*.

   relative pronoun   indefinite pronoun   possessive pronoun

Adjectives

Circle each adjective that tells *what kind*. Underline each adjective that tells *how many*. Draw a box around each article (*a, an, the*). Draw a star above the word each adjective modifies.

28. Kate Shelley lived near a remote bridge in Iowa.

29. During a fierce rainstorm a violent flood washed out the bridge.

30. Shelley knew that a train with many passengers would soon reach the bridge.

Demonstrative Adjectives and Demonstrative Pronouns

Circle each demonstrative adjective. Underline each demonstrative pronoun. Draw a box around the word each demonstrative modifies or replaces.

31. This teenager climbed across another bridge in the heavy rain to warn the train's engineer.

32. Kate Shelley was just in time; she saved many lives on that night.

33. This is the lantern Kate Shelley carried through the dark.

Name _____

Unforgettable Folks

COMMUNITY LEARNING OPPORTUNITIES

In Unit 3 of *G.U.M.*, students learned about **different kinds of nouns, pronouns, and adjectives** and used what they learned to improve their own writing. The content of these lessons focuses on the theme **People Who Overcame Challenges**. As students completed the exercises, they learned about people who have overcome different kinds of challenges. These pages offer activities that reinforce skills and concepts presented in the unit. They also provide opportunities for the students to make connections between the materials in the lessons and the community at large.

Community Services

Find out what services for people facing challenges are available in your community. Look for rehabilitation programs, food distribution centers, shelters, immigrant resource centers, help centers for people with disabilities, and so on. Contact the organizations to find out what services they offer and whom they serve. Then create a descriptive list of helpful organizations. Make sure you include the name of each organization, its phone number and address, and how it helps members of your community. When you have finished, decide whether you think your community has services for all who need them or if other services should also be offered. Add your suggestions for new services to your list.

Any Volunteers?

Choose one organization in your community that helps people overcome challenges, such as a home for the elderly or a help center for people with disabilities. Visit or call the organization to find out about ways you might get involved with the organization as a volunteer. If possible, spend some time volunteering for the organization. Then write an advertisement to convince others to become volunteers for the organization. Include what services the organization offers, what jobs the volunteers do, and why volunteers are important. You may also want to invite a representative from the organization to talk to your class about community needs and the value of volunteers.

Local Heroes

Research people in your community, region, or state who have overcome challenges of any kind. Use what you find out to create a scrapbook of local heroes. In your scrapbook, include a brief biography of each of the people you found. Or, choose two or three of the people and write a short report about each one.

Fund-raising

Plan a fund-raiser, such as a walk-a-thon, to raise money for a good cause. Answer each of these questions to help you formulate a plan:

- What type of fund-raiser will you hold?
- How will the fund-raiser work?
- What organization or group will the money go to?
- What is your target amount for funds raised?
- How many people will you need to participate, and how much will each participant need to raise in order to achieve your target amount?
- How will you get people interested and involved in participating in your fund-raiser?
- Will the participants get any prizes or rewards for their participation? If so, what?

Write the details of your fund-raising plan in a report.

Unforgettable Folks

A Special Person

Interview a family member, friend, or acquaintance about a challenge he or she had to overcome in order to achieve an important goal. Before holding the interview, write a list of questions that you will ask. Take notes during the interview to record the person's responses. After the interview, write a descriptive paragraph about the challenge the person faced and how he or she overcame it.

Work That Helps

Learn about and list some of the job opportunities available for people who want to help others overcome challenges. Look for jobs in education, medicine and science, and social work. Then learn more about one job that interests you. Find out what skills are required for the job, how to get the training required to do the job, and what the job responsibilities are. Use the planner that follows to help you find and organize the information.

Job Information

People/Organizations to call for information:

_____

_____

_____

_____

Information given:

_____

_____

_____

Training needed:

_____

_____

_____

_____

Where to get the training/how long it takes:

_____

_____

_____

_____

Special skills needed/suggested:

_____

_____

_____

Job responsibilities:

_____

_____

_____

Other information:

_____

_____

Name _____

Unforgettable Folks

Read and Discover

The heart is an extraordinary organ.
It pumps blood to all parts of the body.

Underline the verb that shows action. Draw a box around the direct object in that sentence. Circle the verb that links the subject of the sentence to words in the predicate that rename and describe it.

An **action verb** shows action. It usually tells what the subject of a clause is doing, will do, or did. An action verb may include one or more helping verbs in addition to the main verb. A **linking verb** does not show action. It connects the subject of a sentence to a word(s) that describes or renames the subject. Linking verbs are usually forms of *be*. Some common linking verbs are *am, is, are, was, were, been*, and *will be*. The verbs *become, seem, appear,* and *look* can also be used as linking verbs. A linking verb may include one or more helping verbs in addition to the main verb.

See Handbook Sections 18a, 18c

Part 1

Underline each action verb. Circle each linking verb. Be sure to include any helping verbs you find.

1. The human heart is a powerful muscle.

2. It includes four chambers: two atria and two ventricles.

3. The hollow, muscular ventricles are below the atria and are next to each other.

4. In function, the ventricles are similar to pumps.

5. Blood enters the heart's right ventricle from the atrium above it.

6. This blood carries carbon dioxide, a gaseous waste.

7. Poor in oxygen, the blood appears dark in color.

8. The right ventricle pumps this blood into the lungs.

9. The lungs rid the blood of carbon dioxide.

10. While in the lungs, the blood absorbs oxygen.

11. Oxygen is essential to the body's natural processes.

12. The blood now appears bright red; this oxygen-rich blood enters the heart's left atrium.

13. The left atrium squeezes the blood through the mitral valve into the left ventricle.

14. From there, the heart pumps the blood to the rest of the body.

15. This blood is the supplier of oxygen to all parts of the body.

16. It also is a collector and transporter of carbon dioxide, a waste product.

17. After the return of carbon dioxide to the heart and lungs, the cycle of oxygenation begins again.

18. The discovery of this cycle was an important advancement in medicine.

19. The earliest descriptions of the heart's role in blood circulation were the work of William Harvey.

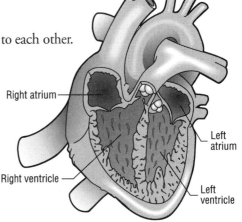

Right atrium

Left atrium

Right ventricle

Left ventricle

Your heart beats more than 100,000 times each day.

The World Outside

Part 2

Look at this diagram of the body's respiratory, or breathing, system. Use the notes to write a paragraph about how the body takes in oxygen. Underline each action verb you use. Circle each linking verb.

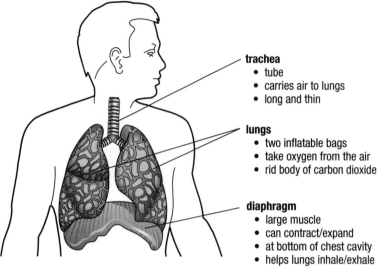

trachea
- tube
- carries air to lungs
- long and thin

lungs
- two inflatable bags
- take oxygen from the air
- rid body of carbon dioxide

diaphragm
- large muscle
- can contract/expand
- at bottom of chest cavity
- helps lungs inhale/exhale

20. _____

_____

_____

_____

_____

_____

_____

_____

Part 3

> Some verbs, such as *appear, look, smell, feel, grow,* and *taste,* can be either action verbs or linking verbs, depending on how they are used in a sentence. You can test whether a verb is a linking verb by substituting a form of the verb *be* (*am, is, are, was, were,* or *been*) in its place. If the form of *be* makes sense, the verb is a linking verb.

In the sentences below, circle each boldfaced verb that is used as a linking verb. Underline each boldfaced verb that is used as an action verb.

21. The box **looked** like a heart.

22. I **smelled** chocolate inside.

23. It **smelled** wonderful.

24. I **looked** inside and found candies.

25. I **tasted** one.

26. It **tasted** better than any I'd tried before.

Name _____

The World Outside

Read   and Discover

Some wasps **lay** their eggs on other insects.

Caterpillars **change** in their cocoons.

Which boldfaced verb says an action the subject did by itself? _____

Which boldfaced verb tells about an action the subject did to something else? _____

A **transitive verb** is an action verb that transfers its action to a direct object. (*Wasps lay eggs.*) An **intransitive verb** does not have a direct object. An intransitive verb shows action that the subject does alone. (*Caterpillars change.*) Many verbs can be either transitive or intransitive, depending on whether or not there is a direct object.

See Handbook Section 18b

Part 1

Underline each transitive verb and draw a box around its direct object. Circle each intransitive verb.

1. Most insects grow in stages.

2. They begin their lives as eggs.

3. The number of eggs and their size, shape, and color vary from insect to insect.

4. Soon a juvenile insect, or *larva,* hatches.

5. Most larvae scarcely resemble the adults of their species.

6. Many live in very different habitats.

7. Mosquito larvae swim in the water.

8. Cicada nymphs devour roots underground for as long as seventeen years.

9. Some wasp larvae live inside the bodies of other insects.

10. Ants feed their colonies' larvae with great care.

11. Some beetle larvae imitate ant larvae for a free meal.

12. Larvae eat constantly for maximum growth.

13. Some enter a *pupal* stage before adulthood.

14. A pupa's tissues dissolve inside its cocoon or shell.

15. The insect emerges from its cocoon as an adult.

16. In time, the female adult lays many eggs.

17. For many insects the entire cycle lasts only a few days.

18. A few insects have a seventeen-year life cycle.

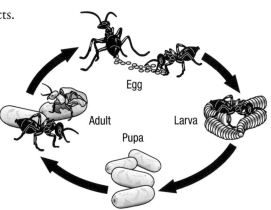

Egg

Adult

Larva

Pupa

Life Cycle of an Ant

The World Outside

Part 2

Write a verb from the word bank to complete each sentence. Then label each transitive verb *T* and each intransitive verb *I*. Circle the direct object of each transitive verb.

begins	lay	live	have	attract	fly

19. Unlike larvae, adult insects often _____ beautiful wings. _____

20. After pumping blood through the new wings, they _____ for the first time. _____

21. Some adults _____ a mate with a scent or a flashing signal. _____

22. Most adult insects do not _____ very long. _____

23. They must _____ their own eggs quickly. _____

24. Then the life cycle _____ again. _____

Part 3

> Many verbs can be transitive or intransitive, depending on whether or not they are used with a direct object.
>
>   D.O.
> The butterfly *grew* wings inside its cocoon. (transitive)
> The wings *grew* inside the cocoon. (intransitive)

Use the verbs *stopped* and *broke* in two sentences. In one sentence, use the verb as a transitive verb with a direct object. In the other, use it as an intransitive verb. Circle the direct object of each transitive verb.

25. stopped (transitive): _____

   _____

   _____

26. stopped (intransitive): _____

   _____

   _____

27. broke (transitive): _____

   _____

   _____

28. broke (intransitive): _____

   _____

   _____

Name _____

The World Outside

Read and Discover

Hot flames scorched the underbrush. _____

The underbrush was scorched by the hot flames. _____

Circle the simple subject in each sentence. Write *X* by the sentence in which the subject does something. Write *O* by the sentence in which something is done to the subject.

> If the subject performs an action, the verb is said to be in the **active voice**. (*Hot flames scorched.*) If the subject is acted upon by something else, the verb is said to be in the **passive voice**. (*The underbrush was scorched.*) Many sentences in the passive voice have a prepositional phrase that begins with the word *by* and follows the verb.
>
> See Handbook Sections 18g, 20

Part 1

Circle the simple subject in each sentence. Draw a box around the simple predicate. Be sure to include helping verbs. Write *A* if the verb is in the active voice. Write *P* if it is in the passive voice.

1. Forest fires consume trees and other vegetation. _____
2. Many animals are killed by the raging flames. _____
3. But a fire's destruction clears the way for new life. _____
4. Small trees and sickly trees have been incinerated by the fire. _____
5. Strong, healthy trees have been saved from damage by their thick bark. _____
6. Sunlight pours through the open spaces between bare branches. _____
7. New grasses, wildflowers, and seedlings sprout in the ashes. _____
8. The number of plant and animal species in a forest may actually increase after a fire. _____
9. In a forest, small fires are sparked frequently by lightning. _____
10. Dead material on the forest floor is eliminated by these small fires. _____
11. Small fires rarely cause serious harm to a forest. _____
12. This natural cycle of destruction and rebirth has been upset by humans. _____
13. Until recently, firefighters fought all forest fires, large and small. _____
14. Flammable dead materials on the forest floor were not eliminated. _____
15. In a region with much dry brush and dead wood on the forest floor, a small fire can quickly grow into an inferno. _____
16. Soon the furious flames incinerate healthy adult trees. _____
17. Today, small natural fires generally are ignored by firefighters. _____
18. They only battle dangerous ones. _____

Some pinecones release their seeds only after a forest fire.

Part 2

Look again at each sentence in Part 1 that has a verb in the passive voice. Rewrite each sentence so the verb is in the active voice.

19. _____

_____

20. _____

_____

21. _____

_____

22. _____

_____

23. _____

_____

24. _____

_____

25. _____

_____

26. _____

_____

Part 3

> The active voice communicates action briefly and powerfully. Some writers believe that the passive voice should be used only when an action is done by an unknown or unimportant agent—for example, *The clock was broken.*

Read the passage below. Notice that all of the sentences are in strong active voice. Then underline each verb in the active voice in the excerpt. (27–36)

> I kicked into the muscles of the horse. Once again it reared and snorted. Then it began to run. I didn't know what to do. Instead of running across the field to the irrigation ditch the horse ran down the road to the vineyard of Dikran Halabian where it began to leap over vines. The horse leaped over seven vines before I fell. Then it continued running.
> —William Saroyan, from "The Summer of the Beautiful White Horse"

Look over a story or a report you have written recently. Find a sentence with a verb in the passive voice. Rewrite the sentence so the verb is in the active voice.

37. _____

Name _____

The World Outside

Read and Discover

Every year, migrating geese pass over my community. In September I watched them on their southward journey. In spring the geese will fly north again.

Circle the verb phrase that tells about something that will happen in the future. Underline the verb that tells about something that happened in the past. Draw a box around the verb that tells about something that happens regularly or is true now.

A **present tense verb** indicates that something happens regularly or is true now. A **past tense verb** tells about something that happened in the past. Regular verbs form the past tense by adding -ed (*watch/watched*). The spelling of most irregular verbs changes in the past tense (*fly/flew*). A **future tense verb** tells what will happen in the future. Add the helping verb *will* to the present tense form of a verb to form the future tense (*pass/will pass*). **Remember to use this information when you speak, too**.

See Handbook Sections 18d, 18e

Part 1

Circle the verb in each sentence. (Don't forget to include helping verbs.) Write whether the verb is in the *present*, *past*, or *future* tense.

1. About sixty percent of all birds migrate to warmer places in the winter. _____

2. This fall you will probably see many migrating birds. _____

3. The arctic tern holds the world record for long-distance yearly migration. _____

4. This hardy bird spends the summer months near the North Pole. _____

5. Each fall it travels to the continent of Antarctica. _____

6. In July of 1951 scientists banded an arctic tern in Greenland. _____

7. The bird traveled 11,000 miles in three months. _____

8. In October the scientists found it in South Africa on its way to Antarctica. _____

9. On their migrations, birds travel invisible routes called *flyways*. _____

10. Billions of birds fly these routes each year. _____

11. I live under one of North America's major flyways. _____

12. Next fall I will borrow some binoculars from my grandmother. _____

13. I will watch the birds on their way south. _____

14. I bought a field guide to Western birds last year. _____

15. I will record my observations carefully. _____

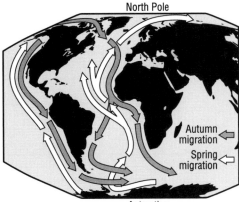

Twice a year, the arctic tern migrates from pole to pole.

The World Outside

G.U.M

Part 2

Write the past, present, or future tense form of a verb from the word bank to complete each sentence. Use a helping verb to form future tense verbs.

watch	take	have	go	photograph	swim

16. Many creatures besides birds _____ both a winter and a summer address.

17. Last year I _____ gray whales on their southern migration.

18. A gray whale typically _____ up to 16,000 miles on its way from the Arctic seas to Baja California.

19. Next year I _____ on a whale-watching expedition.

20. My uncle _____ some gray whales on an expedition last year.

21. I _____ my camera with me the next time I go whale watching.

Part 3

Use these notes about monarch butterflies to write a journal entry about phases of the monarchs' migration. Play the role of a scientist who has observed the monarchs. Use past, present, and future simple tenses in your entry.

- Monarchs—amazing insects (beautiful orange butterflies, black spots)
- Fall—fly to mountains in Michoacan, Mexico
- Spring—fly to Canada
- Journey begins in September in Canada, ends in Mexico in November (3,000 miles)
- Spend winter in Mexico—cover trees with a blanket of color
- Reproduce in spring—begin northward journey again

22. _____

_____

_____

_____

_____

_____

_____

_____

_____

_____

_____

_____

Name _____

The World Outside

Read and Discover

Before I studied ecology, I **had** not **understood** the importance of each individual in a community of living things. Now I **have gained** a better understanding of how living things in an ecosystem affect one another. Before it dies, each organism **will have affected** other creatures, eating some or becoming food for others.

Circle the boldfaced verb phrase that tells about an action that began in the past and continues today. Draw a box around the boldfaced verb phrase that tells about actions that will be complete before a certain time in the future. Underline the boldfaced verb phrase that tells about actions that were completed by a certain time in the past.

The **present perfect** tense (*have gained*) shows action that started in the past and was recently completed or is still happening. The **past perfect** tense (*had understood*) shows action that was completed by a certain time in the past. The **future perfect** tense (*will have affected*) shows action that will be complete by a certain time in the future. To form perfect tenses, use a form of *have* with the past participle of a verb. **Remember to use this information when you speak, too.**

See Handbook Sections 18d, 18e

Part 1

Circle boldfaced verbs in the present perfect tense. Underline boldfaced verbs in the past perfect tense. Draw a box around boldfaced verbs in the future perfect tense. (1–13)

Scientists **have discovered** ecosystems in very small places. Looking into the center of a bromeliad (broh MEE lee uhd), they found that a diverse group of animals **had established** a community there. Bromeliads are pineapple-like plants that trap water that **has fallen** into their leaves. This protected, watery environment is rich in nutrients. By the time it dies, a typical bromeliad **will have supported** thousands of tiny animals in the pools among its leaves.

For example, a tadpole swims in the water that **has collected** in the center of a bromeliad. The tadpole hatched yesterday from an egg a frog **had laid** a few weeks before. By the time the tadpole grows into a frog, it **will have eaten** many mosquito larvae. These larvae **have lived** on one-celled creatures floating in the water, which **have eaten** waste from frogs and other creatures. The cycle of food-web interactions **will have repeated** itself many times before the bromeliad dies.

I **have** just **completed** a report on bromeliads. In the past I **had thought** ecology was boring. This report **has changed** my view.

A universe of creatures may live their entire lives in the tiny ecosystem in a bromeliad.

Part 2

Write the present perfect form (*has* or *have* + past participle), the past perfect form (*had* + past participle), or the future perfect form (*will have* + past participle) of the verb in parentheses to complete each sentence correctly.

14. For the last ten years I _____ bromeliad plants. (study)

15. Before I looked inside my first bromeliad, I _____

     to find only a few bugs inside. (expect)

16. I was astonished by the number of creatures that _____

     their homes inside. (make)

17. Over the past decade I _____ hundreds of tiny

     creatures under my microscope. (examine)

18. By the time my research is finally complete, I _____

     thousands of animals. (count)

Part 3

Authors usually write fiction as if a story's events happened in the past. Actions happening in the "now" of the story are written in the simple past tense. The past perfect tense is often used to indicate events that came before the time in which the story is taking place.

Notice the verb tenses used in this passage.

> He felt that his luck was better than usual today. When he had reported for work that morning he had expected to be shut up in the relief office at a clerk's job, for he had been hired downtown as a clerk, and he was glad to have, instead, the freedom of the streets and welcomed, at least at first, the vigor of the cold and even the blowing of the hard wind.
>
> —Saul Bellow, from "Looking for Mr. Green"

Read the passage again, and write the verbs. Then write whether each verb is in the past tense or the past perfect tense.

19. _____   _____

20. _____   _____

21. _____   _____

22. _____   _____

23. _____   _____

24. _____   _____

25. _____   _____

Name _____

The World Outside

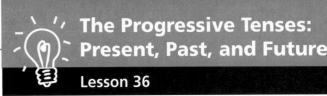

Read and Discover

At midnight last night, Rick **was playing** a video game.
Now he **is snoring** loudly.
Soon his alarm clock **will be ringing**.

Circle the boldfaced verb phrase that tells about an action that is going on now. Underline the boldfaced verb that tells about an action that was happening for a while in the past. Draw a box around the verb phrase that tells about an action that will happen in the future.

Verbs in a progressive tense show continuing action. To form the present progressive tense, add *am, is,* or *are* to the present participle of a verb (usually the present form + *ing*): *is snoring.* To form the past progressive tense, add *was* or *were* to the present participle: *was playing.* To form the future progressive tense, add *will be* to the present participle: *will be ringing.* Remember to use this information when you speak, too.

See Handbook Sections 18d, 18e

Part 1

Write *PR* if the boldfaced verb in a sentence is a progressive tense verb and *X* if it is not.

1. Birds that fly south in the fall **are listening** to their biological clocks. _____

2. Scientists **have shown** that many human activities are controlled by biological clocks. _____

3. Changes in body temperature called *circadian rhythms* **are waking** us up every morning and putting us to sleep every night. _____

4. These natural cycles can cause problems for people who **are trying** to work late at night. _____

5. Scientists **have reset** people's biological clocks successfully by having those people sit under bright lights. _____

6. Every night, biological cycles **are controlling** not only when we sleep but also how we sleep. _____

7. Before 1951, most people **believed** that the brain shut down during sleep. _____

8. That year, a scientist who **was studying** his son's sleep patterns made an important discovery. _____

9. For short periods while the boy **was sleeping,** his eyes moved back and forth quickly. _____

10. Scientists **have labeled** this phase of sleep *REM (rapid eye movement) sleep.* _____

11. During the night, you normally **move** from deep sleep to REM sleep and back several times. _____

12. Your eyes **are moving** constantly during REM sleep, and this is when most dreams occur. _____

13. Some scientists believe that REM sleep **helps** the brain with learning and emotional adjustment. _____

14. By age 70, most people **will have slept** for more than 200,000 hours. _____

15. Tomorrow at 8 A.M. I **will be sleeping** soundly. _____

16. By sleeping late, perhaps I **will be helping** my brain! _____

Part 2

Use a helping verb from the word bank plus a form of the verb in parentheses to complete each sentence. Each verb you write should be in a progressive tense.

am	was	were	will be

17. Last night I dreamed that I _____ through a huge swamp. (walk)

18. In the dream, a big mosquito _____ around my head. (buzz)

19. Its transparent wings _____ me. (tickle)

20. When I woke up, I _____ out loud. (laugh)

21. Now I _____ about my mosquito dream in a journal. (write)

22. If I have my way, tonight I _____ about something else! (dream)

Part 3

Circle the progressive tense verb in each clue. Then write the answers in the puzzle.

Across
2. Scientists are studying this state of deep sleep.
4. When you grow sleepy tonight, this rhythm will be influencing your energy level.
5. You will be doing this tonight.
7. When you look at this, you are checking the time.

Down
1. When you think, you are using this.
3. Some scientists are using bright lights to reset people's __ clocks.
6. One scientist observed that these were moving rapidly at certain times as his son slept.

Name _____

Read  and Discover

The current flows **swiftly**. Salmon must be **very** strong to swim **upstream** against it.

Which boldfaced word tells how the current flows? _____

Which tells where salmon swim? _____

Which modifies an adjective by telling how much? _____

Adverbs modify verbs, adjectives, or other adverbs. They tell **how, when, where,** or **to what extent** (*how much*). Many adverbs end in *-ly*. Other common adverbs are *fast, very, often, again, sometimes, soon, only, too, later, first, then, there, far,* and *now*.

See Handbook Section 19

Part 1

Circle each adverb. There is at least one adverb in each sentence.

1. Some animals almost always bear their young in their own place of birth.
2. Salmon hatch in streams, but they swim steadily to the ocean.
3. After several years at sea, salmon return instinctively to their native streams.
4. The journey upstream is extremely hard.
5. The water flows powerfully in the other direction.
6. The big fish swim forcefully against the current.
7. They leap high in the air over small waterfalls.
8. Finally they reach their birthplace.
9. There, females lay eggs, and males fertilize them.
10. Then the salmon collapse wearily.
11. Their lives usually end near their own birthplace.
12. Tiny salmon soon hatch and begin the cycle again.
13. Sometimes salmon cannot return to their birthplace.
14. Dams can block their journey upstream.
15. Specially built fish ladders in some streams can help salmon safely around obstacles such as dams and power plants.
16. Drought can temporarily turn a river into a dry, sandy path.
17. Many salmon are often caught for sport or for commercial use.
18. Bears thoroughly enjoy fishing in the salmon-rich streams.
19. Fortunately, hatcheries sometimes can restock streams that have been overfished.

Salmon battle upstream to lay eggs where they themselves once hatched.

The World Outside

Part 2

Circle the adverb that tells about each underlined word. Then write *how, when, where, how often,* or *to what extent* to tell what the adverb explains.

20. The ability of salmon to find their birthplace once <u>seemed</u> magical. _____

21. One scientist wisely <u>guessed</u> that smell might guide these fish. _____

22. He plugged the noses of salmon, and the fish were completely <u>unable</u> to find their streams of birth.

    _____

23. He next <u>exposed</u> hatching salmon to a certain chemical smell and let them go free in the water.

    _____

24. He spread the chemical smell in a stream, and all of his salmon <u>swam</u> there. _____

25. The sense of smell is extremely <u>important</u> to salmon. _____

Part 3

Often, adverbs concisely convey information that would otherwise need to be stated in a series of prepositional phrases. Read the sentence below, and circle the eleven adverbs it contains. Remember, adverbs can modify other adverbs. **(26–36)**

> [The river] ran seemingly straight for a while, turned abruptly, then ran smoothly again, then met another obstacle, again was turned sharply and again ran smoothly.
> —Norman Maclean, from *A River Runs Through It*

Now rewrite the sentence, replacing as many adverbs as you can with phrases. Then work with a partner to decide which version—the original or your revision—seems clearer and easier to understand.

37. _____

    _____

    _____

    _____

    _____

    _____

    _____

    _____

    _____

    _____

    _____

    _____

Name _____

The World Outside

Read and Discover

> **During a storm,** rainwater carries small particles **of soil** downhill **into** streams or storm drains.
>
> Which boldfaced word begins a phrase that tells *when*? _____
>
> Which begins a phrase that tells about a noun? _____
>
> Which begins a phrase that tells *where*? _____

A **preposition** shows a relationship between the noun or pronoun that follows the preposition (the **object of the preposition**) and another word or group of words in the sentence. The preposition, its object, and the word(s) between them make a **prepositional phrase**.

See Handbook Section 20

Part 1

Underline each prepositional phrase. Circle the preposition and draw a box around its object.

1. The process of erosion changes the shape of the earth.

2. Water, wind, and ice break solid rock into small pieces.

3. These forces remove soil and rocks from hillsides.

4. After many centuries, a mountain may be reduced to a broad mound.

5. A swift stream can carve a path through a rocky landscape.

6. Creeks in the mountains carry eroded material to wide rivers below.

7. During a flood, rivers deposit tiny grains of soil across low-lying farmlands.

8. Floods destroy homes, but they increase the fertility of the farmlands.

9. A river may spread soil near its mouth, across a triangle-shaped area.

10. The geographic term for such a region is a *delta*.

11. Some particles of eroded material eventually reach the ocean.

12. The sand grains on your favorite beach were probably transported to the sea by rivers.

13. They were possibly then carried along the shoreline by a current.

14. Finally some gentle waves carried the tiny grains onto the beach.

15. Rain in the mountains today may be moving grains of sand that someday will stick between your toes!

The force of water can change the shape of landforms.

Part 2

Fill each blank with an appropriate preposition from the word bank, or use one of your own. You may use a preposition more than once.

of	with	by	among	from	between	in	on	under	along

16. Trees and other plants hold down soil _____ their roots.

17. When people cut down trees and remove bushes _____ hillsides, rains may carry away large amounts _____ soil.

18. Farmers have developed several methods _____ soil conservation.

19. *Strip-cropping* involves planting two different crops _____ alternating strips.

20. A soil-holding crop is planted _____ a strip of land _____ grain fields to reduce the amount of soil carried off _____ the wind.

Part 3

Use the clues to help you complete the crossword puzzle with prepositions. Then circle the object (in the clues) of each preposition you wrote.

Across
1. We looked __ the canyon to the other side.
3. It was thousands __ feet wide.
4. Carolyn rose an hour __ dawn and made hot oatmeal for our breakfast.
6. We decided to start hiking __ seven A.M., while it would still be cool.
7. A narrow trail led __ the edge down into the canyon.
8. We descended carefully __ the canyon.

Down
1. __ a long time, we reached the river at the bottom.
2. The canyon walls loomed __ our heads.
5. We drank from our water bottles and splashed some water __ our faces.
6. The sound of rushing water echoed all __ us.

Now choose one or more prepositions from the puzzle and use them in a sentence about erosion.

21. _____

_____

Name _____

The World Outside

Read and Discover

Kiesha **and** Reiko went outside **because** they wanted to paint a picture of the moon in the night sky. They stared at the sky for hours, **but** they never did see the moon.

Which boldfaced word links two nouns? _____

Which links two independent clauses? _____

Which begins a dependent clause? _____

Coordinating conjunctions (*and, but, or*) connect words or groups of words (including independent clauses) that are similar. Subordinating conjunctions such as *although, because, since, so, if,* and *before* show how one clause is related to another. Subordinating conjunctions are used at the beginning of adverb clauses.

See Handbook Section 22

Part 1

Underline each coordinating conjunction. Circle each subordinating conjunction.

1. The moon often lights up the sky, but sometimes it is not visible at all.

2. The moon's appearance changes nightly, and the times at which it is in the sky vary also.

3. The moon may look like a half circle one night, and a few nights later it may look like a crescent.

4. Over 29½ days, the moon changes from a thin sliver to a full round disc and back again.

5. These changes, or *phases,* are called *new, crescent, quarter, gibbous,* and *full.*

6. People once associated the moon with unreliability because they saw it changing constantly.

7. The moon may have a reputation for unreliability, but it is actually very consistent.

8. Although the moon's appearance varies, it never turns different sides toward Earth.

9. As the moon revolves around Earth, one side permanently faces us.

10. Before lunar probes visited the moon, humans had never seen its far side.

11. The moon's phases occur because the sun's light hits different parts of its face.

12. If you look at a crescent moon through a telescope, you can see the dark part dimly lit by Earth's reflected light.

13. Because that dim light has been reflected by Earth, it is called *earthshine.*

14. When Earth passes between the sun and the moon, a lunar eclipse occurs.

15. In a partial lunar eclipse, Earth blocks part of the sun's light for a short period of time, and a portion of the moon temporarily becomes dark.

The Moon's Phases

Part 2

Complete each sentence with a conjunction from the word bank. Write *C* if you used a coordinating conjunction or *S* if you used a subordinating conjunction.

because	but	although	as	and

16. _____ the earth rotates, the moon's gravity pulls on the water in the oceans. _____

17. _____ the moon's gravity is too weak to pull water off the earth, it is strong enough to create bulges. _____

18. _____ the earth is constantly rotating, these bulges move steadily across the face of the earth. _____

19. The bulges of water create high tides _____ low tides. _____

20. Tides are highest during the new moon, when the sun _____ the moon pull the waters in the same direction. _____

21. There are also tides in the air, _____ they can be detected only with sensitive machines. _____

Part 3

Subordinating conjunctions are commonly used in proverbs, aphorisms, and other wise sayings. In many of these, the subordinating conjunction introduces a clause that tells the conditions under which something is true.

Underline the subordinate clause in each wise saying below; circle each subordinating conjunction.

When the well's dry, we know the worth of water.

Don't throw stones at your neighbors', if your own windows are glass.

Three may keep a secret, if two of them are dead.

—Benjamin Franklin, from *Poor Richard's Almanac*

Now try your hand at writing a proverb, aphorism, or wise saying of your own that includes a subordinating conjunction.

22. _____

_____

_____

_____

Name _____

The World Outside

Read and Discover

For your report on how one creature can benefit from a symbiotic relationship with another, focus on either the <u>cattle egret</u> or the <u>clownfish</u>.

Circle the word that joins the two underlined nouns. Underline another word that helps this word show how the nouns are linked.

Correlative conjunctions always appear in pairs. They connect words or groups of words and provide more emphasis than coordinating conjunctions. Some common correlative conjunctions are *both...and, either...or, neither...nor, not only...but (also),* and *whether...or.*

See Handbook Section 22

Part 1

Circle the correlative conjunctions and coordinating conjunctions in these sentences. If a sentence contains correlative conjunctions, write *COR*. Write *X* if the sentence does not contain correlative conjunctions.

1. When two animal species not only live together but also have a very close relationship, we call them *symbiotic.* _____

2. Symbiotic relationships can be either *parasitic, commensal,* or *mutual.* _____

3. Parasites may hurt their hosts or even kill them. _____

4. In a commensal relationship, the host is neither hurt nor helped by its neighbor. _____

5. Mutual symbiotic relationships involve a cycle of give and take. _____

6. For example, both the cattle egret and the African buffalo benefit from their relationship. _____

7. A buffalo might be infested with skin parasites, but the egret cleans them off. _____

8. In return, the egret gets a tasty meal of both the parasites and the insects the buffalo kicks up from the grass. _____

9. The sea anemone's sting is not only painful but also deadly to most fish. _____

10. Only the clownfish is able to build up immunity to the sting and live in harmony with this dangerous predator. _____

11. The clownfish both lures prey for the anemone and chases away fish that might damage it. _____

12. In return, the anemone provides the clownfish with protection and scraps from its meals. _____

13. If you study either biology or environmental science, you may learn about lichens. _____

14. Lichens, gray-green organisms that live on rocks and trees, appear to be plants but are actually a combination of an alga and a fungus. _____

15. Neither the alga nor the fungus can survive alone. _____

16. The alga produces food for the fungus, and the fungus protects the alga from the drying effects of sun and wind. _____

Part 2

Rewrite each sentence pair as one new, shorter sentence using the correlative conjunctions in parentheses.

17. Swollen-thorn acacia trees provide food for acacia ants. The trees provide a home for the ants. (not only/but also) _____

_____

_____

18. The ants protect the tree from harmful insects. They clear other plants away from it. (both/and)

_____

_____

_____

19. Swollen-thorn acacia trees benefit from their mutual relationship with acacia ants. Acacia ants benefit from the mutual relationship, too. (both/and) _____

_____

_____

_____

20. Acacia ants will be the subject of my oral report. Maybe clownfish will be the subject of my oral report instead. (either/or) _____

_____

_____

Part 3

Circle the correct correlative conjunction in each clue. Use information from the lesson to label each symbiotic relationship.

21. (Both/Neither) the host creature and its neighbor benefit in this kind of relationship.

_____ _____ _____ _____ _____ _____

22. The host may be (either/neither) hurt or killed in this kind of relationship.

_____ _____ _____ _____ _____ _____ _____ _____

23. The host is (either/neither) harmed nor helped in this kind of relationship.

_____ _____ _____ _____ _____ _____ _____ _____

Name _____

The World Outside

Diagraming Linking Verbs

Notice the difference between these two sentence diagrams.

Hawks eat rodents.   Hawks | eat | rodents   *Rodents* is the object of the action verb, *eat*.

Hawks are predators.   Hawks | are \ predators   *Predators* is a predicate noun that follows the linking verb *are* and renames the subject, *hawks*.

Diagram these sentences yourself. Make a slanting line after each linking verb and a vertical line after each action verb.

1. Hawks are capable hunters.

2. Small animals fear them.

3. Young animals are frequent victims.

Diagraming Predicate Nouns and Predicate Adjectives

You have learned that a predicate noun follows a linking verb and renames the subject of the sentence. Notice the way a predicate noun is diagramed.

The osprey is a **hawk**.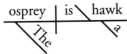

You have learned that a predicate adjective follows a linking verb and describes the subject of the sentence. Here's how to diagram a predicate adjective.

Ospreys are **powerful**.   Ospreys | are \ powerful

Diagram these sentences on another sheet of paper.

4. Carp are bottom-feeders.
5. Many mature carp are orange.
6. That osprey is hungry.
7. Its cry is shrill.

Diagraming Adverbs

You have learned how to diagram sentences containing adjectives (page 29). Like adjectives, adverbs are diagramed on slanted lines. An adverb is connected to the word it modifies. This model shows how to diagram an adverb.

The osprey circled the river **slowly**.

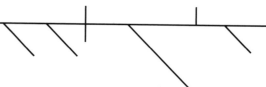

Diagram these sentences to show where the adverb belongs.

8. The big bird watched the water intently.

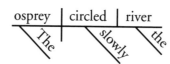

9. Suddenly it dove.

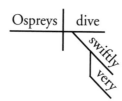

10. It deftly seized a glistening carp.

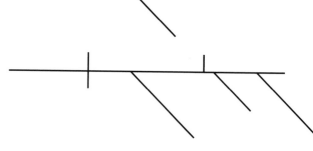

Some adverbs modify other adverbs. Notice how these adverbs are diagramed.

Ospreys dive **very** swiftly.

Use what you have learned to diagram these sentences on another piece of paper. Look back at the lesson to recall how to diagram action and linking verbs, adverbs, predicate nouns, and predicate adjectives.

11. Steelhead are large trout.
12. Many steelhead inhabit coastal streams.
13. Steelhead are migratory.
14. They are powerful swimmers.
15. I hooked a large steelhead once.

16. It fought desperately.
17. The steelhead was the uncontested victor.
18. It swam upstream.
19. I was disappointed, but I was impressed.

Name _____

The World Outside

Writing Sentences

Revise each sentence written in the passive voice so that it is in the active voice. Revise each sentence in which the coordinating conjunction and the dependent clause are misplaced so that the sentence makes sense.

1. Although springtime is still months away, days grow longer after the winter solstice. _____

   _____

   _____

2. Because animals shed their winter coats, the air temperature grows warmer. _____

   _____

   _____

3. The cycle of the seasons is demonstrated by longer days, warmer temperatures, and renewed plant life.

   _____

   _____

4. The landscape looks alive again, so new buds form on the trees. _____

   _____

   _____

5. Every year the winter solstice is celebrated by people in some cultures. _____

   _____

   _____

6. The longer, warmer days of spring are welcomed by most people. _____

   _____

   _____

A well-written paragraph has a topic sentence, at least two or three supporting sentences, and a concluding sentence. Your reader will understand your writing more easily if you use correct verb tenses, time-order words, and clear transitions. Notice how this model paragraph is written.

topic sentence —————————⌈ *Every year my family celebrates the coming of summer with a camping trip.* Last year we *went* to Yellowstone National Park in June. This year we *will go* to Crater Lake, Oregon. **Although sleeping out in the open is fun, what I like best about our camping trips is fishing.** My sister and I *have caught* trout, steelhead, and salmon in some of America's most beautiful streams. *Nothing beats wide-open spaces, clean air, and the smell of fish sizzling over the fire.*

time-order words

verb tense

transition sentence

concluding sentence —————————⌈

Writing a Paragraph

The sentences you revised on page 121 can be used to make a paragraph. Decide what order the sentences should be in. If necessary, add transition words to make the sentences flow more easily. Write the paragraph on the lines below.

_____

_____

_____

_____

_____

_____

_____

Write a personal narrative about what you do at your favorite annual event. A personal narrative is a passage about a real experience you have had in which you refer to yourself as *I*. Make sure you use verb tenses correctly. Also, make sure you use clear transitions and time-order words to help your reader follow changes in place, time, or idea. Use the paragraph at the bottom of page 121 as a model.

_____

_____

_____

_____

_____

_____

_____

_____

Reread your paragraph. Use this checklist to make sure it follows the style of a personal narrative.

- ❏ Does my paragraph have a topic sentence?

- ❏ Have I written in the first-person voice?

- ❏ Have I included time-order words and clear transitions to make my personal narrative easy to follow?

- ❏ Have I used verb tenses correctly?

- ❏ Does my paragraph have a concluding sentence?

Name _____

The **World** **Outside**

Proofreading Others' Writing

Read this passage about a mini-ecosystem that exists inside an acorn and find the mistakes. Use the proofreading marks below to show how each mistake should be fixed.

Proofreading Marks

Mark	Means	Example
✄	delete	Many creatures maked their home inside an acorn.
∧	add	Many creatures make their home inside a acorn.
≡	make into a capital letter	many creatures make their home inside an acorn.
(sp)	fix spelling	Many creetures make their home inside an acorn.
⊙	add a period	Many creatures make their home inside an acorn⊙
/	make into a lowercase letter	Many creatures make their home inside an Acorn.

More Than Just an Acorn

Would you beleive that the humble acorn is responsible for the survival of numerous creatures in the wild? If you don't. Just crack open an acorn. Inside you will find all kinds of creatures flourishing. Living off the acorn but also one another. Even before an acorn is full ripe, insects burrow or gnaw their way into its shell. Acorn weevils dig holes with their tiny, sharp teeth? After dining on the nutmeat. The females lay their eggs inside the shell. The eggs hatch, and the larvae had fed on the soft flesh within the acorn. Once the acorn falls to the ground, the now fully grown larvae emerge, squeezing through a whole they gnaw in the shell!

A whole host of creatures, looking for sustenance, may find their way into a fallen acorn. These creatures, as well as the parasites that live off them, make they're home inside it. They enter the shell through holes and cracks created by previous insect residents. Or by the fall from the tree. The nutmeat offer them nourishment, and the shell offers shelter from the sun the wind.

even decaying acorns attract a variety of creatures. Scavengers look for remains left by other insects Carnivores had gone from acorn to acorn looking for prey inside the shells Empty acorn shells serve as houses for both small insects, such as the tiny fungus beetle, and larger ones, such as the slug

Birds and animals hoard acorns for the winter by burying them in the soil. More than a few are forgotten. Some of these luckily survivors take root and grow into oak trees. in doing so they beginning a new cycle, and in time they will produce acorns that will sustain new generations of tiny creatures.

Proofreading Your Own Writing

You can use the list below to help you find and fix mistakes in your own writing. Write the titles of your own stories or reports in the blanks at the top of the chart. Then use the questions to check your work. Make a check mark (✓) in each box after you have checked that item.

Proofreading Checklist for Unit 4

Titles

Have I used colorful action verbs in sentences?				
Have I used the simple tenses, the perfect tenses, and the progressive tenses correctly?				
Have I used adverbs and prepositions effectively?				
Have I used correlative conjunctions correctly?				

Also Remember . . .

Have I written complete sentences?				
Does each sentence begin with a capital letter?				
Have I included correct end punctuation?				
Have I spelled each word correctly?				

Your Own List

Use this space to write your own list of things to check in your writing.

Name _____

The World Outside

Verbs

Circle each linking verb. Underline each action verb. Then label each action verb as *transitive* (with *T*) or *intransitive* (with *I*).

1. Nature's most celebrated cycle is the yearly cycle of seasons. _____

2. Most temperate regions experience four seasons each year. _____

3. The seasons are spring, summer, fall, and winter. _____

4. With each new season, weather and temperatures change. _____

5. In autumn the days become shorter and cooler. _____

6. Winter brings early darkness and cold. _____

7. The days lengthen again in spring. _____

8. Summer is the hottest season in most areas. _____

9. Long summer days often provide hours of sunshine. _____

10. I like the days of early summer best. _____

Verb Tense

Circle the word or phrase in parentheses that identifies the tense of each boldfaced verb.

11. In the Southern Hemisphere, summer **begins** in late December. (present/present perfect)

12. Many tourists **will visit** Australia next January. (future/future perfect)

13. Some already **have reserved** hotel rooms. (present/present perfect)

14. Here in the Northern Hemisphere, many of us **will be shoveling** snow in January.
    (present progressive/future progressive)

15. Last year snow **fell** throughout the Northeast in mid-April. (past/present)

16. During that snowstorm, we **were dreaming** of flying to South America for a long visit.
    (past perfect/past progressive)

17. A shipment of delicious grapes from Chile **had arrived** in our markets just a few days earlier.
    (past perfect/past progressive)

18. Chilean farmers **are growing** more fruits and vegetables each year for sale in the United States during
    our winter and spring months. (simple present/present progressive)

19. By the middle of next March, those farmers **will have harvested** most of their crops.
    (future perfect/future progressive)

Active and Passive Voice

Write *A* after each sentence with a verb in the active voice. Write *P* after each sentence with a verb in the passive voice.

20. In the mountains, snow is melted by the warm sunshine. _____

21. At the beach, sunbathers lie on towels and mats. _____

22. In the forest, deer browse on fresh green leaves. _____

23. In the desert, most creatures are driven from open areas by the fierce heat. _____

Adverbs and Prepositions

Draw a star above each boldfaced word that is an adverb. Circle each boldfaced word that is a preposition. Underline the prepositional phrase it begins and draw a box around its object.

24. Knowledge of the cycle of seasons was **very** important to many ancient peoples.

25. **In** some cultures, astronomers understood the relationships between the length of days and the progression of seasons.

26. These ancient scientists **also** learned to use the angle of the sun's rays to identify the longest and shortest days of the year.

27. **On** winter's shortest day, people celebrated the approach of spring.

28. In some regions people **joyfully** danced around bonfires.

29. They knew that lengthening days would **eventually** bring spring.

30. Some cultures **still** celebrate this day, which is called the *winter solstice*.

Conjunctions

Circle each coordinating conjunction. Underline each subordinating conjunction. Draw boxes around the two parts of each correlative conjunction.

31. Plants sense the changing seasons; they sprout, bloom, and drop their leaves according to the seasonal cycle.

32. Not only plants but also people can be affected by the seasons.

33. If people continually feel sad in winter, they may have *winter depression*.

34. A lack of sunlight can produce feelings of sadness, anger, or despair.

35. Because the sun shines very little in the far north during winter, people there commonly experience winter depression.

36. Since the condition is brought on by reduced amounts of sunlight, doctors renamed it *light deprivation syndrome*.

37. Doctors use either medication or bright sunlamps to treat this condition.

Name _____

COMMUNITY LEARNING OPPORTUNITIES

In Unit 4 of *G.U.M.*, students learned about **verbs, adverbs, prepositions,** and **conjunctions** and used what they learned to improve their own writing. The content of these lessons focuses on the theme **Cycles in Nature**. As students completed the exercises, they learned about things in the natural world that follow a cyclical pattern, from ocean tides to the human circulatory system. These pages offer a variety of activities that reinforce skills and concepts presented in the unit. They also provide opportunities for students to make connections between the materials in the lessons and the community at large.

Animal Migrations

Conduct research about animal migrations in the United States to find out what animals, if any, pass through or near your community as they migrate. Follow these steps to aid your research:

- Find out if you live near any major paths of bird migration, especially one of the four main flyways (the Pacific, Central, Mississippi, or Atlantic flyway).
- Learn about the routes that are followed by other long-distance migrants, such as monarch butterflies or gray whales.
- Look for migratory patterns of animals indigenous to your region or state. Keep in mind that some animals migrate over relatively short, or native, distances. For instance, mule deer migrate between mountains in the summer and valleys in the winter.

If you discover that some animals come near your community during migration, find out when they are most likely to be nearby. If possible, try to see the animals as they pass through your area.

Unnatural Cycles

In imitation of nature, people have created cyclical systems to organize or regulate human activities. For example, the repeated green-yellow-red cycle of a traffic light is used to control the flow of traffic. List as many artificial cycles as you can; describe what purpose each one was invented to serve.

The Cycle of Life

Insects develop in one of three basic ways: through simple growth, incomplete metamorphosis, or complete metamorphosis. Research the life cycle of one insect from each of these three groups:

Simple growth: silverfish, springtail

Incomplete metamorphosis: grasshopper, roach, dragonfly, cicada

Complete metamorphosis: butterfly, moth, beetle, bee, ant

Develop a chart that illustrates the descriptions of the life cycles of the three insects you have chosen.

Healthy Habits

The human circulatory system can be affected by human behavior in both positive and negative ways. Contact a doctor or another health official to talk about habits—both healthy and unhealthy—that can affect your circulatory system over time. Also find out what makes those habits good or bad for your circulatory system. Summarize your findings in a report. Or design a poster showing the do's and don'ts for optimum circulatory health. Use the Healthy Habits Worksheet on page 128 to organize your research.

The World Outside

Healthy Habits Worksheet

Person I spoke with: _____

Job title: _____

Place of employment: _____

Good habits for circulatory health: Why:

_____	_____
_____	_____
_____	_____
_____	_____
_____	_____
_____	_____
_____	_____
_____	_____
_____	_____
_____	_____
_____	_____

Bad habits for circulatory health: Why:

_____	_____
_____	_____
_____	_____
_____	_____
_____	_____
_____	_____
_____	_____
_____	_____
_____	_____
_____	_____

Name _____

The World Outside

Read and Discover

Grab **your** pan! **You're** coming to the National Gold Panning Championships with me.

Circle the boldfaced word that means "you are." Underline the boldfaced word that shows ownership.

> The words *your* and *you're* sound almost alike but have different spellings and meanings. *Your* is a possessive pronoun and shows ownership. *You're* is a contraction made from the words *you* and *are*.
>
> **See Handbook** Section 33

Part 1

Read the conversation below. Circle the word in parentheses that completes each sentence correctly. (1–16)

"It's great that we can stay at (your/you're) grandparents' house near Coloma this weekend, Alexa," said Desiree. "I hope (your/you're) going to show me some of the historic sites up there in the gold country."

"It's (your/you're) lucky day," Alexa replied. "The U.S. National Gold Panning Championships are being held this weekend. They'll be taking place on the stretch of the American River where James Marshall discovered gold in 1848."

"(Your/You're) planning to compete in the championships, aren't you?" said Desiree.

"Yes," said Alexa, "and I hope (your/you're) going to compete, too. It's a lot of fun."

"(Your/You're) going to have to help me prepare," said Desiree. "(Your/You're) first job as coach is to tell me how gold panning works."

"The original forty-niners used the panning method to separate gold dust from sand," said Alexa. "This is the way you pan for gold: First, you put sand from a stream bed into a wide, shallow pan. Then you fill (your/you're) pan with water and swirl it around, letting the sand flow out with the water. Grains of sand are much lighter in weight than flakes of gold. If (your/you're) careful and lucky, you'll be left with heavy flakes of gold in the bottom of the pan."

The National Gold Panning Championships commemorate the California Gold Rush.

"Did you find any gold in (your/you're) pan in last year's championships?" asked Desiree.

"Yes," said Alexa. "For the championships everyone starts out with the same number of gold flakes hidden in a bucket of sand and gravel. (Your/You're) given twenty minutes to pan for the gold in (your/you're) bucket. If (your/you're) the first one to find all the hidden flakes, (your/you're) the winner. Even if you don't win, you can keep (your/you're) gold flakes. You'll have a good time! (Your/You're) also going to enjoy the demonstrations of Gold Rush cooking and crafts."

Grab Bag

Part 2

Imagine that you are at the Gold Panning Championships and a friend asks you these questions. Answer each question with a complete sentence. Use *your* or *you're* in each answer.

17. Do you want to borrow my pan? _____
_____

18. Do you think I'm good at panning for gold? _____
_____

19. How do you like my panning technique? _____
_____

20. Do you think I'm going to win the Panning Championships? _____
_____

21. Would you like to be on my team? _____

22. Have you seen my flakes of gold? _____

23. Am I the first person to show you how to pan for gold? _____
_____

24. Am I a good teacher? _____

25. Are you going to beat my record someday? _____
_____

Part 3

Words like *your* and *you're* that sound alike but have different spellings and meanings are called *homophones*. Each sentence below uses one or more homophones incorrectly. Circle the misused word(s) in each one. Then write the correct words on the line.

26. The warm sand felt good on her bear feat. _____

27. He likes the cent of freshly baked cookies. _____

28. I am learning to fly a plain. _____

29. You'll hurt your eyes if you stair at the son. _____

30. For dinner we eight spaghetti with meet sauce. _____

31. First we painted the walls, and then we painted the sealing. _____

32. That dear has a beautiful white tale. _____

33. The bluejay poked a whole in another bird's nest and tried to steel eggs. _____

34. We went to here the band play. _____

Name _____

Grab Bag

Read and Discover

Many citizens of Kyoto, Japan, are very busy this week. **They're** preparing for the Gion Matsuri parade. Look at the floats over **there**. **Their** decorations are beautiful!

Which boldfaced word means "belonging to them"? _____

Which means "they are"? _____

Which means "in that place"? _____

> The words *their*, *they're*, and *there* sound the same but have different meanings and spellings. *Their* is a possessive pronoun that means "belonging to them." *They're* is a contraction that means "they are." *There* is an adverb and means "in that place." *There* may also be used as an introductory word.
>
> **See Handbook Section 33**

Part 1

Circle the word in parentheses that correctly completes each sentence.

1. The people of Kyoto begin (their/they're/there) summers with a festival called Gion Matsuri.

2. This ancient celebration has been held (their/they're/there) since A.D. 869.

3. In that year (their/they're/there) was a terrible plague that swept through Japan.

4. The people of Kyoto carried sacred carriages through the streets and prayed that the plague would depart from (their/they're/there) country.

5. The plague did end, and ever since then the people of Kyoto have remembered (their/they're/there) good fortune by staging similar parades.

6. If you visit (their/they're/there) on July 17, you will see this colorful commemoration.

7. (Their/They're/There) are two kinds of floats in the Gion Matsuri parades, the *Hoko* and the *Yama*.

8. The people of Kyoto spend long hours decorating the floats with beautiful things brought (their/they're/there) from all around the world.

9. When (their/they're/there) finished, Persian carpets, Dutch embroidery, and Chinese tapestries adorn the floats.

10. The people who create the floats take great pride in (their/they're/there) work.

11. Each year (their/they're/there) are eight Hoko floats in the parade; these look like gigantic wagons.

12. (Their/They're/There) wooden wheels are almost ten feet in diameter!

13. (Their/They're/There) pulled through the streets by groups of strong people.

14. In addition to the eight Hoko floats, (their/they're/there) are twenty-three Yama floats in the parade, each of which is mounted on long wooden posts.

15. Sixteen marchers grasp the poles of each Yama and carry the heavy float on (their/they're/there) shoulders!

Grab Bag

Part 2

Rewrite each sentence, replacing the boldfaced words with *their, they're,* or *there.*

16. The Gion Matsuri is celebrated **in Kyoto** every year. _____

_____

17. A parade of historic floats is the highlight of **the Kyoto citizens'** celebration. _____

_____

18. A few days before the parade, the floats are displayed **on two city streets.** _____

_____

19. A lottery is held to decide **the floats'** order in the parade. _____

_____

20. **The floats are** only one feature of the Gion festival, which lasts for the entire month of July. _____

_____

_____

Part 3

Find the mistakes in the dialogue in this cartoon. Then rewrite the dialogue, correcting the errors, on the lines below.

21. _____

_____

22. _____

_____

Name _____

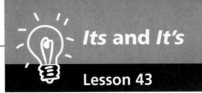
Read  and Discover

It's more fun to visit a country if you can speak the language most commonly spoken there. Often the first step in learning a language is becoming familiar with **its** alphabet.

Circle the boldfaced word that means "it is." Underline the boldfaced word that shows ownership.

Its and *it's* sound the same but are spelled differently and have different meanings. *Its* is a possessive pronoun; it means "belonging to it." *It's* is a contraction that means "it is" or "it has." The apostrophe takes the place of the missing letter(s).

See Handbook Section 33

Part 1

Circle words in parentheses to complete these sentences correctly. (1–14)

Five hundred years ago the Korean language did not have (it's/its) own alphabet. Instead, Koreans wrote with Chinese characters. Since these languages are different, (it's/its) not surprising that the Chinese characters did not match Korean words very well. This problem was solved when a special Korean alphabet was invented. (It's/Its) called Hangul, and (it's/its) inventor was King Sejong the Great, a famous Korean ruler. The king announced his invention on October 9, 1446. Koreans of many generations have shown their appreciation for the king's invention. (It's/Its) commemorated each year on October 9 by a national holiday called *Hangul Nal,* which means "Alphabet Day." School is not held on Hangul Nal; instead, (it's/its) traditional for children to compete in calligraphy contests on that day. (Calligraphy is the art of writing beautifully.) (It's/Its) possible for the winners to be awarded a considerable amount of prize money!

In many Asian cultures, calligraphy is a highly respected art form.

Bulgaria also has a day to celebrate the invention of (it's/its) language's alphabet. Have you ever heard of Cyrillic? (It's/Its) the alphabet that Bulgarian, Russian, and several other Slavic languages are written in. (It's/Its) said that in the ninth century, two brothers named Methodius and Cyril developed this alphabet. (It's/Its) name comes from the name *Cyril.* Every year Bulgaria celebrates (it's/its) culture and the legendary achievement of these brothers on a special holiday. (It's/Its) called Slavic Script and Bulgarian Culture Day, and (it's/its) held on May 24.

Part 2

Write *its* or *it's* to complete each sentence correctly. Remember to capitalize a word that begins a sentence.

15.   The Japanese have a holiday to honor writing. _____ celebrated on the second day of the new year.

16.   _____ name, *Kakizome,* means "first writing."

17.   Each family prepares _____ calligraphy supplies, including long papers and sticks of ink.

18.   _____ up to each person to choose a favorite poem or proverb to copy.

19.   _____ traditional to create calligraphy with brushes and ink.

20.   The best piece of calligraphy is hung in a prominent place for the next year so people will be inspired

to try to make their own writing match _____ elegance.

Part 3

> Charles Lutwidge Dodgson, who used the pen name Lewis Carroll, wrote two immensely popular fantasies, *Alice's Adventures in Wonderland* and *Through the Looking-Glass.* In these works Dodgson, who was a mathematician by profession, presented many humorous arguments between characters having to do with whether particular statements are nonsensical.

The passages below have been printed without apostrophes. Read each passage and add apostrophes to the contractions. Then work with a partner to decide whether what each character is saying makes sense.

"Take some more tea," the March Hare said to Alice, very earnestly.

"Ive had nothing yet," Alice replied in an offended tone: "so I cant take more."

"You mean you cant take *less,*" said the Hatter: "its very easy to take *more* than nothing."

—*Alice's Adventures in Wonderland*

"Theres no use trying," she said: "one cant believe impossible things."

"I daresay you havent had much practice," said the Queen. "When I was your age, I always did it for half-an-hour a day. Why, sometimes Ive believed as many as six impossible things before breakfast."

—*Through the Looking-Glass*

"The rule is, jam tomorrow, and jam yesterday—but never jam today."

"It must come sometimes to 'jam today,'" Alice objected.

"No, it cant," said the Queen. "Its jam every other day: today isnt any other day, you know."

—*Through the Looking-Glass*

Name _____

Grab Bag

Read and Discover

"**Whose** red balloons are these?"

"They're Kim's. **Who's** going to help me carry this Tet tree home?"

Underline the boldfaced word that means "who is." Circle the boldfaced word that shows ownership.

Who's and *whose* sound alike but are spelled differently and have different meanings. *Whose* shows ownership or possession. *Who's* is a contraction of "who is" or "who has."

See Handbook Section 33

Part 1

Circle the correct word in parentheses.

1. Anyone (whose/who's) culture bases its calendar on the cycles of the moon celebrates the new year at a different time than people in Western cultures.

2. The Vietnamese, (whose/who's) new year holiday is *Tet Nguyen Dan,* celebrate for at least three days.

3. Anyone (whose/who's) familiar with the customs of Vietnam can tell you how festive this holiday is.

4. No season is busier than Tet for merchants, (whose/who's) customers all seem to want to buy special holiday foods, gift items, and cloth for new clothing.

5. People buy and bring home Tet trees; a person (whose/who's) tree has its branches covered with miniature oranges is considered fortunate.

6. To ensure good luck in the next year, families try to make sure that their first visitor on this holiday is someone (whose/who's) rich, happy, and prestigious.

7. (Whose/Who's) home will you visit this morning?

8. Children (whose/who's) relatives give them red envelopes filled with money certainly feel lucky.

9. The youngest child is the one (whose/who's) the most lavishly rewarded, because he or she receives envelopes from older brothers and sisters as well as from adults.

Fireworks announce the new year in many Vietnamese Tet celebrations.

10. (Whose/Who's) the youngest in your family?

11. The Chinese, (whose/who's) new year traditions are similar to those of the Vietnamese, also give children money in red envelopes.

12. Almost everyone (whose/who's) celebrating Tet honors his or her ancestors with a special feast.

13. (Whose/Who's) the best cook in your family?

14. Families (whose/who's) members closely follow traditions prepare chicken, sticky rice, a special soup, boiled pork, and duck eggs for this feast.

15. (Whose/Who's) recipe did you use to prepare this wonderful soup?

Grab Bag

Part 2

Write a question to go with each answer below. Use *who's* or *whose* in each question you write.

16. My sister is sewing a new dress for herself. _____
_____

17. That Tet tree belongs to me. _____
_____

18. Your tree has the most oranges on it. _____
_____

19. Everyone in our family is celebrating the new year today. _____
_____

20. Mr. Tang is going to be their first lucky visitor. _____
_____

21. Mai-Lan is going to cook the duck eggs for the celebration. _____
_____

22. Those red envelopes of lucky money are my cousin's. _____
_____

23. I am taking my cousin to the zoo this afternoon. _____
_____

Part 3

Circle *who's* or *whose* to complete this joke. Then write an original knock-knock joke. Try it out on a friend.

Knock, knock.

(Who's/Whose) there?

Justin.

Justin who?

Justin time! I thought you would never come to the door.

24. _____
_____
_____
_____
_____

Name _____

Grab Bag

Read and Discover

Have you ever traveled **to** Texas? I have **two** friends there. My uncle lives there, **too**.

Which boldfaced word names a number? _____ Which means "in the direction of"? _____ Which means "also"? _____

The words *to, too,* and *two* sound the same but have different meanings and spellings. *To* can be a preposition that means "in the direction of." *To* can also be used with a verb to form an *infinitive*, as in the sentence *We like to celebrate holidays. Too* is an adverb and means "also" or "excessively." *Two* means the number 2.

See Handbook Section 33

Part 1

Circle the word in parentheses that correctly completes each sentence.

Abraham Lincoln signed the Emancipation Proclamation, which led to the Thirteenth Amendment.

1. General Gordon Granger of the United States Army traveled (to/too/two) Galveston, Texas, on June 19, 1865.

2. He went there (to/too/two) inform the people of Texas of the Thirteenth Amendment, which outlawed slavery in their state and throughout the nation.

3. This amendment (to/too/two) the United States Constitution had been proposed six months earlier in Washington, D.C.

4. It was soon (to/too/two) be ratified by all the states.

5. Some African Americans in Texas were almost (to/too/two) happy to speak when they heard the news.

6. They decided (to/too/two) celebrate this event by creating a new holiday.

7. They combined (to/too/two) words, *June* and *nineteenth,* to create the name "Juneteenth" for this holiday.

8. Barbecues and baseball games are (to/too/two) traditional Juneteenth activities.

9. Rodeos and parades are often held, (to/too/two).

10. (To/Too/Two) symbols that are seen in many Juneteenth parades are torches, which represent freedom, and axes, which symbolize the death of slavery.

11. In Texas, where Juneteenth is an official holiday, many people do not go (to/too/two) work on June 19.

12. Juneteenth has been an official holiday in Texas for almost (to/too/two) decades now.

13. These days, people in many other states celebrate Juneteenth, (to/too/two).

14. Some people return (to/too/two) their hometowns every year for the celebration.

15. When people celebrate Juneteenth, they commemorate an important moment in our history and have fun, (to/too/two)!

Part 2

Write *too, to,* or *two* to complete each sentence correctly.

16. "I'm going home _____ Houston, Texas, for Juneteenth," announced Pattie.

17. "I am, _____," said Angela. "My family always has a big celebration."

18. "So does mine. In fact, _____ of my cousins will be marching in the parade this year," Pattie said.

19. "That's wonderful," Angela replied. "Will you have a baseball game, _____?"

20. "Yes, we always do," said Pattie. "And I'm going _____ be in charge of the barbecue."

21. "Don't talk about barbecues," Angela giggled. "You're making me _____ hungry!"

22. "Okay," said Pattie, "I won't tell you about the _____ kinds of barbecue sauce I plan to make."

23. "My brother always assigns a job to each person in the family _____ months ahead of time," said Angela.

24. "This year he put me in charge of telling the history of Juneteenth _____ the younger children," she continued.

25. "You'll do a great job with that," said Pattie. "You know all the facts, and you're a great storyteller, _____."

Part 3

> *To, too,* and *two* are *homophones:* they sound the same but are spelled differently. These riddles are based on other homophones.
>
> Question: Why was the race rough?   Question: How much does it cost to mail perfume?
> Answer: The course was coarse.   Answer: A scent can be sent for a dollar and a cent.

Choose three of the following sets of homophones to create your own riddles. Write them on the lines below. Use a dictionary to check the meaning of any word you don't know.

to/too/two	nose/knows	vain/vein	whale/wail	bored/board
bolder/boulder	peace/piece	pair/pear	heal/heel	see/sea

26. _____

    _____

27. _____

    _____

28. _____

    _____

Name _____

Grab Bag

Read  and Discover

"First we'll march in the Carnival parade, and **then** we'll go to a party. I like this holiday more **than** any other!" said Ana as she and Keenan made their way through the crowded streets.

Which boldfaced word is used to make a comparison? _____

Which is used to talk about time? _____

Than and *then* sound similar but are different words with different spellings and meanings. *Than* is a subordinating conjunction used to make comparisons, as in the sentence *Kim is taller than Rolf*. *Then* can be an adverb that tells about time. It can also mean "therefore."

See Handbook Section 33

Part 1

Circle the correct word in parentheses to complete each sentence.

1. "At Carnival time, people put on masks and elaborate costumes, and (than/then) they parade in the streets, singing and dancing," Ana explained.

2. (Than/Then) she said, "These festivals are part of the Christian calendar in many cultures."

3. "People celebrate Carnival, and (than/then) comes the season of Lent, when it is a tradition for people to give up sweets and luxuries," she continued.

4. "I know Carnival was first celebrated in Europe and (than/then) came to the Americas," said Keenan.

5. "In the Caribbean and South America, Carnival became livelier (than/then) it was in Europe," he added.

6. "Yes, the celebration here in Rio de Janeiro, Brazil, is bigger (than/then) any other Carnival festival in the world," replied Ana.

7. "In my opinion, Carnival is more exciting (than/then) any other holiday," said Keenan.

8. "Members of the samba schools work for months trying to make costumes and floats that are more elaborate (than/then) all the others," Ana said as the two of them reached the main parade route.

9. "(Than/Then) they show off their handiwork in the annual parade," she finished.

10. Just (than/then), drum rolls filled the air and the parade started.

11. "Look at the person on that float," said Keenan. "His costume has more feathers (than/then) I've ever seen in one place."

12. "If you like his costume, (than/then) you'll really like the one on the dancer on the next float," Ana said.

13. "It's even more elaborate (than/then) the first one!" she exclaimed.

14. (Than/Then) the samba music started, and everyone began to dance.

15. "For dancing, I like samba music more (than/then) any other kind!" said Keenan.

16. "And dancing samba yourself is even more fun (than/then) watching the samba schools dance," he added.

17. "(Than/Then) let's dance!" suggested Ana.

Grab Bag

Part 2

Write a sentence that follows each direction. Use *than* or *then* in each answer.

18. Compare two costumes you have worn. _____

    _____

19. Write simple instructions for making a mask out of a paper bag. _____

    _____

20. Compare two kinds of music. _____

    _____

21. Imagine that you are watching a Carnival parade. In order, tell about three things you see pass by.

    _____

    _____

22. Describe two things you would do after attending the Carnival parade. _____

    _____

23. Describe one difference between how you celebrate two different holidays. ____

    _____

24. Think about one thing that would be easy for you to give up for Lent and one thing that would be difficult to give up. Tell why giving up the one would be harder than giving up the other.

    _____

    _____

Part 3

People often confuse words that sound similar. Decide which word should be used in place of each boldfaced word. Then write the correct word on the line.

condemned	conscience	formally	contempt	tureen	declined	declaimed	inhabits

25. Polishing our shoes and putting on our best clothes, we dressed **formerly** for my brother's graduation ceremony. _____

26. He finally admitted his guilt because his **conscious** bothered him. _____

27. Because he spoke rudely to the judge, he was held in **content** of court. _____

28. The waiter brought the soup in a large silver **terrain**. _____

29. A family of ducks **inhibits** the boathouse during the winter. _____

30. After thanking the committee for its nomination, Mr. Newhart politely **reclined** to serve as chairperson. _____

Name	

Grab Bag

Negatives

Lesson 47

Read and Discover

a. I haven't never visited a Hopi village before.
b. I don't want to distract the dancers, so I won't take any flash photographs.

Which sentence uses too many negative words? _____

Which uses negatives correctly? _____

A **negative** is a word that means "no" or "not." The words *no, not, nothing, none, never, nowhere,* and *nobody* are negatives. The negative word *not* is found in contractions such as *don't* and *wasn't.* Use only one negative in a sentence to express a negative idea. Use the contraction **doesn't** with singular subjects, including *he, she,* and *it.* Use the contraction **don't** with plural subjects, including *we* and *they.* Use *don't* with *I* and *you,* too. 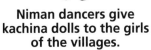 **Remember to use this information when you speak, too.**

See Handbook Section 26

Part 1

Circle the correct expression in parentheses to complete each sentence. Be careful. Some sentences express ideas that require the use of two negative words.

1. The Hopi Indians of the American Southwest wouldn't be able to raise (any/no) crops without rain.

2. (No/Any) large rivers or lakes furnish water to their high desert homeland.

3. It shouldn't surprise (anyone/no one) that many Hopi celebrations focus on rain and fertility.

4. In some of these ceremonies, dancers don't wear (their/none of their) regular clothes; instead, they wear costumes and masks representing sacred spirits called *kachinas.*

5. According to Hopi beliefs, for half the year the kachinas don't come (anywhere/nowhere) near Hopi villages.

6. Just before the start of winter, the kachinas come to visit, and they don't (never/ever) come empty-handed.

7. Kachinas are believed to bring good health and rain with them; no year could be a good year (with/without) these two things.

8. Not all kachinas arrive at the same time; chief kachinas appear in late December, but others (arrive/don't arrive) until January or February.

9. Although most kachinas are serious, (some/none) are clown figures.

10. But don't think that dances with funny kachinas have (any/no) meaning.

11. The clown's example of bad behavior shows people how (to/not to) act.

12. The kachinas (don't/don't never) leave until after the Niman Dance is held in July.

13. The Niman Dance isn't (an/no) easy thing to do: it means dancing and singing for most of a day.

14. After this "going-home" ceremony, the kachinas do not return to the lands of (the Hopi/none of the Hopi) until December.

15. The Hopi hold dances between late July and December, but none of these involve (no/any) kachinas.

Niman dancers give kachina dolls to the girls of the villages.

Grab Bag

G.U.M.

Part 2

Rewrite each sentence so that it uses negatives correctly. There is more than one way to change each one.

16. Nowhere is not more interesting than the desert of northern Arizona. _____
    _____

17. A ranger told us that nobody shouldn't never hike into no desert canyons without no guide. _____
    _____

18. She did say, though, that we wouldn't need no guide if we hiked on marked trails in a national park.
    _____

19. She also said that hiking without no hat wasn't a good idea. _____
    _____

20. I didn't want to spend no more than a dollar, so I decided to stop at a garage sale on our way through
    Flagstaff, Arizona. _____
    _____

21. The hat I found there looked as if it hadn't never been worn by no one. _____
    _____

22. Because I kept my hat on all the time, I didn't suffer from no sunstroke on none of the hikes we took.
    _____
    _____

Part 3

Fill in the crossword puzzle with negatives. Use the clues to help you.

Across
2. We missed the Hopi Snake Dance because we were ___ at the pueblo at the right time.
4. This "non-masked" ceremony ___ involve kachinas.
6. ___ photography is allowed.
7. Hopi gather snakes from the desert, but they ___ keep the snakes for long.
8. They would ___ harm the snakes because they believe the snakes help bring rain.

Down
1. Hopi dancers hold the snakes in their mouths, but they ___ worry about being bitten.
3. Usually ___ is bitten because other dancers stroke the snakes with feathers to keep them from striking.
5. ___ the arrival of European settlers nor conflicts with the Navajo have destroyed Hopi traditions.

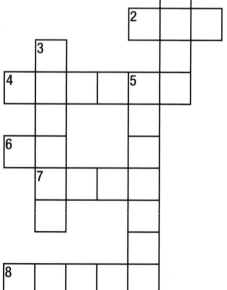

Name _____

Grab Bag

Read and Discover

I go, "I can't wait for this year's River Festival!"
Marcus is like, "*What* are you talking about?"
So then Janisa goes, "It's a really big festival in Wichita, Kansas."

Has this conversation been written in formal language or informal language?_____ Cross out the words that indicate that someone is speaking. Write *said* above the words you crossed out.

> **Go** and **went** mean "move(d)." **Is like** means "resembles something." **All** means "the total of something." In your written work and in polite conversation, avoid using *goes, is all,* or *is like* to mean "said." Also be careful not to insert the word *like* where it doesn't belong, as in the sentence *This is, like, the best festival of the year.* 📢 **Remember to use this information when you speak, too.**
>
> **See Handbook Section 32**

Part 1

Cross out *go, went, all,* or *like* if these words are used incorrectly. (If the word *was* is part of the incorrect expression, cross that out also.) (1–15)

Janisa was like, "My family goes to Wichita each spring to see the festival. We can't stay for the whole thing, though; it lasts for, like, a week or more."

Marcus was all, "What do they do for a whole week?"

Then I go, "You wouldn't believe all the different activities at the festival. People fly kites, build sandcastles, and race in boats made out of, like, antique bathtubs."

"But the best part is the Windwagon," Janisa added.

"What's a *windwagon*?" Marcus asked.

I was like, "It's a covered wagon with sails like the ones on boats. It moves by wind power."

The Windwagon sails the prairie at the Wichita River Festival.

Janisa explained, "Some inventors in the 1800s thought wind-powered wagons would, like, revolutionize cross-country travel because they'd be faster and cheaper to use than wagons pulled by animals."

I went, "The Windwagon at the River Festival is a re-creation of a huge wagon that a pioneer named Mr. Thomas tried to sail in Kansas in 1853."

"What happened?" went Marcus.

Janisa goes, "It went out of control and crashed, but, like, no one was hurt."

I was like, "Now each year the festival organizers choose an honorary leader of the festival who goes by the title 'Admiral Windwagon Smith.' The admiral dresses in a fancy uniform with, like, tons of braid and gold medals and rides in the Windwagon with a crew of high school students."

Janisa was all, "My cousin in Wichita was a Prairie Schooner Mate last year. He had, like, so much fun! I'd like to be a Mate someday."

Part 2

Rewrite each sentence to eliminate incorrect expressions. There is more than one way to rewrite each sentence.

16. Janisa wanted us to, like, enter the bathtub boat race. _____
_____

17. I was all, "Where are we going to get a bathtub to use?" _____
_____

18. Janisa went, "My grandmother has a really old one in her basement." _____
_____

19. Marcus was like, "Do you know how to turn a bathtub into a boat?" _____
_____

20. Janisa said that her cousin, like, showed her how last year. _____
_____

21. So then I go, "Let's do it!" _____

22. Marcus was, like, more reluctant. _____

23. He was all, "Won't we sink?" _____

24. Janisa convinced him that the race is, like, totally safe. _____
_____

Part 3

Many verbs, including *asked, answered, replied, added, exclaimed, remarked, suggested, began, continued, cried, whispered, grumbled,* and *yelled,* may be used to tell how a character is speaking. Using a variety of verbs for this purpose not only makes writing more interesting but also has a dramatic effect on the mood of direct quotations.

Choose verbs from the word bank to complete the sentence frame in six different ways. Notice how each verb gives the sentence a different mood.

muttered	shouted	gasped	boomed	wailed	sighed	mumbled	breathed
growled	thundered	hissed	grumbled	whispered	giggled	screeched	sniffed

25. "I know," he _____.   28. "I know," he _____.

26. "I know," he _____.   29. "I know," he _____.

27. "I know," he _____.   30. "I know," he _____.

Name _____

Grab Bag

Read and Discover

The Queen of May will **sit** on this throne.
I will **set** the flower crown on her head.
I **laid** my guidebook on the chair, but it isn't there anymore.
After all the singing and dancing around the maypole, I will need to **lie** down and rest.

Which boldfaced word means "move your body into a chair"? _____
Which means "recline"? _____ Which boldfaced words mean "place or put something somewhere"? _____ _____

Lie and *Lay* are different verbs. *Lay* takes a direct object and *lie* does not. *Lie* means "to recline." *Lay* means "to put something down somewhere." The past-tense form of *lie* is *lay*, and the past participle form of *lie* is *lain*. The past-tense form of *lay* is *laid*, and the past participle form of *lay* is also *laid*. *Set* and *sit* are different verbs. *Set* takes a direct object and *sit* does not. If you're about to use *set*, ask yourself, "Set what?" If you can't answer that question, use *sit*. Also, remember that you can't *sit* anything down—you must *set* it down. The past-tense form of *sit* is *sat* and the past participle form (the form used with *have*) is also *sat*. *Set* is one of the few verbs that does not change in past or past participle form. **Remember to use this information when you speak, too.**

See Handbook Section 32

Part 1

Underline the word in parentheses that correctly completes each sentence.

1. You have (laid/lain) in bed all morning.

2. Come with me and (lie/lay) flowers by the paths in a village called Padstow in Cornwall, Great Britain.

3. Yesterday you (lay/laid) on the couch all day watching cartoons and music videos.

4. May Day will be here soon, and we should not (sit/set) at home and miss the festivities.

5. Did you see where I (sit/set) the letter from Aunt Ethel?

6. She wants us to visit her in Padstow, and if we will (sit/set) in the least expensive seats, she will pay our way.

7. I have (sat/set) a brochure about the Padstow 'Obby 'Oss celebration on the table.

8. You should read it while you (lie/lay) on the sofa.

9. It tells how a huge hobby horse dances in the streets on May Day, while people stand or (sit/set) and watch.

10. The Hobby Horse (lays/lies) down and "dies" many times during its strange dance.

11. Finally, late in the evening, this creature is (lay/laid) to rest.

12. According to the brochure I (sat/set) on the table, the dance recalls an occasion in the fourteenth century when raiders from France were frightened off by a hobby horse at the entrance to the town's harbor.

13. Other traditions, such as the dancing and (laying/lying) the Hobby Horse to rest, have become a part of local May Day celebrations over the centuries.

14. If you will stop (laying/lying) in bed and start packing, we can see some of these traditions for ourselves.

Grab Bag

Part 2

Rewrite each sentence using a form of *sit, set, lie,* or *lay.* There is more than one way to rewrite each sentence.

15. Miguel placed flower garlands on the path. _____

_____

16. He took a seat nearby and began talking with another tourist. _____

_____

17. His sister Lupe told him about the food she had put inside the picnic basket. _____

_____

18. Then Lupe put the basket down in a protected place and began to dance around the maypole.

_____

_____

19. Miguel had already placed his backpack in a safe place, so he joined the dance, too. _____

_____

_____

20. As the day wore on, Miguel's feet and legs became very sore. He began to wish he could recline.

_____

_____

21. Finally the musicians put down their instruments. _____

_____

22. Lupe invited Miguel to take a seat beside her on the bench. _____

_____

Part 3

Even professional writers sometimes make mistakes with word choices. Look at the following examples from published works. Correct each sentence by replacing the boldfaced word.

23. From a book review: "Rosa roams afield while Julie **lays** and writes." _____

24. From a story about basketball players: "…they **laid** on the floor." _____

25. From an ad for bathing suits: "Choose from one or two pieces in all these exciting styles for the

beach or **laying** in the sun." _____

Name _____

Grab Bag

Read and Discover

Many cultures have **holded** festivals to celebrate the middle of winter. Last year we **held** a midwinter party at my house.

Cross out the boldfaced word that is an incorrect verb form.

Many verbs are **irregular;** they do not add *-ed* in the past tense. Here are some of those verbs:

Verb	Past	Past with *has, have,* or *had*
hold	held	held
build	built	built
sing	sang	sung
bring	brought	brought
lie	lay	lain
lay	laid	laid

📢 **Remember to use this information when you speak, too.**

See Handbook | Section 18d

Part 1

Circle the correct verb form in parentheses in each sentence.

1. On the shortest day of each year, ancient Druids in Britain (builded/built) huge bonfires with a Yule log.

2. They (singed/sang) and danced around the fire to awaken the sun god, who was said to be asleep for winter.

3. They believed that this ceremony (brought/brang) back the season of spring.

4. Iroquois False Face Society members have traditionally (weared/worn) masks for their midwinter ceremony.

5. By the end of the ceremony, members will have (shook/shaken) rattles at the doors of many Iroquois homes.

6. After the False Faces have (blown/blowed) ashes around a home, they are given gifts.

7. For many years, Tibetan monks have (builded/built) enormous sculptures out of yak butter to celebrate the new year.

8. The sculptures are (litten/lit) with butter lamps.

9. After the celebration the sculptures are (thrown/threw) away to demonstrate the Buddhist belief that everything is impermanent.

10. Every winter, people in the state of Oaxaca, in Mexico, carve sculptures from radishes that have (grown/growed) into unusual shapes.

11. The ones that are (thought/thinked) to be the best are awarded prizes.

12. Have you ever (heared/heard) someone blow a wooden horn?

Hanukkah, the Jewish Festival of Lights, is celebrated with candles.

13. Each year, wooden horns are (blowed/blown) in parts of the Netherlands to chase away evil winter spirits.

14. Perhaps you have (cut/cutted) an evergreen tree to decorate as part of the celebration of Christmas.

15. In Russia, a different winter tradition involving evergreen trees has (arised/arisen).

16. For many years, Russians have (maked/made) decorating an evergreen tree part of celebrating the new year.

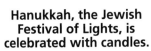

Grab Bag

Part 2

Fill in the blank with a past-tense form of the verb in parentheses. Remember to capitalize a word that begins a sentence.

17. Last Christmas Eve my neighbors came to my house and _____ Christmas carols. (sing)

18. I _____ them coming even before they _____ the bell. (hear/ring)

19. When I opened the door, I _____ that each caroler _____ a candle. (see/hold)

20. The candles _____ their way as they went from house to house. (light)

21. I _____ the carolers they sounded wonderful. (tell)

22. Then I _____ them each a candy cane. (give)

23. Unfortunately, the wind _____ very hard! (blow)

24. The carolers should have _____ warmer clothing. (wear)

25. I _____ out some hot cocoa to warm them up. (bring)

26. In return, they _____ a piece of mistletoe on my porch. (lay)

27. Then they _____ for the next house. (leave)

Part 3

Use forms of the verbs in the word bank to complete the crossword puzzle.

blow	know	bring	wear	write	build	ring

Across
2. I have ___ a short story about midwinter.
4. I should have ___ that it would be cold.
7. I should have ___ along my camp stove.
8. The wind had never ___ so hard.

Down
1. I ___ that there was no time to lose.
3. A little bell ___ in my head.
5. I had ___ my coat with the matches in the pocket!
6. I ___ up a pile of wood and lit a fire.

Name _____

Grab Bag

Diagraming Prepositions and Prepositional Phrases

You have learned that many adverbial prepositional phrases tell *when, where,* or *how.* You have also learned that most adjectival prepositional phrases describe nouns. Note how the adverbial prepositional phrase is diagramed in the first example. Then observe how the adjectival prepositional phrase is diagramed in the second example.

We celebrate the harvest **in early October**.

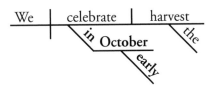

We serve fresh foods **from local farms**.

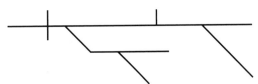

Where does the diagonal line for the preposition connect in the first example? Circle your answer.

    a. to the verb   **b.** to a noun

Where does the diagonal line for the preposition connect in the second example? Circle your answer.

    a. to the verb   **b.** to a noun

Diagram these sentences. Connect adjectival prepositional phrases to the noun they tell about and adverbial prepositional phrases to the verb they tell about.

1. I invited thirty people to the party.

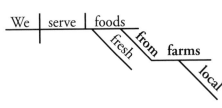

2. Margie brought a plate of sandwiches.

3. I bought twelve red hats with gold tassels.

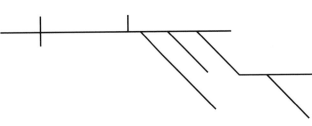

4. We decorated the table with dried leaves.

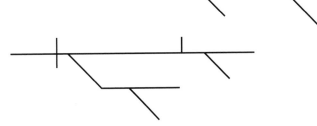

Grab Bag

Diagraming Indirect Objects

You have learned where to place a direct object in a sentence diagram. Here's how to diagram an indirect object. (The indirect object is in boldfaced type in this example.)

I sent my **cousin** an invitation.

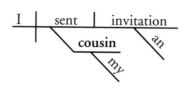

Try diagraming these sentences.

5. Giselle brought me a huge pumpkin.

6. I lent Giovanni my binoculars.

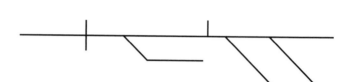

7. He gave me some lettuce seeds.

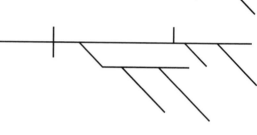

8. Colleen gave the muddy puppy a good bath.

Diagraming Sentences with *There*

When the word *there* is used to begin a sentence, place it on a separate line above the subject.

There are ripe tomatoes on the vine.

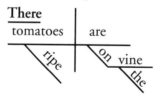

Diagram these sentences.

9. There are apples in the orchard.

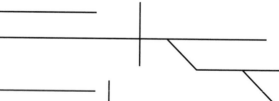

10. There is a bee on your watermelon!

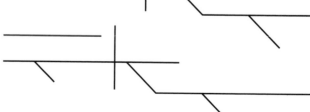

Name

Grab Bag

Writing Sentences

These sentences need your help. Rewrite each one so that homophones, problem words, and irregular verbs are used correctly.

1. So join in our Arbor Day celebration: the tiny seedling your about to plant may grow even taller then those trees one day. _____
_____

2. People planted more then one million trees on the first Arbor Day, in 1872. _____
_____

3. Now its celebrated in like most states of the United States. _____
_____

4. Arbor Day is a holiday when everyone is encouraged too plant a tree. _____
_____

5. A Nebraska settler who's name was Julius Sterling Morton first came up with the idea for this holiday.
_____
_____

6. Imagine how tall the trees planted on that first Arbor Day have growed! _____
_____

An informative paragraph's purpose is to inform readers. It should contain several interesting facts about a particular topic. The paragraph begins with an introductory sentence and ends with a concluding sentence. In between are sentences providing more information about the topic. Read this informative paragraph.

introductory sentence

sentences that give more information about the topic

concluding sentence

For people who love to eat clams, there is no event quite as wonderful as the annual Clam Festival in Pismo Beach, California. This festival, held on the third weekend of February, lures visitors to "The Clam Capital of the World" with the promise of free clam chowder on the municipal pier on Sunday as well as an amazing array of clam delicacies served up by local chefs. The festival is not just about eating, however. Featured activities include sack races on the beach, kite flying, a Saturday morning parade, a fishing derby, sand casting, and an art show, as well as a clam pitch contest and a clam shell dig. The scenic beauty of the central California coast and the generally mild February weather in the region are further attractions. **So if you hate cold winter weather and love playing on the beach and eating hot clam chowder, you should make plans now to attend next year's Clam Festival.**

Grab Bag

Writing a Paragraph

The sentences you repaired on page 151 can be reordered to make an informative paragraph. Decide which sentence is the introductory sentence, which sentences provide more information, and which sentence is the concluding sentence. Reorder the sentences, and write the paragraph below.

_____

_____

_____

_____

_____

_____

_____

Write an informative paragraph about one of the celebrations described in Unit 5 or about a holiday you and your family celebrate at home. Use the model paragraph on page 151 as a guide.

_____

_____

_____

_____

_____

_____

_____

_____

_____

_____

Reread your paragraph. Use this checklist to make sure it is complete and correct.

- ❑ My paragraph contains an introductory sentence and a concluding sentence.
- ❑ My paragraph provides several interesting facts about a topic.
- ❑ I have used homophones and problem words correctly.
- ❑ I have used irregular verbs correctly.
- ❑ I have used negatives correctly.

Name _____

Grab Bag

Proofreading Others' Writing

Read this passage about the Butterfly Parade and find the mistakes. Use the proofreading marks below to show how each mistake should be fixed.

Proofreading Marks

Mark	Means	Example
ℒ	delete	A monarch butter̶fly's wings are orange and black.
∧	add	A monạch butterfly's wings are orange and black.
≡	make into a capital letter	a̲ monarch butterfly's wings are orange and black.
⊙	add a period	A monarch butterfly's wings are orange and black⊙
sp	fix spelling	A monarch butterfly's wings are ⓢᵖawrange and black.
⌄	add an apostrophe	A monarch butterfly⌄s wings are orange and black.
/	make into a lowercase letter	A monarch butterfly's W̸ings are orange and black.

A Colorful Festival Honors a Beautiful Insect

Every october, millions of monarch butterflies begin to arrive in Pacific Grove on Californias Monterey Peninsula. These butterflies, who's ability to undertake long journeys is well known, begin they're migration south from the Canadian Rockies. And southern Alaska at the end of the summer. They leave to exape the cold winter in those regions.

Each year the people of Pacific Grove throw a kind of wellcome party for the buterflies. Called the Butterfly Parade. Children dress up in monarch butterfly costumes and than march in a parade through the streets of Pacific Grove. The festival ends with like a school bazaar, feachering arts and crafts, food, and games. The people celibrate the beauty of these butterflies that favor trees native to this area, such as the Monterey pine and the Monterey cypress Throughout the Winter the butterflies can be found in huge clusters, hanging of the branches off those trees in and near Pacific grove.

If your looking for something new and interesting to do for you're next vacation, you might consider taking a trip to Pacific Grove to help welcome the monarch butterflies. Theirs no other festival nowhere quite like the Butterfly Parade.

Proofreading Your Own Writing

You can use the list below to help you find and fix mistakes in your own writing. Write the titles of your own stories or reports in the blanks at the top of the chart. Then use the questions to check your work. Make a check mark (✓) in each box after you have checked that item.

Titles

Proofreading Checklist for Unit 5

Have I used *your* and *you're* correctly?				
Have I used *their*, *they're*, and *there* correctly?				
Have I used *its* and *it's* correctly?				
Have I used *who's* and *whose* correctly?				
Have I used *to*, *too*, and *two* correctly?				
Have I used *than* and *then* correctly?				
Have I used correct forms of irregular verbs?				
Have I used *go, went, like,* and *all* correctly?				
Have I used negatives correctly in sentences?				

Also Remember . . .

Does each sentence begin with a capital letter?				
Have I spelled each word correctly?				
Have I used commas correctly?				

Your Own List

Use this space to write your own list of things to check in your writing.

Name _____

Grab Bag

Your and You're; Their, They're, and There; Its and It's; Who's and Whose; To, Too, and Two; Than and Then

Circle the word in parentheses that correctly completes each sentence.

1. If (your/you're) looking for an interesting way to celebrate the beginning of spring, here are some ideas.

2. If you go (to/too/two) India in the spring, you might see a Hindu festival called Holi.

3. Everyone (whose/who's) participating throws water and brightly colored powder.

4. Soon (their/there/they're) all covered with the colors of spring.

5. Those of you (whose/who's) relatives live in Egypt may know about the holiday called *Sham al-Neseem,* which means "Smell the Spring Day."

6. People in Egypt have celebrated this festive holiday for more than (to/too/two) thousand years.

7. Many people go to the countryside and have picnics (their/there/they're).

8. People in many parts of Europe show (their/there/they're) joy at the coming of spring by celebrating May Day on the first day of May.

9. Each community puts up (it's/its) own maypole and decorates it, and then people dance around the pole.

10. Many people decorate their homes with flowers on this day, (to/too/two).

11. The Japanese holiday called *Setsubun* is more (than/then) just a celebration of spring.

12. According to tradition, (it's/its) also a day to drive away evil spirits.

13. If you want to follow tradition, you put sardine heads and branches on (your/you're) door on this day.

14. (Than/Then) you throw beans in every corner of the house.

15. (Their/There/They're) are also several significant holidays that are celebrated near the end of spring.

16. (Your/You're) probably familiar with Memorial Day, which traditionally is celebrated on May 30.

17. (Its/It's) a legal holiday in most states and territories of the United States.

18. This holiday has special meaning for people (whose/who's) relatives and ancestors lost their lives fighting for the United States.

19. (Whose/Who's) going to fly an American flag on Memorial Day?

20. If people fly a flag on May 30, (their/there/they're) likely to fly it on June 14 as well.

21. They will fly the flag (then/than) because that day is Flag Day.

22. Let's buy a larger flag; this one is (to/two/too) small to be seen by passersby.

Grab Bag

Negatives

Circle each error. Write *C* on the line if the sentence is written correctly.

23. The Fourth of July is nearly here, and I haven't made no plans to celebrate yet. _____

24. I haven't never had as much fun as I did at last year's celebration. _____

25. I hope nobody gets hurt by fireworks this year. _____

Words Often Misused

Cross out each incorrect use of *go, went, like,* and *all.* (If the word *was* is part of the incorrect expression, cross that out also.) Write a correct word to replace the incorrect expression, if a replacement is needed. Try not to use a word more than once as a replacement.

26. My brother Ali was like, "We need some new holidays. The ones we have are all really old."

    _____

27. I was all, "They're not all old. President's Day is only about 30 years old." _____

28. Then Ali went, "President's Day is not a new holiday. It's a combination of two old holidays, Washington's Birthday and Lincoln's Birthday." _____

29. I was, like, surprised to learn that Washington's Birthday has been celebrated as a holiday for, like, more than 200 years. _____

Lie and *Lay, Sit* and *Set*

Circle the correct word in parentheses to complete each sentence.

30. Last year Osamu (sat/set) up a snow cave for Kamakura, the Snow Cave Festival in Yohoto, Japan.

31. After he had finished, he (lay/laid) a straw mat on the floor.

32. He invited his friends and family to (sit/set) inside and talk with him.

33. After they left, he (lay/laid) on the mat, covered himself with blankets, and went to sleep.

Irregular Verbs

Circle the correct form of the verb in parentheses.

34. Loy Krathong, or the Festival of the Floating Leaf Cups, has been (held/holden) in Thailand for more than six thousand years.

35. Tiny boats called *krathongs* are (built/builded) out of banana leaves, lotus, or paper.

36. Inside the boats people place candles, incense, coins, or gardenias they have (brung/brought) to the river's edge.

37. Then people launch the boats, (litten/lit) by candles, on the river.

38. It is (thought/thinked) that a wish will come true if the krathong disappears before the candle goes out.

Name _____

Grab Bag

COMMUNITY LEARNING  OPPORTUNITIES

In Unit 5 of *G.U.M.*, students learned how to **use words that are easily confused** when writing. The content of these lessons focuses on the theme **Celebrations of Many Cultures**. As students completed the exercises, they learned about different cultural festivals and celebrations around the world. These pages offer a variety of activities that reinforce skills and concepts presented in the unit. They also provide opportunities for the student to make connections between the material in the lessons and the community at large.

Festival Calendar

Use the entertainment section of a local newspaper, fliers posted around your community, and other sources to find out what cultural events are happening in your community this season. Then create a calendar of cultural events to organize the information. If possible, arrange to go to one of the events with a friend or family member. You may also want to display your calendar in your school or community center for others to see.

Traditions

Interview an elderly person in your community who came to the United States from another country. Use his or her responses to write a report to summarize important festivals in that culture. Make sure you correctly use words that are easily confused, such as *their* and *there*.

Party Time

Think about what kind of festival you would like to see in your community, and make a plan for holding one. Try to answer these questions when making your plan.

- What will the theme of this festival be?
- Is your community known for a particular crop or product that could be celebrated?
- Is there an event in your community or region that deserves to be commemorated?
- What other kinds of themes might your festival have?
- What kind of entertainment would the festival feature? What individuals or groups would you invite to participate?
- Would the festival have food, arts and crafts, or anything else? Whom would you have provide these things?
- When and where would the festival be held?
- How would you advertise the festival? Be specific.
- How much would you need to charge to offset the costs of putting on the festival?

When you have finished working out your plan, develop a flier you could use to advertise the event. Include the important details about the event on the flier.

The Planning Stage

To hold a festival, planners must make sure they follow local laws governing community events. Research the laws and rules you would need to comply with in order to hold a festival in your community. Make sure you also find out about any permits you would need. Use the Festival Planner on the next page to help you organize what you learn.

Grab Bag

Festival Planner

Phone number of City Hall: _____

Other numbers to call: Whom to speak to:

_____   _____

_____   _____

_____   _____

_____   _____

_____   _____

Permits needed:

_____

_____

_____

Other laws/regulations to follow:

_____

_____

_____

_____

Notes:

_____

_____

_____

_____

_____

_____

_____

_____

_____

_____

Name _____

Grab Bag

Read and Discover

a. Laluah and Bonsu tricked Anansi.
b. They tricked **him**.

Which boldfaced word replaces the word *Anansi*? _____

Which boldfaced word replaces the phrase *Laluah and Bonsu*? _____

Which pronouns would you use in sentence b. if Anansi tricked Laluah and Bonsu? _____ _____

Subject pronouns include *I, he, she, we,* and *they*. (Subject pronouns are in the *subjective case*.) Subject pronouns can be the subject of a clause or sentence. **Object pronouns** can be used after an action verb or a preposition. Object pronouns include *me, him, her, us,* and *them*. (Object pronouns are in the *objective case*.) The pronouns *it* and *you* can be either subjects or objects. **Remember to use this information when you speak, too.**

See Handbook Section 17b

Part 1

Circle the correct pronoun in parentheses. Write *S* if you circled a subject pronoun. Write *O* if you circled an object pronoun.

1. My aunt used to tell (I/me) stories about Anansi. _____

2. (She/Her) says Anansi is the central folktale character of the Ashanti people of West Africa. _____

3. The stories (they/them) tell about (he/him) teach moral lessons. _____ _____

4. In some stories Anansi is a spider, and in others (he/him) is a man. _____

5. Anansi is called a *trickster character* because (he/him) is always trying to swindle others. _____

6. Anansi is sometimes clever and sometimes foolish, but either way, another character usually gets the better of (he/him). _____

7. (I/Me) remember a story in which Anansi says (he/him) wants to start a business but not do any work. _____ _____

8. Anansi's wife tells her friend Laluah about Anansi's plan, and (she/her) tells her husband, Bonsu. _____

9. Bonsu tells (she/her) that (he/him) will trick Anansi into doing all the work instead. _____ _____

10. It's not surprising that (he/him) succeeds in tricking Anansi. _____

11. Anansi's wife tells (he/him) at the end of the story that when (he/him) digs a hole for someone else, (he/him) will fall into it himself. _____ _____ _____

12. My friend Vanessa and I have started telling stories about Anansi when (we/us) baby-sit. _____

13. (We/Us) think (they/them) help kids learn the consequences of trying to cheat others. _____ _____

14. Telling these stories is fun for (we/us), too. _____

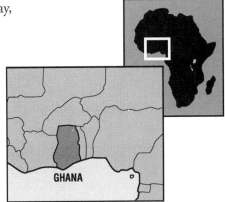

Anansi tales are popular in the West African nation of Ghana.

Part 2

Rewrite each sentence. Replace each boldfaced phrase with a pronoun. Circle the subject pronouns you write. Draw a box around the object pronouns.

15. **Anansi tales** have been carried all over the world by people of African descent. _____
    _____

16. As new storytellers have told **Anansi tales, the tales** have changed in some ways. _____
    _____

17. For example, **Anansi** has had his name changed to "Aunt Nancy" in some Caribbean countries. _____
    _____

18. **The plants and animals in a story** might change from African ones to those found in the Caribbean
    or in North or South America. _____
    _____

19. **The message of the stories** has remained the same, however. _____
    _____

20. **Anansi** always tries to take advantage of **other people or animals in the forest**, but **others** usually
    teach **Anansi** a lesson in the end. _____
    _____

Part 3

Forms of personal pronouns in English have changed over the years. Until the sixteenth century, the word *thou* was used as a subject pronoun to indicate the person being spoken to, and the word *thee* was used as the object form. Since that time, people have used the word *you* as both a subject and an object pronoun to indicate the person being spoken to. Yet many writers continued to use *thou* and *thee* well into the eighteenth century.

Read the following passage. Circle each pronoun that is no longer commonly used. Then write the modern English pronoun that would be used instead of each of these archaic pronouns.

ROMEO: By a name
I know not how to tell thee who I am:
My name, dear saint, is hateful to myself,
Because it is an enemy to thee;
Had I written it, I would tear the word.

JULIET: My ears have not yet drunk a hundred words
of thy tongue's uttering, yet I know the sound:
Art thou not Romeo, and a Montague?

ROMEO: Neither, fair maid, if either thee dislike.
—William Shakespeare, from *Romeo and Juliet*

21. _____

22. _____

23. _____

24. _____

25. _____

Name _____

Timeless Tales

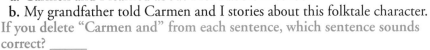

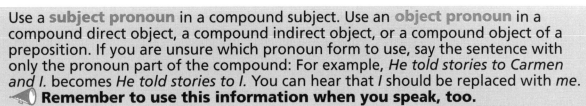

Read and Discover

  a. Carmen and I learned about Brer Rabbit in school.
  b. My grandfather told Carmen and I stories about this folktale character.
If you delete "Carmen and" from each sentence, which sentence sounds correct? _____

Use a **subject pronoun** in a compound subject. Use an **object pronoun** in a compound direct object, a compound indirect object, or a compound object of a preposition. If you are unsure which pronoun form to use, say the sentence with only the pronoun part of the compound: For example, *He told stories to Carmen and I.* becomes *He told stories to I.* You can hear that *I* should be replaced with *me*.
  📢 **Remember to use this information when you speak, too.**

See Handbook Section 17b

Part 1

Circle the correct pronoun in each pair. Write *S* if you chose a subject pronoun and *O* if you chose an object pronoun.

1. Last week Carmen, Bobby, and (I/me) visited my grandparents. _____

2. Bobby had asked me to arrange the visit because (he/him) and Carmen hoped Grandfather would tell them about Brer Rabbit for their school folklore project. _____

3. Carmen knows a lot about Anansi the Spider, and our teacher had told Bobby and (she/her) that Brer Rabbit stories are similar to Anansi stories. _____

4. (She/Her) and Bobby explained that enslaved African Americans developed the Brer Rabbit stories. _____

5. Grandfather told Grandmother and (we/us) that he heard Brer Rabbit stories when he was little. _____

6. (He/Him) and Grandmother talked about the ways Brer Rabbit outsmarts more powerful animals. _____

7. Grandfather told Carmen, Bobby, and (I/me) that these stories helped enslaved people think about outsmarting slaveholders. _____

8. Carmen asked Grandfather to tell a Brer Rabbit story that (she/her) and Bobby had never heard. _____

9. Grandfather told Grandmother and (we/us) about Brer Rabbit and Brer Fox. _____

10. (He/Him) and Brer Rabbit were always trying to trick one another. _____

11. Bobby took notes as Grandfather told Carmen and (he/him) that Fox caught Rabbit with some tar. _____

12. Grandmother and (I/me) said we had heard this story many times before. _____

13. Everyone listened to Grandmother and (I/me) as we told how Brer Rabbit got stuck to the Tar Baby. _____

14. Grandfather turned to Carmen and asked Bobby and (she/her) what Brer Fox did to Brer Rabbit. _____

15. Grandmother and (I/me) said Brer Rabbit tricked Brer Fox into throwing him into the briar patch. _____

16. Carmen laughed and said (she/her) and Bobby could guess the ending: Brer Rabbit got away easily since he had been born and raised in the briar patch. _____

Part 2

Rewrite these sentences. Substitute a pronoun for each boldfaced noun. Circle the subject pronouns you write. Draw a box around the object pronouns.

17. **Bobby** and Carmen collected stories about Brer Rabbit. _____

_____

18. Grandmother and Grandfather told Bobby and **Carmen** most of the stories. _____

_____

19. Ramona and **Carmen** read other stories in a book. _____

_____

20. Ramona discovered lots of stories about Brer Fox and **Brer Rabbit.** _____

_____

21. Bobby, Carmen, and **Ramona** gave an oral report on folktales to the class. _____

_____

22. **The students** and the teacher were especially interested in the Tar Baby. _____

_____

23. The story of how **the Tar Baby** and **Brer Rabbit** met made everyone burst out laughing. _____

_____

24. Bobby and **Carmen** acted out a few stories. _____

_____

25. Everyone gave **Bobby** and Carmen a big round of applause. _____

_____

Part 3

When *I* and *me* are used in a pair with a noun or another pronoun, the pronouns *I* and *me* should always come last (*Grandfather and me*, NOT *me and Grandfather*).

Circle the choice that completes each sentence correctly.

26. (I and Carmen/Carmen and I) presented what we had learned about Brer Rabbit to the class.
27. The class had lots of questions for (Carmen and me/me and Carmen).
28. (Me and Carmen/Carmen and I) answered all the questions we could.
29. The questions we couldn't answer gave (Carmen and me/me and Carmen) a great idea.
30. (Bobby, I, and Carmen/Carmen, Bobby, and I) are going to start up a folktales club at school.

Name _____

Read  and Discover

Scheherazade is a mythical Arabian queen. **She** narrates the stories of *The Thousand and One Nights.*

Circle the proper noun that the boldfaced pronoun replaces. Draw an arrow from the pronoun to that name.

An **antecedent** is the word or phrase a pronoun refers to or takes the place of. The antecedent always includes a noun. When you write a pronoun, be sure its antecedent is clear. A pronoun must also **agree** with its antecedent. An antecedent and pronoun agree when they have the same number (singular or plural) and gender (male or female). For example, *women,* a plural noun naming females, would never be the antecedent of *he,* a singular masculine pronoun.
📣 **Remember to use this information when you speak, too.**

See Handbook Section 17c

Part 1

Circle the antecedent of each boldfaced pronoun.

1. *The Thousand and One Nights* is a famous piece of Arabic literature. **It** was written around A.D. 1500.

2. There are about 200 folktales in this collection. **They** originally came from Arabia, Egypt, India, Persia, and other countries.

3. The first story tells of a cruel king. **He** does not trust women.

4. Each evening the king marries a new bride. Then, the next morning, he executes **her**.

5. The wise and beautiful Scheherazade volunteers to marry the king. **She** has a plan to stop his cruelty.

6. On the night of the wedding, Scheherazade's sister asks the king if Scheherazade can tell a story. **He** gives his permission.

7. Scheherazade begins telling the king a story, but she does not finish **it**.

8. The king has to spare Scheherazade's life if **he** wants to find out how the story ends.

9. The next night, Scheherazade finishes the story. Then right away **she** tells the beginning of another story.

10. Scheherazade's stories tell about genies, princesses, and talking animals. **They** are wonderful fairy tales.

11. Every night, Scheherazade tells a story to her husband, and every morning **he** lets her live so that she can finish it.

12. Scheherazade tells stories for one thousand and one nights. By this time, the king has fallen in love with **her**.

13. Scheherazade's stories are so entertaining that **they** save her life.

The story of Aladdin's lamp is in *The Thousand and One Nights*.

14. Jean Antoine Galland made it possible for people in France to enjoy *The Thousand and One Nights.* **He** translated **it** into French in the early 1700s.

15. English translations of these tales were not generally available until the 1880s. **They** were prepared by Sir Richard Francis Burton, who was a famous explorer as well as a skillful translator.

Part 2

Write the pronoun that could replace or relate to each antecedent in boldface. Capitalize a word that begins a sentence.

16. **The stories in** *The Thousand and One Nights* are hundreds of years old, but people still enjoy telling and listening to _____ today.

17. One of the most popular stories tells of **a poor boy named Aladdin.** _____ finds a genie in a magic lamp.

18. When Aladdin rubs the lamp, **the genie** appears. _____ grants Aladdin's wishes.

19. Aladdin later meets **a princess** and falls in love with _____.

20. **A cartoon film version of Aladdin's tale** was released in the early 1990s. _____ quickly became one of the most popular films ever shown.

21. **Sinbad the Sailor** also appears as a character in some of these stories. Incredible things happen to _____ during seven long sea voyages.

22. **Real Arab sailors** regularly sailed as far as China in the Medieval period (about A.D. 500–1500). Some scholars think the character of Sinbad was based on _____.

23. Another popular character in *The Thousand and One Nights* is **Ali Baba.** _____ finds a sealed cave filled with treasure.

24. To open **the treasure-filled cave,** Ali Baba stands in front of _____ and says the magic words.

25. Unfortunately, the treasure belongs to **forty thieves.** _____ will do anything to protect it.

Part 3

Ante means "before." A pronoun's antecedent should come before the pronoun so that the reader knows for sure what noun the pronoun replaces. Rewrite the paragraph below so that every pronoun has a clear antecedent. There is more than one correct way to do this. You'll want to replace some pronouns with nouns, but remember that using pronouns with clear antecedents helps the flow of your writing.

She tells about him in the story "Ali Baba and the Forty Thieves." In it, Ali Baba hides from them. While hidden in the tree, he overhears them opening it with the password "open sesame." He later says the password himself and is able to enter their treasure cave and take it for himself. They try to kill him, but he gets away with it in the end. It has remained a favorite tale for centuries, and several exciting movie versions of it have been made.

_____

_____

_____

_____

_____

Name _____

Read and Discover

Some folk heroes are based on people **who** actually lived. _____

John Henry was a real African American worker about **whom** many folk songs and stories have been written. _____

Underline the clause in each sentence that includes who *or* whom. *Which boldfaced word is a subject?* _____ *Which boldfaced word begins a clause that is the object of a preposition?* _____ *After each sentence, write whether* who *or* whom *is a subject or an object.*

Use **who** as the **subject** of a sentence or a clause. Use **whom** as the **object** of a verb or of a preposition. **Remember to use this information when you speak, too.**

See Handbook Sections 17b, 17h

Part 1

Underline the clause in each sentence that includes the words in parentheses. Decide whether the word in parentheses will be a subject or an object. Circle *who* or *whom* to complete each sentence correctly.

1. John Henry is a folk hero (who/whom) is legendary for his strength of body and will.

2. He was one of a group of workers (who/whom) a railroad company had hired to dig a tunnel in the 1870s.

3. The workers, (who/whom) had to be very strong, used heavy sledgehammers to pound drills into solid rock.

4. They were followed by other workers (who/whom) put sticks of dynamite into the holes to blast a tunnel through the rock.

5. John Henry could swing a hammer harder and faster than any of the other men with (who/whom) he worked.

6. One day a man came (who/whom) had built a steam-powered drill.

7. He claimed it could dig a hole faster than twenty workers (who/whom) used regular hammers.

8. The workers were worried: if the steam drill was so fast, (who/whom) would need workers to pound drills anymore?

9. To (who/whom) could they turn?

10. John Henry was the only one (who/whom) was willing to accept the challenge of competing against the steam drill driver.

11. The winner would be the one (who/whom) drilled a hole faster.

12. (Who/Whom) won the contest? John Henry did, but he died soon after.

13. According to legend, John Henry died of exhaustion, but the people (who/whom) witnessed the contest said he was crushed by falling rock.

14. The workers made a hero of John Henry, (who/whom) they buried with a hammer in his hand.

15. John Henry, (who/whom) came to symbolize the workers' struggle against machinery that could replace them, has been the subject of both stories and songs.

John Henry beat a machine in a race.

Part 2

Complete a question to go with each statement. Be sure to end each sentence with a question mark.

16. The folktale character John Henry was based on a real person. On whom _____

    _____

17. The real John Henry was an African American worker. Who _____

    _____

18. He was working with other laborers to build the Big Bend Tunnel and the Ohio Railroad. Who ____

    _____

19. Songs and stories have been written about him. About whom _____

    _____

20. John Henry was given the task of competing with a mechanical steam drill. To whom _____

    _____

21. John Henry won the race. Who _____

22. Workers especially admired him. Who _____

23. For many, he is an important American hero. For whom _____

    _____

Part 3

Circle *who* or *whom* to complete each quotation correctly.

No man is an island....never send to know
for (who/whom) the bell tolls; it tolls for thee.
—John Donne

He (who/whom) learns but does not think,
is lost. He (who/whom) thinks but does not learn
is in great danger.
—Kong Qiu (Confucius)

I am only a public entertainer (who/whom)
has understood his time.
—Pablo Picasso

If your lips would keep from slips,
Five things observe with care:
To (who/whom) you speak; of (who/whom) you
    speak;
And how, and when, and where.
—William Edward Norris

No! the two kinds of people on earth that I mean
Are the people (who/whom) lift and the people
    (who/whom) lean.
—Ella Wheeler Wilcox

Now write your own saying using *who* or *whom*.

24. _____

    _____

Name _____

Read and Discover

Jewish **tales** of a helpful **monster** have been told and retold for centuries. Circle the boldfaced noun that is the simple subject of this sentence. Is this noun singular or plural? _____ Underline the auxiliary verb that agrees with the subject. What form of this verb would be used if the simple subject of this sentence was *tale*? _____

The **subject** and its **verb must agree**. Add *s* or *es* to a regular verb in the present tense when the subject is a singular noun or *he, she,* or *it*. Do not add *s* or *es* to a regular verb in the present tense when the subject is a plural noun or *I, you, we,* or *they*. Some verbs have irregular forms. Singular forms of *be* are *is, am, was*. Plural forms are *are* and *were*. Be sure the verb agrees with its subject and not with the object of a preposition that comes before the verb. **Remember to use this information when you speak, too.**

See Handbook Section 18f

Part 1

Circle the simple subject in each sentence. Then underline the correct form of the verb in parentheses.

1. Stories about the golem (is/are) still told and read today.

2. According to legend, the body of a golem (is/are) made of clay and dust.

3. Only a person very learned in the ways of magic (is/are) able to bring the clay golem to life.

4. These monsters, human in form, (is/are) very strong but unable to speak.

5. One of the most famous golem stories (is/are) "The Golem of Prague."

6. At the time in which this tale is set, the sixteenth century, Jewish people (was/were) terribly persecuted in many parts of eastern Europe.

7. In the story, the rabbi of Prague, a religious leader known for his great knowledge, (creates/create) a golem to guard his people.

8. This protector of the Jews (roams/roam) the streets of the city at night, stopping crime.

In legends of the golem, a clay figure comes to life.

9. Some parts of the story (is/are) humorous.

10. The wife of the rabbi (asks/ask) the golem to carry water from the well to fill a washtub.

11. The obedient golem (carries/carry) buckets of water so fast that the tub is soon overflowing.

12. (Is/Are) the persecutors of the Jews brought to justice with the help of the golem?

13. Yes, a plot to make false accusations against the Jewish residents (is/are) revealed by the golem, who has been disguised as a night watchman.

14. The king, hearing news of the cruel plot, (issue/issues) an order protecting the Jewish people.

15. When the help of the golem is no longer needed, the rabbi (turns/turn) the giant back into clay.

16. According to legend, the clay form of the golem still (lies/lie) hidden, waiting to be brought to life if needed.

Timeless Tales

Part 2

Circle the simple subject in each sentence. Then write the correct form of the verb in parentheses to complete the sentence.

17. A book of folktales _____ the power to entertain adults as well as children. (have)

18. A favorite story of my parents _____ "Strongheart Jack and the Beanstalk," an early version of the story we know as "Jack and the Beanstalk." (be)

19. In this version, a hot desert filled with cactus plants _____ the first thing Jack sees when he reaches the top of the beanstalk. (be)

20. Then a yellow turtle in a pond _____ Jack to answer a riddle. (challenge)

21. A calico cat named Octavia _____ Jack defeat the giant. (help)

22. The prisoners in the giant's castle _____ very happy to be free. (be)

23. Any story about giants _____ my brother. (scare)

24. One of my assignments in art class this week _____ to mold a clay figure. (be)

25. _____ the name "golem" a good one for a large clay figure? (be)

Part 3

> Folktales are one way wisdom has been passed from one generation to another. *Aphorisms,* brief truths about human behavior, are another.

Read these three aphorisms from Benjamin Franklin. Underline the correct verb form in each. Then write a brief explanation of each saying's message.

26. The cat in gloves (catch/catches) no mice. _____

_____

_____

27. A word to the wise (is/are) enough, and many words won't fill a bushel. _____

_____

_____

28. They that can give up essential liberty to obtain a little temporary safety (deserve/deserves) neither liberty nor safety. _____

_____

_____

_____

Name _____

Timeless Tales

Read and Discover

a. Neither the wolf's big eyes nor its big mouth makes Red Riding Hood suspicious.

b. Fortunately, Red and her grandmother escape from the wolf in the end.

Circle the compound subject in each sentence. Underline the verb in each sentence. Which sentence has a verb that goes with a singular subject? _____

A **compound subject** and its verb must agree. If a compound subject includes the conjunction *and*, the subject is plural and needs a plural verb. If a compound subject includes *or* or *nor*, the verb must agree with the last item in the subject. **Remember to use this information when you speak, too.**

See Handbook Sections 11, 18f

Part 1

Look at the compound subject in each sentence. Draw a box around the conjunction. Then underline the correct verb in parentheses.

1. Lin and Rick (collect/collects) information about wild canine characters in folktales.

2. Wolves, foxes, and coyotes (is/are) all closely related to dogs.

3. A wolf or a coyote (act/acts) more like a dog than a fox does.

4. Native American cultures and European cultures (has/have) very different ideas about wild canine characters.

5. When a fox or a wolf (appears/appear) in a European fairy tale, it is usually the villain.

6. "Little Red Riding Hood" and "The Three Little Pigs" (is/are) two good examples.

7. Neither Red Riding Hood nor the pigs (regrets/regret) the evil wolf's death.

8. Although the real animals may be similar, the evil fairy tale wolf and the coyote of Native American tales (is/are) totally different from one another.

9. Native American stories and a favorite Mexican folktale of mine (portrays/portray) Coyote as a lovable trickster figure.

10. Greed, arrogance, or selfishness (gets/get) Coyote into trouble.

11. Fox, Bear, or all the other animals (laughs/laugh) at his misadventures.

12. But neither injury nor even death (stops/stop) Coyote.

13. The power to come back from the dead and the power to create anything he can imagine (belongs/belong) to Coyote.

14. This laughable fool or powerful creator (is/are) one of the most complicated characters in Native American folklore.

The Coyote character lived in a legendary time before humans.

Part 2

Write the correct present-tense form of the verb in parentheses to complete each sentence.

15. Lin and Alvin, a friend of hers, _____ the story of Coyote's name best. (like)

16. The Great Spirit, or Spirit Chief, _____ to rename all the animals. (decide)

17. Coyote and all the other animals _____ to line up first thing the next morning for their new names. (agree)

18. "Grizzly Bear" or "Salmon" _____ to Coyote as a new name. (appeal)

19. Coyote's ambition and cunning _____ him think of a scheme for being first in line: he'll stay up all night. (help)

20. Boasts and selfish wishes _____ from the mouth of Coyote almost all that night. (pour)

21. Finally, either laziness or just plain exhaustion _____ Coyote, and he falls asleep. (overwhelm)

22. While Coyote sleeps, the real Grizzly Bear and the real Salmon _____ their own names. (choose)

23. By the time the tired Coyote wakes up, neither "Grizzly Bear" nor "Salmon" _____ a possibility for a new name. (remain)

24. Coyote and his old name _____ to stick together. (have)

Part 3

Use information in this lesson and in earlier lessons in this unit to fill in the puzzle. Each answer will be part of a compound subject. Then circle the correct verb in parentheses to complete each clue.

Across
3. Aladdin, Ali Baba, and __ the Sailor (is/are) all characters in *The Thousand and One Nights*.
4. Either the steam drill driver or John __ (wins/win) the race.
5. The Great Spirit and the Spirit __ (is/are) both Native American names for the same deity.
6. Wolves and __ (is/are) often villains in European fairy tales.

Down
1. Bonsu and __ the Spider (goes/go) fishing together, and they try to trick each other.
2. Brer Rabbit and the Tar __ (sticks/stick) to each other.
5. Either Brer Rabbit, Anansi, or __ (makes/make) a good example of a trickster character.

Name _____

Timeless Tales

Read and Discover

The Folkways Club meets on Thursdays. **"Cinderellas from Many Cultures"** is the title of this week's discussion. **Everybody** has a different version of the story to read.

Look at the boldfaced subjects of these sentences. Circle the proper noun that refers to a group of people but does not end in *s*. Underline the story title. Draw a box around the indefinite pronoun. Do the verbs that follow these subjects agree with singular subjects or with plural subjects? _____

The **subject** and its **verb must agree**. There are special rules for certain kinds of subjects. **Titles** of books, movies, stories, or songs are considered singular even if they end in -s. (*"The Three Little Pigs"* is my little brother's favorite story.) A **collective noun,** such as *collection, group, team, country, kingdom, family, flock,* and *herd,* names more than one person or object acting together as one group. These nouns are almost always considered singular. (*Katie's <u>team</u> wins every game.*) Most **indefinite pronouns,** including *everyone, nobody, nothing, something,* and *anything,* are considered singular. (*<u>Everyone</u> likes pizza.*) A few indefinite pronouns, such as *many* and *several,* are considered plural. (*<u>Many</u> like spaghetti.*) **Remember to use this information when you speak, too.**

See Handbook Sections 17f, 18f

Part 1

Underline the simple subject in each sentence. Then circle the correct form of each verb in parentheses.

1. "Cinderella and the Little Glass Slipper" (is/are) a story with a fascinating history.

2. Almost every culture (has/have) a collection of folktales it passes from generation to generation.

3. Many (seems/seem) to have their own version of a Cinderella story, in which a poor mistreated girl wins the love of a prince.

4. My favorite folktale collection (include/includes) versions of this tale from Russia, Appalachia, Egypt, and Vietnam.

5. "Mufaro's Beautiful Daughters" (is/are) a version from Zimbabwe.

6. "Boots and the Glass Mountain" (comes/come) from Norway.

The footwear in the Cinderella stories reflects different cultures.

7. Something (is/are) unique about each version of the story.

8. Cinderella's footwear (is/are) sometimes made of glass, sometimes of fur, and sometimes of gold.

9. In some versions Cinderella makes friends with the birds, and a flock (helps/help) her with difficult chores.

10. *Grimm's Fairy Tales* (includes/include) the grisly German version, in which Cinderella's sisters cut off their toes to try to fit into her shoe.

11. But everyone easily (recognizes/recognize) each of these stories as a Cinderella story.

12. In almost every version, Cinderella's family (mistreats/mistreat) her.

13. A prince finds the slipper of a beautiful, mysterious woman, and the whole kingdom (tries/try) it on for size.

14. Nobody (fits/fit) into the slipper but Cinderella.

15. When the prince and Cinderella marry, the whole country (rejoices/rejoice)—except Cinderella's family.

Part 2

Write the correct present-tense form of the verb in parentheses to complete each sentence.

16. An ancient Chinese story collection _____ the earliest known version of the Cinderella story. (include)

17. The beautiful Yeh-hsien's wicked stepmother _____ her dress in rags and do dangerous chores. (make)

18. Yeh-hsien has a magic fish who _____ in a nearby pond, but her stepmother kills the fish. (live)

19. The pile of magic fish bones _____ Yeh-hsien's wishes, giving her gorgeous clothes to wear to a festival. (grant)

20. "Wishbones" _____ one title for the story. (be)

21. Unlike many versions of the Cinderella story, no royal men _____ the festival. (attend)

22. But, just as in other versions, one of Yeh-hsien's golden slippers _____ lost as she hurriedly leaves the festival. (get)

23. The richest merchant in the land _____ Yeh-hsien's lost golden slipper after the festival. (find)

24. No one _____ more beautiful than Yeh-hsien when she tries on the slipper. (look)

25. In the end, the beautiful Yeh-hsien _____ the merchant. (marry)

Part 3

Flock and *herd* are not the only collective nouns that can refer to a group of animals. Groups of certain kinds of animals can be named by special collective nouns. Some of these nouns may be familiar to you, but others are used very rarely.

Match the collective nouns below with the animal groups they refer to. Write the correct letter in the blank.

a. cats	**d.** zebras	**g.** jellyfish	**i.** grasshoppers
b. lions	**e.** dogs or wolves	**h.** bees	**j.** ants
c. seals or whales	**f.** fish		

26. school _____   29. swarm _____   32. army _____   34. pack _____

27. cloud _____   30. zeal _____   33. clutter _____   35. pod _____

28. pride _____   31. fluther _____

Now use one of these collective nouns in a sentence. Remember that a collective noun is singular even when it is followed by a prepositional phrase. (*A herd of horses <u>is</u> coming toward us.*)

36. _____

_____

Name _____

Read and Discover

    a. Always getting into trouble, Juan Bobo is a classic "noodlehead" character.

    b. When telling stories to children, Juan Bobo tales are popular in Puerto Rico.

Who is getting into trouble in sentence a.? _____

Does sentence b. say exactly who is telling stories? _____

> Verbal phrases must always refer to, or modify, a noun or a pronoun in the main part of a sentence. **Dangling modifiers** are phrases that do not clearly refer to any particular word in the sentence. Dangling modifiers make your writing unclear, so avoid them in your writing. When you begin a sentence with a verbal phrase such as "When telling stories to children," make sure that the question "<u>Who</u> is telling?" is answered clearly in the first part of the rest of the sentence.
>
> See Handbook **Sections 25, 31**

Part 1

Underline the verbal phrase that begins each sentence. If the phrase is a dangling modifier, write *dangling* on the line. If the phrase is used correctly, circle the word it modifies and write *C* on the line.

1. While doing the housework, Mama often calls Juan Bobo to help her with the chores. _____

2. Needing his help, Juan Bobo only wants to play. _____

3. Doing everything wrong, even easy tasks spell disaster. _____

4. Needing water for the dishes, Mama asks Juan Bobo to fill buckets of water at the stream. _____

5. Not wanting to carry heavy buckets, baskets are chosen instead. _____

6. Woven from strips, the baskets are not waterproof. _____

7. Dripping through holes in the baskets, Juan Bobo walks home. _____

8. Arriving at the house, no water is left. _____

9. When leaving for church, Mama asks Juan Bobo to stay home and take care of the pig. _____

10. Listening to the pig's squealing, Juan Bobo thinks it must want to go to church, too. _____

11. Dressing the pig in Mama's new dress, the sight is hilarious. _____

Juan Bobo creates chaos and produces laughter in stories.

12. Letting the pig go free, the people laugh or shriek. _____

13. Rolling in the mud with its snout in the air, Mama's dress is ruined. _____

14. Seeing the pig in her dress and shoes, Mama could not have been angrier. _____

15. Reading a Juan Bobo story, laughter is unavoidable. _____

Part 2

Use the noun in parentheses to rewrite each sentence correctly and avoid the dangling modifier. There is more than one way to rewrite each sentence.

16. While creating chaos for everyone else, trouble is sometimes made for himself as well. (Juan Bobo)

_____

_____

17. Warning him to be polite, Juan Bobo is taken to Señora Soto's house for lunch. (Mama) _____

_____

18. Trying not to sneeze, his head shakes from side to side. (Juan Bobo) _____

_____

19. Seeing Juan Bobo shake his head, it is assumed that he doesn't want any beans and rice. (Señora Soto)

_____

_____

20. Not wanting to scratch at an itchy mosquito bite, a squeal of frustration is heard. (Juan Bobo) _____

_____

21. Hearing the squeal, the assumption is made that Juan Bobo doesn't like fried bananas, either. (Señora Soto)

_____

_____

22. Going home hungry, it is very disappointing. (Juan Bobo) _____

_____

Part 3

Introductory verbal phrases delay the message a sentence has to communicate. A writer might avoid introductory verbal phrases in a business letter in order to make the message more direct. Sometimes, though, writers want to delay the message of a sentence while they create an image or give important information.

Read the passage below; notice how the long introductory verbal phrase evokes Johnny Appleseed's long journey and the trees he planted.

> Planting the trees that would march and train
> On, in his name to the great Pacific,
> Like Birnam Wood to Dunsinane,
> Johnny Appleseed swept on.
>   —Vachel Lindsay, from "In Praise of Johnny Appleseed"

Now look for a sentence beginning with a long verbal phrase in a book you are reading. On another sheet of paper, explain why the writer might have decided to construct the sentence this way.

Name _____

Timeless Tales

Read and Discover

Tall tales are **more exaggerated** than folktales. In fact, tall tales are the **most exaggerated** stories of all.

Circle the boldfaced words that compare tall tales with one other type of story. Underline the boldfaced words that compare tall tales with more than one other type of story.

The **comparative form** of an **adjective** or **adverb** compares two people, places, things, or actions. Add -*er* to short adjectives or adverbs to create the comparative form. Use the word *more* before long adjectives and adverbs (generally three or more syllables) to create the comparative form (*more exaggerated*). The **superlative form** compares three or more people, places, things, or actions. Add -*est* to create the superlative form. Use the word *most* before long adjectives and adverbs to create the superlative form (*most exaggerated*). Use *better* and *less* to compare two things. Use *best* and *least* to compare three or more things.

📣 **Remember to use this information when you speak, too.**

See Handbook Section 27

Part 1

Think about how many things are being compared in each sentence. Then underline the correct form of the adjective or adverb in parentheses.

1. (More often/Most often) than not, folktale characters have qualities that make them different from others.

2. Rapunzel's hair grows (longer/longest) than any ordinary person's hair ever grows.

3. Snow White's troubles arise from the fact that she is "the (fairer/fairest) of them all."

4. Tom Thumb gets his name because he is (shorter/shortest) than his father's thumb.

5. Thumbelina is the (smaller/smallest) of all: she is only half as big as a thumb.

6. Folktale giants, of course, are (taller/tallest) than normal.

7. In one English story, the (meaner/meanest) giant in the land captures three sisters and plans to eat them.

8. Molly Whuppie, the (younger/youngest) of the three, is very clever.

9. She is (smarter/smartest) than the giant, and she tricks him and steals his gold.

10. After Molly tricks him, the giant keeps watch (more carefully/most carefully) than before.

11. He captures her when she returns to steal his ring, but she tricks him again, even (more cleverly/most cleverly) than the first time.

12. The folktale giant known (better/best) is Paul Bunyan, the legendary North American lumberjack.

13. Stories about Paul Bunyan's adventures on the frontier are the (more outrageous/most outrageous) tall tales I have ever heard.

14. According to legend, Bunyan cleared all the trees from North Dakota and South Dakota, and, even (more incredible/most incredible) than that, he created all five Great Lakes.

15. He dug the lakes to provide water for his blue ox, Babe, who was much (larger/largest) than any real ox.

Timeless Tales

Part 2

Write the correct form of the adjective or adverb in parentheses. (You may need to add *more* or *most*.)

16. Is Goldilocks the _____ character in any folktale? (rude)

17. She may be the _____ of all: she breaks the baby bear's chair. (clumsy)

18. She wants her porridge to be _____ than the father bear's porridge. (cool)

19. She wants her porridge to be _____ than the mother bear's porridge. (hot)

20. She eats all of the baby bear's porridge because she thinks it is the _____ of all. (good)

21. If I were a bear in a folktale, I would lock my cottage _____ than those bears did! (carefully)

Part 3

> Some adjectives are *absolute*: either they describe a thing or they do not. They cannot properly be put into the comparative form. For example, a plant is either dead or alive; it does not make sense to say "That plant is the *deadest*."

Read each of the sentences below. Think about the italicized adjectives. Decide whether putting that adjective in the comparative or superlative form in which it appears is logical and correct. If it is not logical and correct, rewrite the sentence so it gives accurate information.

22. Paul Bunyan is the *most unique* character in American folklore. _____
_____

23. Snow White's stepmother seems even *more wicked* than Cinderella's stepmother. _____
_____
_____

24. The clothes made for the emperor in Hans Christian Andersen's tale "The Emperor's New Clothes" are the *most invisible* clothes any emperor has ever worn. _____
_____
_____

25. "Rumpelstiltskin" is one of the *most difficult* fairy tale names to spell. _____
_____

26. Goldilocks thought that the baby bear's bed was the *most perfect*. _____
_____

Name _____

Timeless Tales

Read and Discover

I **will tell** you about Mother Goose.
She **might be** the best-known nursery rhyme character.

Circle the main verb in boldface in each sentence. Underline the auxiliary verb in boldface that works with each main verb.

> An **auxiliary verb,** or **helping verb,** works with a main verb. Auxiliary verbs have a variety of purposes. Some auxiliary verbs, such as *could, should, might,* and *may,* show how likely it is that something will happen. Some auxiliary verbs, such as *did, is, will,* and *would,* indicate the tense of the main verb.
>
> See Handbook Sections 18c, 18e

Part 1

Underline the auxiliary verb or verbs in each sentence.

1. No rhyme or story has ever been written about Mother Goose.

2. But for many years nursery rhyme collections have displayed the name of Mother Goose on their covers. Why?

3. Some scholars think Mother Goose may have been inspired by a real storyteller.

4. Some say the original Mother Goose might have been Queen Bertha of France.

5. This ancient queen was often called "Goose-Footed Bertha."

6. Others say Mother Goose could have been an American invention.

7. A woman named Elizabeth Goose, who lived in colonial Boston, may have collected stories in a book called *Mother Goose's Melodies.*

8. Nowadays most experts do not believe this explanation.

9. They say that if this were true, someone would have found the book by now, but no such book has ever been found.

10. Many say Mother Goose did not exist in real life; they say she is a made-up character.

11. No one can say for sure how Mother Goose began.

12. Even though she seems to be a fictitious character, she has had a consistent and recognizable appearance for generations.

13. Most illustrators have drawn Mother Goose as an old woman in a pointed hat.

14. In many pictures she is riding on a huge goose.

15. She can often be seen reading to a group of children, too.

We may never know if Mother Goose was a real person.

Part 2

Complete each sentence with an auxiliary verb or verbs. Some sentences have more than one correct answer.

16. The Mother Goose rhyme "Rock-a-Bye-Baby" _____ have been inspired by a Native American custom.

17. At one time, some Native Americans _____ hang babies' cradles safely from trees.

18. Some historians believe the rhyme's writer _____ have been a pilgrim who came to North America on the Mayflower.

19. This rhyme _____ be the earliest poem written in English on the North American continent.

20. The rhyme that mentions "four-and-twenty blackbirds baked in a pie" _____ probably inspired by real-life recipes.

21. Sixteenth-century chefs _____ sometimes hide live birds in "pies" as an amusing surprise.

22. "Little Miss Muffet" _____ written in the 1500s by a scientist who studied spiders.

23. Perhaps he _____ be surprised to discover how long his poem has lasted.

24. Many modern readers _____ been confused by the rhyme's references to a "tuffet."

25. That's because most people today _____ not know that *tuffet* was a name for a three-legged stool.

26. You _____ be surprised to learn that *curds and whey* was a name for a type of custard.

27. Some of our modern expressions _____ probably sound just as odd to people in the future.

28. If you want to learn more about Mother Goose rhymes, you _____ read an annotated Mother Goose collection.

Part 3

Find eight helping verbs in the puzzle and circle them.

Q	W	K	D	M	G	M	C	O
J	A	H	W	I	L	L	R	H
G	S	M	T	R	H	N	S	A
X	W	I	K	Q	U	J	D	V
I	R	G	C	O	U	L	D	E
J	M	H	C	J	B	F	N	W
M	C	T	V	Z	Q	W	L	H
A	B	S	H	O	U	L	D	T
Y	W	F	S	B	D	O	E	S

Now imagine how the story of "Little Miss Muffet" would have been different if Miss Muffet were not arachnophobic (afraid of spiders). On another sheet of paper, write two sentences about the story, using helping verbs you found in the puzzle.

Name _____

Diagraming Subject and Object Pronouns

You have learned how to diagram the simple subject and the direct object in a sentence.

Paul Bunyan liked fluffy **pancakes**.

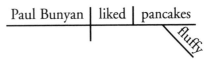

Subject and object pronouns are placed in the same places in a sentence diagram as the nouns they stand for would be placed.

He liked **them**.

Diagram these sentences. Refer to the models if you need help.

1. I have a book about Paul Bunyan.

2. It contains twelve folktales.

3. My brother and I read them yesterday.

Diagraming Adjective Clauses

You have learned that an adjective clause is a dependent clause that describes a noun or pronoun and begins with a relative pronoun such as *who, that,* or *which*. Notice the way an adjective clause is diagramed. In this sentence, the relative pronoun *that* is the direct object of the verb *found.*

The huge ox **that Paul Bunyan found** was blue.

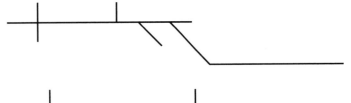

4. What sentence elements does the dashed slanted line connect? _____
   a. the two verbs in the sentence   b. the direct object and the relative pronoun *that*
            c. the relative pronoun *that* and the noun to which it refers

In this example, the relative pronoun *that* is the subject of the adjective clause.

An ox **that is blue** attracts attention.

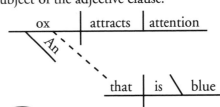

Try diagraming these sentences. Be sure to decide whether the relative pronoun is the *subject* of the adjective clause or the *direct object* of its verb.

5. Babe had a body that resembled a blue mountain.

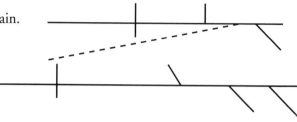

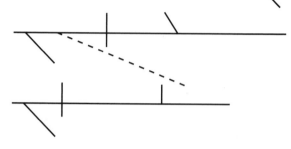

6. The strength that this ox possessed was tremendous.

Diagraming Adverb Clauses

You have learned that an adverb clause is a dependent clause that tells about a verb, an adjective, or an adverb and that an adverb clause often begins with a subordinating conjunction such as *although, because, when,* or *where.* Here's how to diagram a sentence that contains an adverb clause:

When Babe bellowed, people listened.

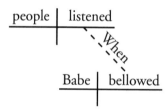

7. Where is the subordinating conjunction *when* placed in this diagram? _____
    a. on a slanted line below the simple subject
    b. on a slanted dotted line connecting the verb in the clause to the word the clause modifies
    c. on a slanted dotted line connecting two subjects

Diagram these sentences. Refer to the model if needed.

8. Although Babe was powerful, he obeyed Paul's commands.

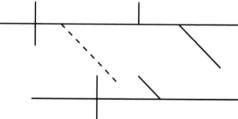

9. Whenever Paul called, Babe appeared.

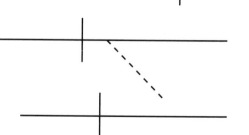

Name _____

Timeless Tales

Writing Sentences

These sentences need your help. Rewrite each one so that the subject and verb agree.

1. Nobody are sorry when the wolf falls into the soup pot as he is climbing down the chimney to eat the pigs.
   _____
   _____

2. Attitudes toward canine characters is more favorable in Native American tales than in European ones.
   _____
   _____

3. Thoughts of a wonderful new name makes Coyote drift off to sleep, however, and he ends up last of all.
   _____
   _____

4. "The Three Little Pigs" are a good example of a European folktale with a villainous wolf. _____
   _____

5. When a fox or a wolf appear in a European fairy tale, that animal is usually the villain. _____
   _____
   _____

6. "Coyote Gets His Powers" tell how Coyote tries to stay awake all night in order to be first in line on
   the day all the animals are to be given names. _____
   _____
   _____

7. In contrast, Native American folklore portray Coyote as a rascal, not a villain. _____
   _____

A piece of writing comparing two characters may be divided into two paragraphs. The first paragraph describes how the characters are alike. The second paragraph might describe the characters' differences. Each paragraph should have a topic sentence stating its main idea. Notice this structure in this model.

    At first glance, the character Sleeping Beauty and the character Beauty from "Beauty and the Beast" might seem to be very similar. Both are young and beautiful. Magic spells cause problems for both: Sleeping Beauty is put under a spell that makes her sleep endlessly, while Beauty meets a prince who has had a spell cast on him that makes him appear to be a monster. Finally, both characters fall in love.

    A closer look shows these characters to be very different, however. Sleeping Beauty is completely helpless. She must wait for someone else to break the spell she is under. In contrast, Beauty herself bravely breaks the spell that traps the Beast. While Sleeping Beauty falls in love at first sight with a handsome prince, Beauty falls in love slowly over time. She recognizes the inner goodness of the ugly Beast. She does not know until after she has fallen in love with him that the Beast is actually a handsome prince. Sleeping Beauty is weak and superficial; Beauty is brave and wise.

G.U.M.

Writing a Paragraph

The sentences you repaired on page 181 can be reordered to make one paragraph describing differences between Coyote and Wolf. Decide which sentence is the topic sentence and which sentences are the supporting sentences. Reorder the sentences, and write the paragraph on the lines below.

_____

_____

_____

_____

_____

_____

_____

_____

Write two paragraphs of your own in which you compare two folktale characters. In the first paragraph, tell how the characters are alike. Be sure to use a topic sentence and supporting examples. In the second paragraph, describe differences between the characters. Use the model paragraph on page 181 as a guide. Continue writing on a separate sheet of paper if you need more room.

_____

_____

_____

_____

_____

_____

_____

_____

_____

_____

Read your paragraphs again. Use this checklist to make sure they are complete and correct.

- ❏ My composition has a topic sentence.
- ❏ Each paragraph contains a topic sentence and supporting details.
- ❏ I have described both similarities and differences.
- ❏ The subject and verb in each sentence agree.
- ❏ My composition has a concluding sentence.

Name _____

Timeless Tales

Proofreading Others' Writing

Read this passage about Hans Christian Andersen and find the mistakes. Use the proofreading marks below to show how each mistake should be fixed.

Proofreading Marks

Mark	Means	Example
�	delete	Hans Christian Andersen's fairy tales are famous throughout the the world.
∧	add	Hans Christian Andersen's fairy tals are famous throughout the world.
≡	make into a capital letter	Hans Christian andersen's fairy tales are famous throughout the world.
∨	add apostrophe	Hans Christian Andersens fairy tales are famous throughout the world.
(sp)	fix spelling	Hans Christian Andersen's phary tales are famous throughout the world.
/	make into a lowercase letter	Hans Christian Andersen's fairy tales are Famous throughout the world.

A Master Storyteller

Before the invenshin of the printing press. Folklore were passed from generation to generation orally. Once the printing press made it possible for storys to be shared and preserved in print, writers began setting these tales down on paper, some writers proved to be most skillful storytellers than others, perhaps the more skillful of all was the Danish writer Hans Christian Andersen, whom took characters and plots from folktales and developed them into long, complecks storys.

Andersens lively tales is full of beautiful images noble characters and inspiring triumphs. It captures some of the best elements of the human spirit. Yet andersen's own life was filled with hardships and sadness. Born too poor parents in Odense, Denmark, Andersen lost his father when he was 11 years old. At the age of 14 he left home and moved to the capital, copenhagen, to try to make a life for him. After finishing school, Andersen began writing Poems, Plays, and Novels. He enjoyed some success, but life remained difficult? Hoping to add to his meager income, stories for children, which he called "trifles," were written. Them proved to be extremly poplar, but for a long time he considered these less importanter than his writings for adults.

Andersen eventually wrote and publish more than 160 tails for children. Many of his storys continues to be popular today. More than a century after his death. In fact, some is now been translated into more than one hundred languages.

Proofreading Your Own Writing

You can use the list below to help you find and fix mistakes in your own writing. Write the titles of your own stories or reports in the blanks at the top of the chart. Then use the questions to check your work. Make a check mark (✓) in each box after you have checked that item.

Titles

Proofreading Checklist for Unit 6

Have I used the correct subject and object pronouns?				
Have I made sure that all pronouns agree with their antecedents in number and gender?				
Does every verb agree with its subject?				
Have I avoided dangling modifiers?				

Also Remember . . .

Does each sentence begin with a capital letter?				
Have I spelled each word correctly?				
Have I used commas correctly?				

Your Own List

Use this space to write your own list of things to check in your writing.

Name _____

Timeless Tales

Subject and Object Pronouns

Circle each boldfaced word that is a subject pronoun. Underline each boldfaced word that is an object pronoun.

1. **I** am doing a report on animal characters in folktales.

2. Keesha is working with **me** on the report.

3. **We** are going to act out some stories.

Pronouns in Pairs

Circle the correct pronoun or pronouns in parentheses.

4. Keesha and (I/me) are going to act out the story of Coyote and Horned Toad.

5. (Her and I/She and I) have made masks for our performance in the school folktale contest.

6. I hope first prize will go to Keesha and (I/me).

Antecedents

Underline the antecedent or antecedents of each boldfaced pronoun.

7. The story tells about an argument between Coyote and Horned Toad and explains why **they** don't like each other.

8. Coyote gets mad at Horned Toad and swallows **him** whole.

9. Trapped inside Coyote, Horned Toad begins kicking and scratching **him**.

10. Keesha is playing Horned Toad, so **she** will hide behind me and pretend to be inside my stomach.

Who and *Whom*

Write *who* or *whom* to complete each sentence correctly.

11. I made up my own folktale character, _____ is a talkative squirrel named Slim.

12. Slim tells predators _____ plan to eat him long, boring stories.

13. The animals to _____ Slim tells his stories fall asleep, and he gets away.

Verbs

Circle the correct form of each verb in parentheses.

14. "The Bremen Town Musicians" (is/are) a terrific animal folktale.

15. This story about four old animals (makes/make) me smile every time I read it.

16. An old donkey no longer able to carry heavy loads (goes/go) off to make his fortune.

17. He thinks he (might/has) be able to get a job as a musician in the town of Bremen.

18. A dog, a cat, and a rooster (joins/join) the donkey along the road to Bremen.

19. Nobody (wants/want) these animals any more, so they must take care of themselves.

20. Neither the donkey, nor the dog, nor the cat, nor the rooster (sings/sing) very well.

21. But the group (makes/make) music that saves the day.

22. A gang of robbers (is/are) hiding out in a house in the forest along the way to Bremen.

23. All the animals sing together, and the robbers are convinced the racket (must/is) be made by a scary ghost.

24. The sound of the animals (frightens/frighten) the robbers away, and the animal musicians live happily ever after in the little house in the forest.

Dangling Modifiers

Underline the verbal phrase that begins each sentence. If the phrase is a dangling modifier, write *dangling* on the line. If the phrase is used correctly, circle the word it modifies and write *C* on the line.

25. Traveling to Bremen, the animals discover robbers hiding out in a little house. _____

26. Crowing, barking, and making a big racket, the robbers are driven out of the house. _____

27. Relaxing and eating the robbers' food, it is a perfect home. _____

Adjectives and Adverbs

Circle the correct form of the adjective or adverb in parentheses.

28. Those animals are the (noisier/noisiest) musicians I have ever heard.

29. The donkey sings even (worse/worst) than the cat.

30. The rooster is the (louder/loudest) singer of all.

Revising Sentences

Rewrite each sentence so it is correct.

31. In the tale "bremen Town musicians," the dog the cat the rooster and the donkey makes an unusual entourage. _____

_____

32. The four of them becomes friends in their quest for a happy life and allies. _____

_____

33. The terrible sounds of their music who run away frightens a band of robbers. _____

_____

34. The story of how they outsmart the robbers prove that talent isn't everything. _____

_____

35. Coyotes, foxes, and wolves is all popular folktale characters. _____

_____

36. Wolfes in real life is smart, but they usually is the losers in Folktales. _____

_____

37. Kindness in folktales from most cultures, and cleverness generally wins out over greed. _____

_____

Name _____

Timeless Tales

COMMUNITY LEARNING  OPPORTUNITIES

In Unit 6 of *G.U.M.*, students learned more about **grammar,** and they used what they learned to improve their own writing. The content of these lessons focuses on the theme **Folktale Characters.** As students completed the exercises, they learned about some traditional folktale characters from different parts of the world. These pages offer a variety of activities that reinforce skills and concepts presented in the unit. They also provide opportunities for students to make connections between the content of the lessons and the community at large.

The Storyteller's Craft

Invite a local storyteller to your class to share some of the stories he or she has collected over time. After the storyteller has finished, identify and evaluate different methods the storyteller used to help bring the stories alive for the listeners.

Sharing Stories

Many people who find it difficult to read for themselves enjoy listening to stories read aloud. Share your storytelling skills by volunteering as a reader at a nearby library, children's hospital, or nursing home. You may want to ask your listeners whether they liked each story you read and why. Use their responses to create a list of appropriate stories for that type of audience.

Community Tales

Talk to several people of different ages and cultural backgrounds about traditional folktales their families tell. Ask each person to tell one story to you. You may wish to tape record the stories people tell and transcribe them (write them down) later. Use the stories to create a community folktale collection. Make notes that indicate the origin of each story you have collected, the name of the storyteller, and the date the story was recorded. Share the completed collection with your classmates. You may wish to donate your collection to the school library or to a public library in your community.

New Directions

Select one of the folktale characters you read about in Unit 6. Write an original tale in which that character plays the leading role. Adapt the setting so that the story takes place in the modern day, in your own community. Make sure you follow all the rules of grammar you learned in Unit 6 when writing the story. Read the completed story aloud to your class or to a group of friends. You may want to submit it to a magazine or local newspaper for publication.

A Storied Event

Plan a storytelling gala for younger children in your school or community. Begin by making these decisions:
- Where and when will the gala be held?
- What stories will be included in the gala?
- Who will tell each story?
- What children will you invite to the gala?
- How will you announce the event?

Use the Storytelling Gala Planner on the following page to help you organize your ideas and plan the event.

Storytelling Gala Planner

When the gala will take place:

_____

What stories will be included:

_____

_____

_____

_____

Where it will take place:

_____

Who will tell each story:

_____

_____

_____

_____

Whom to invite to the gala:

_____

_____

_____

How to advertise the event:

_____

_____

_____

Things to bring (props, food, books):

_____

_____

_____

Notes:

_____

_____

_____

_____

Name _____

Timeless Tales

Read and Discover

When tourists think about the **island** of **Jamaica**, most of them picture sun-drenched beaches and an aqua sea. Many people do not know that this **Caribbean** nation is home to a unique mix of cultures.

Circle the boldfaced word that names any body of land surrounded by water. Underline the boldfaced word that names one specific island. Draw a box around the boldfaced word that is an adjective.

A common noun names a person, place, thing, or idea. A **proper noun** names a specific person, place, thing, or idea. The important words in proper nouns are **capitalized**. **Proper adjectives** are descriptive words formed from proper nouns. They must be capitalized. A **title of respect,** such as *Mr.* or *Judge*, is used before a person's name. This title is also capitalized. The names of the months, the names of the days of the week, and the first word of every sentence are always capitalized.

See Handbook Sections 1, 15

Part 1

Draw three lines (≡) under each lowercase letter that should be capitalized. (1–35) Then circle each proper noun and draw a box around each proper adjective.

The caribbean sea is part of the atlantic Ocean. Dozens of islands lie in the Caribbean. Trinidad and tobago are two separate islands that form one country. Haiti and the dominican republic are two countries that share the same island. other caribbean island countries include Jamaica, barbados, antigua, and grenada.

The region's first inhabitants were the Carib, arawak, and warahuns. in october 1492, columbus landed on an island in the Caribbean that he named san salvador. During the decades that followed, spanish explorers established colonies on many of the islands. Most of the native peoples died as a result of diseases brought by the europeans. Many others perished in wars waged against these invading colonial powers.

By 1750, the English, dutch, swedish, and french had settled in parts of the caribbean. Barbados, jamaica, and haiti became sugar plantation colonies. Sugar cane thrived in the fertile volcanic soil. Workers from Africa were forced into labor on the plantations. Laborers from china and india were also brought to the Caribbean. In the 1800s, slavery was abolished by most european countries. During that century, the islands fought for their independence, one by one.

Today's caribbean islanders are the proud descendants of Carib, african, European, east indian, middle Eastern, and chinese cultures. These cultures have combined to create a vibrant mix of traditions found nowhere else.

Great Getaways

Part 2

Draw three lines (≡) under each lowercase letter that should be capitalized. Draw a line (/) through each capital letter that should be lowercase. (36–52)

The celebration of Carnival is perhaps the most famous caribbean festival. carnival has its roots in the traditions of african tribal celebrations and european religion. Carnival occurs in the Week before easter. music, dancing, parades, and costumes are part of the celebration.

Paraders wear colorful and elaborate Costumes made of feathers, mirrors, animal horns, shells, and beads. Modern-day costumes might include beach balls, colored light bulbs, and headdresses shaped like satellite dishes. Traditional Characters such as moco jumbie, Midnight Robber, and Pitchy Patchy appear at Carnival festivals throughout the Caribbean. During Carnival, the sound of Steel Drums fills the air as dancers fill the street. The celebration continues nonstop for two days and two Nights. Carnival celebrations also occur in london, toronto, and New york City.

Part 3

A character called "archy the cockroach" was created in the 1920s by American humorist Donald Robert Perry Marquis. archy was a very talented insect; he typed out wise sayings and poems by hopping from one key to another on Don Marquis's typewriter. With his method of typing, though, archy could not capitalize words because he could not use the shift key. He also could not punctuate sentences.

Read this passage by archy. Then rewrite it with correct capitalization and punctuation. Afterward, discuss with a partner the effect you think the absence of capitalization and punctuation has on the reader.

i have noticed that when chickens quit quarreling over their food they often find that there is enough for all of them i wonder if it might not be the same with the human race
—*archys life of mehitabel*
random thoughts by archy

53. _____

_____

_____

_____

_____

_____

Name _____

Great Getaways

Read and Discover

Dr. James L. Waihee, an expert on Hawaii, visited our class. Our teacher, Mr. Yamaguchi, invited him to speak about Hawaii and show us slides. Mr. Yamaguchi posted a sign that said: "Tues., Jan. 26—Dr. Waihee."

Underline a short way to write *Doctor*. Draw a square around a short way to write *Mister*. Circle short ways to write *Tuesday* and *January*. Underline a letter that stands for a name.

An **abbreviation** is a shortened form of a word. **Titles of respect** are usually abbreviated. So are words in **addresses,** such as *Street* (*St.*), *Avenue* (*Ave.*), and *Boulevard* (*Blvd.*). The names of **days,** the names of some **months,** and certain words in the names of **businesses** are often abbreviated in informal notes. These abbreviations begin with a capital letter and end with a period. An **initial** can replace a person's or a place's name. It is written as a capital letter followed by a period.

See Handbook Section 2

Part 1

Draw three lines (≡) under each lowercase letter that should be a capital letter. Draw a line (/) through each capital letter that should be a lowercase letter. Add periods where they are needed. (1–20)

Dr James l Waihee described the eight main islands of Hawaii. He discussed them in order from east to west. The largest Island is Hawaii, which is often called the *Big Island.*

West of Hawaii is a cluster of four main islands. Maui, the largest of these, is called the *Valley Island* because much of its land lies in a fertile valley between two large volcanoes. Nearby is Molokai, called the *Friendly Island* because of the hospitality of its people. South of Molokai is Lanai, the *Pineapple Island.* Castle & Cook, inc grows and processes pineapples on Lanai. The Company owns 98 percent of the island. Kahoolawe, the smallest of the Main islands, is now dry, windy, and uninhabited. In the early part of the century it was used for cattle raising.

The island of Oahu, which lies to the northwest of the cluster of four islands, is sometimes called the *Gathering Place.* About 75 percent of the state's people live there. Dr Waihee said that his brother, mr Merrill k Waihee, lives on Oahu. He has a house on Ulukani st. in the Town of Kailua.

Because of its many colorful gardens and beautiful greenery, the island of Kauai is called the *Garden Island.* Mt Waialeale, near the center of Kauai, is one of the world's rainiest places, with an average rainfall of 460 inches a year!

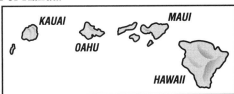
Hawaii's eight main islands

Niihau, the westernmost main island, is called the *Forbidden Island.* No one can visit Niihau without the permission of its owners, the Robinson Family. The Robinson family is descended from mrs Elizabeth Sinclair, who bought the island in 1864. Most of Niihau's Residents are native Hawaiian people.

Great Getaways

Part 2

Rewrite each item below, using abbreviations and initials for the underlined words.

21. <u>Doctor Helen Marie</u> Kealoha _____

22. <u>Mount</u> Kaala _____

23. <u>Mister David Glenn</u> Ariyoshi _____

24. <u>Mistress</u> Ellen <u>Claire</u> Takai _____

25. 19 Lahaina <u>Street</u> _____

26. 212 Kalakaua <u>Avenue</u> _____

27. The Koele <u>Company, Incorporated</u> _____

28. <u>Thursday, February</u> 14 _____

29. 2222 Bradley <u>Boulevard</u> _____

30. Haleakala <u>Drive</u> _____

31. <u>Monday, March</u> 22 _____

32. <u>Mistress Ellen Mae</u> Kanata _____

33. Tropic Isles, <u>Incorporated</u> _____

34. <u>Friday, October</u> 30 _____

35. The White Sands <u>Corporation</u> _____

36. <u>Wednesday, January</u> 20 _____

37. <u>Doctor Ralph Peter</u> Shuster _____

Part 3

Use information from Part 1 to fill in the puzzle.

Across
1. The Gathering Place
6. The Valley Island
7. The Garden Island
8. The Pineapple Island

Down
2. The Big Island
3. Smallest main island
4. The Friendly Island
5. The Forbidden Island

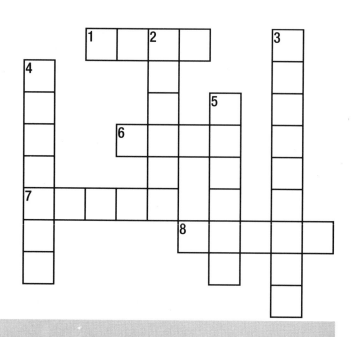

Name _____

Great Getaways

Read and Discover

In class we saw a movie titled <u>Hawaii: The 50th State</u>. We also read a poem called "A Hawaiian Memory."

Circle the movie title. Draw a box around the title of the poem. How are they written differently? _____

Underline the **titles** of **books, magazines, newspapers** and **movies (or videos)**. These are written in italics in printed text. Use quotation marks around the titles of **songs, stories,** and **poems.** **Capitalize** the first word and the last word in titles. Capitalize all other words except articles, short prepositions, and coordinating conjunctions. Remember to capitalize short verbs, such as *is* and *are*.

See Handbook Section 3

Part 1

Draw three lines (≡) under each lowercase letter that should be a capital letter. Underline or add quotation marks to titles.

1. The state song of Hawaii is hawaii ponoi, which means "Hawaii's Own."

2. Last night we watched a movie called the wettest place on Earth.

3. I just finished reading a book titled kings and queens of hawaii.

4. My sister can play a Hawaiian song called the new hawaiian blues.

5. I learned a lot of Hawaiian words from a book titled you
   can speak hawaiian.

6. After visiting Hawaii, I wrote a poem called aloha hawaii.

7. We watched a short movie in class called lanai: the pineapple island.

8. My mother is reading a book called the mystery of the sleeping volcano.

9. Last night she rented a musical comedy titled honolulu holiday.

10. She bought a travel book called from hawaii to maui in twenty days.

11. Bethany wrote a short story about Hawaii titled the big hurricane.

12. She hopes that a magazine called the voice of hawaii will print her story.

13. She is working on another story titled the sea turtles are gone.

14. I think a great title for a book about Hawaii would be the islands of sunshine and rain.

15. The poem let's save the nene is about Hawaii's state bird.

16. The video Habits of the hawaiian goose shows the nene in its natural environment.

17. Have you seen the movie islands of light?

18. The theme song for the movie is titled rain song.

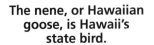

The nene, or Hawaiian goose, is Hawaii's state bird.

Part 2

Read the titles of the works on the library shelf and then answer each question by writing a complete sentence. Use correct capitalization and punctuation.

19. Which book probably contains information about Hawaii's natural environment? _____
_____

20. Which book might give historical information about ancient Hawaii? _____
_____

21. Which book would likely be a good place to find traditional tales about Hawaii? _____
_____

22. Which book would probably give information about surfing? _____
_____

23. Which movie might be a humorous mystery? _____

24. Which video would probably give information about Hawaiian history during the last fifty years?
_____

25. Which video might show viewers how to make mango salsa? _____
_____

26. Which book might inform visitors of the best places to go snorkeling? _____
_____

27. Which video probably describes the process of growing, harvesting, and shipping mangos? _____
_____

Part 3

A famous Hollywood producer is interested in turning your book about Hawaii into a major motion picture. On another sheet of paper, write a paragraph to convince her to do so. Include the title of the book and create an exciting movie title. Use correct capitalization and punctuation.

Name _____

Great Getaways

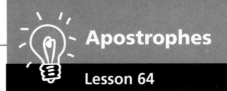

Apostrophes

Lesson 64

Read  and Discover

Ellis Island in New York Harbor was the first stop for most of **America's** immigrants between 1892 and 1924. Immigrants **couldn't** enter the United States until they had passed several inspections there.

Which boldfaced word shows possession or ownership? _____
Which boldfaced word is a combination of two words? _____

To form the **possessive** of a singular noun, add an **apostrophe** and **s** (*girl's shoe*). For plural nouns that end in *s*, add an apostrophe (*birds' nests*) to form the possessive. For plural nouns that do not end in *s*, add an apostrophe and *s* (*children's boots*). **Apostrophes** are also used in **contractions,** two words that have been shortened and combined.

See Handbook Sections 7, 26, 28, 30

Part 1

Underline the correct word in parentheses. If the answer is a possessive, write *possessive*. If the answer is a contraction, write the two words from which the contraction was made.

1. In the early nineteenth century, Samuel Ellis was the (island's/islands') owner. _____

2. The United States government bought the island from Mr. Ellis in 1808 but (did'nt/didn't) start using it as an immigrant station until 1892. _____

3. More than 12 million people entered the United States through (Ellis Island's/Ellis Islands') elegant Main Building, which opened in 1900. _____

4. The dining room seated 1,200 people, but pleasing that many (wasn't/was'nt) easy. _____

5. The dietary preferences of various (country's/countries') emigrants differed greatly. _____

6. The (immigrant's/immigrants') journeys by ship took weeks or months. _____

7. Many passengers (weren't/were'nt) in good health when they arrived in America. _____

8. The (stations'/station's) Contagious Disease Hospital had eleven wards. _____

9. They were usually filled with immigrants who had contracted diseases in a (ships'/ship's) damp, crowded quarters. _____

10. Persons with infectious diseases (couldn't/couldnt') enter the United States. _____

11. In addition to undergoing medical exams, newcomers had to answer immigration (inspector's/inspectors') questions. _____

12. Inspectors wanted to make sure applicants (wouldn't/would'nt) be a burden to society. _____

13. The restrictions did not spoil (newcomer's/newcomers') dreams: only about two percent of all people processed at Ellis Island were refused admission to the United States. ____ _____

14. Those who (didn't/did'nt) pass inspection were detained, often for weeks. _____

15. Detainees stayed in big dormitories; (mens'/men's) and (women's/womens') areas were separate.

_____ _____

Great Getaways

Part 2

Rewrite these sentences. Replace boldfaced words with possessives or contractions.

16. In 1924 the **passage of the immigrants** through Ellis Island started to decrease. _____

_____

17. In 1954 the **buildings of the station** were closed completely. _____

_____

18. Sadly, the government **did not** maintain the elegant old buildings. _____

_____

19. The historic structures **could not** withstand the damp, salty air, and they decayed. _____

_____

20. In the 1980s, the National Park Service began major repairs on the **buildings of the island**. _____

_____

21. Today Ellis Island is a museum honoring all **the immigrants of America**. _____

_____

Part 3

Writers sometimes use apostrophes to change the spellings of certain words to reflect the way the words are actually pronounced in informal speech. This technique is used quite often in representing a *dialect*, or regional speech pattern, in writing.

With a partner, read aloud this stanza of a poem about the famous explorer Sir Francis Drake. Circle the words for which the poet created new spellings, either by changing letters or by replacing letters with apostrophes, to make the words mirror the way they would have been spoken. Then, on another sheet of paper, write the words correctly. (22–44)

Drake he's in his hammock an' a thousand miles away,

(Capten, art tha sleepin' there below?)

Slung atween the round shot in Nombre Dios Bay,

An' dreamin' arl the time o' Plymouth Hoe.

Yarnder lumes the Island, yarnder lie the ships,

Wi' sailor lads a-dancin' heel-an'-toe,

An' the shore-lights flashin', an' the night-tide dashin',

He see et arl so plainly as he saw et long ago.

—Sir Henry Newbolt, from "Drake's Drum"

Name _____

Great Getaways

Read and Discover

a. Manhattan Island, the legend goes, was purchased by Dutch settlers in 1626.
b. The settlers paid a group of Native Americans cloth, beads, and small trinkets worth about $24.00.
c. Today Manhattan is the center of the teeming, bustling city known as New York.

Circle the commas in sentence a. Circle the commas in sentence b.
In which sentence do the commas separate three items in a series? _____
Circle the comma in sentence c. What kind of words does it separate? _____

A **series** is a sequence of three or more words, phrases, or clauses. A **comma** is used to **separate items in a series**. The last comma in a series goes before the conjunction (*and, or*). A comma is also used to separate **pairs of similar adjectives** (*teeming, bustling city*). To decide whether to put a comma between adjectives, read the sentence with the word *and* inserted between the adjectives. If the word *and* sounds natural, use a comma.

See Handbook Sections 8, 16

Part 1

Add commas where they are needed in these sentences.

1. New York City is a great center of culture finance entertainment and trade.

2. Central Park Times Square and the Empire State Building are world famous.

3. These and other landmarks are on the busy crowded island of Manhattan.

4. Manhattan is the smallest of New York City's five boroughs.

5. The other boroughs are the Bronx Queens Brooklyn and Staten Island.

6. Ferries tunnels and bridges connect Manhattan to the other boroughs.

7. Many thousands of clerks secretaries executives laborers professionals and job-seekers commute to Manhattan every day.

8. Some work in sunny spacious offices high in the sky.

9. Others labor in dark windowless rooms.

10. Manhattan is home to the World Trade Center the New York Stock Exchange and the United Nations headquarters.

The Empire State Building was once the world's tallest skyscraper.

11. Several of America's largest publishing companies and banks have headquarters there.

12. Harlem has been a center of African American business and culture for almost a century.

13. Duke Ellington, a suave cosmopolitan bandleader considered by many to be America's greatest jazz composer, made his home in Harlem.

14. Many musicians actors and dancers come to New York City with high hopes.

15. Some seek experience some want to study and some hope to find work in the theater.

16. Only a few are able to achieve all their goals in this wealthy worldly city.

17. Many others spend years on this glittering island chasing bright elusive dreams.

Part 2

Rewrite each group of sentences as a single sentence. Use *and* or *or* to join the last two items in a series. Add commas where you need them.

18. New York's Greenwich Village is home to poets. Greenwich Village is home to artists. Many dancers live there, too. _____

_____

19. Greenwich Village is known for its trendy boutiques. It is known for its charming restaurants and art galleries. _____

_____

20. We could go shopping. We could see a play. We could visit the World Trade Center. _____

_____

21. Central Park has a large skating pond. The pond is picturesque. _____

_____

22. Noisy subway trains whisk people from place to place on Manhattan Island. These subway trains are crowded. _____

_____

Part 3

Skillful public speakers often use items in a series to emphasize points they wish to make and to stir listeners' emotions. Read each quotation below. Circle the commas that set off items in a series. Then, with a partner, choose one quotation and explore its meaning.

…government of the people, by the people, for the people, shall not perish from the earth.
—Abraham Lincoln, from Address at Gettysburg

We shall not flag or fail. We shall go on to the end. We shall fight in France, we shall fight on the seas and oceans, we shall fight with growing confidence and growing strength in the air, we shall defend our island, whatever the cost may be, we shall fight on the beaches, we shall fight on the landing grounds, we shall fight in the fields and in the streets, we shall fight in the hills; we shall never surrender.
—Winston Churchill, from Speech on Dunkirk

Let every nation know, whether it wishes us well or ill, that we shall pay any price, bear any burden, meet any hardship, support any friend, oppose any foe to assure the survival and the success of liberty.
—John F. Kennedy, from Inaugural Address

Given what you know about each speaker quoted above, what would you say the three quotes have in common?

23. _____

_____

Name _____

Read and Discover

"Mariko, will you tell us about Japan?" Mrs. Harris asked.
"Yes, I'd be happy to, but I don't know where to start," she answered.

Circle the name of the person being spoken to in the first sentence.
What punctuation mark comes after it? _____

Draw a line under the word that introduces the second sentence.
What punctuation mark follows it? _____

Draw a box around the conjunction that joins the two parts of the second
sentence. What punctuation mark comes before it? _____

Commas tell a reader where to pause. A comma is used to separate an **introductory word,** such as *yes* or *well,* from the rest of a sentence. It is also used to separate **independent clauses** in a **compound sentence** and to separate a **noun of direct address** from the rest of a sentence. A noun of direct address names a person who is being spoken to.

See Handbook Sections 8, 13, 14, 23

Part 1

Add the missing comma to each sentence. Then decide why the comma is needed. Write *I* for introductory word, *C* for compound sentence, *D* for direct address, or *S* for items in a series.

1. "Well Japan is made up of four large islands and thousands of smaller ones," Mariko began. _____

2. "Honshu is the biggest island and most of Japan's people live there." _____

3. "Japan isn't one of the biggest countries in the world but it is one of the most crowded," Raj added. _____

4. "Yes Japan has 11 cities with a population of over a million," Mariko said. _____

5. "Mrs. Harris is it true that Tokyo has 50 million people?" Raj asked. _____

6. "No that's an exaggeration. Tokyo has more than eight million people," she said with a smile. _____

7. "Japan's cities are crowded but even big cities have many peaceful gardens," Mariko continued. _____

8. "Raj would you hold up this picture?" she asked. _____

9. "This traditional garden is hundreds of years old and it's right in the middle of Tokyo!" she said. _____

10. "Mrs. Harris is it true that Japan has few natural resources?" Julie asked. _____

11. "Yes Japan must import most of the raw materials it uses in industry," she answered. _____

12. "Nonetheless Japan is one of the world's leading industrial nations," Mariko said. _____

13. "Mariko what does Japan export besides cars?" Mrs. Harris asked. _____

14. "Well computers, calculators, and other electronic items are made in great quantity," she replied. _____

15. "Julie can you name Japan's other three major islands?" asked Mrs. Harris. _____

16. "They are Hokkaido Kyushu and Sakhalin," replied Julie. _____

17. "You've named two of the three correctly but Sakhalin is not part of the nation of Japan,"
    answered Mrs. Harris. _____

18. "The correct answer is Shikoku Hokkaido and Kyushu," she continued. _____

Great Getaways

Part 2

Rewrite the sentences, adding the words in parentheses. Be sure to use commas correctly.

19. Is it true that raw fish is popular in Japan? (Mariko) _____

_____

20. Many people like sashimi. (yes) _____

_____

21. I like sea urchin eggs. (but I also like hamburgers) _____

_____

22. Yellowfin tuna is delicious in sushi. (and shrimp is also excellent) _____

_____

23. The green paste in the little bowl is really hot! (wow) _____

_____

24. That paste is called *wasabi.* (Raj) _____

_____

25. It's made from horseradish. (and it's traditionally served with sushi and sashimi) _____

_____

Part 3

An *interjection* is a word used to express strong or sudden feeling. Interjections are sometimes used as introductory words. (The word *wow,* which you have encountered in this lesson, is an interjection.) If an interjection is said with force or strong feeling, it is followed by an exclamation mark; if a sentence follows it, the first word of the sentence begins with a capital letter. If an interjection is not said with force or strong feeling, it is followed by a comma, and the word after the comma is not capitalized.

Choose an interjection from the word bank to complete each item. Add appropriate punctuation. Draw three lines (≡) under the first letter of any word that should be capitalized.

Alas	Bravo	Eureka	Hooray	Ahoy	Ugh	Halt	Shh

26. _____ the baby is asleep!

27. _____ this area is closed to the public!

28. _____ this soup tastes terrible.

29. _____ who's in command of this ship?

30. _____ what a magnificent performance!

31. _____ I'm afraid that book is no longer available.

32. _____ we've struck gold!

33. _____ we're all done!

Name _____

Great Getaways

Read and Discover

a. The Galápagos Islands are located 600 miles west of Ecuador, they lie along the equator.
b. These isolated islands are home to many unusual creatures: penguins, giant tortoises, and swimming iguanas are just a few of these.
c. Scientists have studied Galápagos wildlife for centuries; they study not only the habits of certain species but also the interactions among them.

In which sentence are two independent clauses separated incorrectly with only a comma and no conjunction? _____

What punctuation marks are used to separate the independent clauses in the other two sentences? _____ _____

A **semicolon** (;) can be used instead of a comma and conjunction to separate the independent clauses in a **compound sentence**. A **colon** (:) can be used to separate two independent clauses when the second explains the first. It can also be used to introduce a list at the end of a sentence, to separate parts of references in a bibliography, and to separate hours and minutes in an expression of time.

See Handbook Sections 8, 13

Part 1

Write a colon or a semicolon to separate the clauses in each sentence. Note: Four sentences require a colon.

1. About five million years ago the Galápagos Islands rose from the sea they are the result of volcanic explosions deep under the water.

2. These volcanic islands are barren and harsh initially they were lifeless.

3. Scientists have a theory about how wildlife came to the Galápagos creatures from South America rode there on "sea rafts" of vegetation.

4. These creatures were undisturbed for centuries over time they adapted to the environment in unique ways.

5. The marine iguana is quite unusual it swims in the rough surf.

6. Adult marine iguanas can dive forty feet they can stay underwater for thirty minutes.

7. Hundreds of years ago pirates stopped in the Galápagos some hid treasure there.

8. Whalers and seal hunters filled their ships with giant tortoises they used them for food during long voyages.

9. The Spanish name for the tortoises is *galápagos* the islands got their name from this word.

10. The tortoises are huge they can weigh up to 600 pounds.

11. At one time there were 250,000 tortoises in the Galápagos today there are fewer than 15,000.

12. Predators are responsible for much of this decrease they have eaten tortoise eggs and killed adult tortoises.

13. Human beings have caused animal predation we are now trying to protect the remaining tortoises.

14. Humans introduced dogs, pigs, and rats to the islands these animals prey on the tortoises' eggs.

15. Scientists have taken action to save the tortoises from extinction they have built a captive-breeding station.

Great Getaways

Part 2

Draw a line from each sentence on the left to a sentence on the right to make a compound sentence. Then rewrite each pair of sentences as one sentence. Use a semicolon or a colon to separate independent clauses.

Cormorants first flew to the Galápagos many centuries ago.

According to scientists, these birds' bodies changed over time.

Swimming became more important than flying.

Their feet became stronger, and their bodies became more streamlined.

In time, they lost their flying skills.

They adapted to island life.

16. _____

_____

17. _____

_____

18. _____

_____

Part 3

The colon has many uses in writing. Think about how the colon is used in these examples. Then draw a line from each example to the rule it matches.

RAMÓN: Look at that iguana!
CARLO: It's coming closer!

The game will begin at 7:15 P.M.

Remember the first rule of the Wildlife Observation Club: "Never touch a wild animal."

O'Dell, Scott. *Cruise of the Arctic Star*. Boston: Houghton Mifflin, 1973.

We saw fourteen iguanas: three adult males, six adult females, and five juveniles.

Use a colon to introduce a list or series at the end of a sentence.

Use a colon after the speaker's name in a play.

Use a colon to separate the place of publication and the name of the publisher in a book reference in a bibliography.

Use a colon to separate hours and minutes in an expression of time.

Use a colon to introduce a quotation.

Now write an example of your own to match each rule.

19. _____

20. _____

21. _____

22. _____

23. _____

Name _____

Great Getaways

Read and Discover

a. Gibraltar (pronounced juh BRAHL ter) is not an island, but it is like an island in many ways. Gibraltar is on the southwestern tip of Spain. A barren strip of no-man's-land separates Gibraltar from Spain.

b. Gibraltar-pronounced-juh BRAHL ter is not an island, but it is like an island in many ways. Gibraltar is on the southwestern tip (of Spain). A barren strip of no man's land separates Gibraltar from Spain.

In which paragraph are parentheses ( ) used to enclose information that explains a word in the sentence? _____ In which paragraph are hyphens used to link words that form a compound word? _____

Hyphens and parentheses are used to make writing clearer. Use a **hyphen** to:
- separate the syllables in a word when you must break a word at the end of a line of text
- link the parts of some compound words, such as *no-man's-land*
- link some word pairs or groups of words that precede a noun and act as an adjective, such as *best-known attraction*
- link the parts of numbers (written as words) between twenty-one and ninety-nine.

Use **parentheses** to set off an explanation or example.

See Handbook Section 9

Part 1

Write *C* beside each sentence in which hyphens and parentheses are used correctly. Cross out hyphens and parentheses that are used incorrectly. If you are unsure whether a hyphen should be used to link parts of a compound word or adjective phrase, check a dictionary.

1. Gibraltar's inhabitants (who call themselves *Gibraltarians*) are citizens of Great Britain. _____

2. The government of Spain believes that (because Gibraltar is physically attached to Span-ish soil), it should be part of Spain. _____

3. In 1967 Gibraltarians were asked whether they wanted to become part of Spain; only forty-four people out of twelve thousand voted in favor of the idea. _____

4. The Rock of Gibraltar is 1,398 feet (426 meters) tall; it rises almost vertically from the sea. _____

5. The Rock is one of the (world's) most recognizable and visually-arresting-natural features. _____

6. The ancient Romans named the rock *ne plus ultra* (the end of the world). _____

7. The Moors (people from North Africa) captured Gibraltar from Spain in-the-700s. _____

8. Since then, this two-and-a-half-square-mile outcropping of land has undergone 14 sieges. _____

9. In 1779 the Spanish and the French began a four-year siege. _____

10. This attempt, which was unsuccessful, led to the expression ("safe as the Rock of Gibraltar"). _____

11. Gibraltar is also a real-life classroom for archeologists. _____

12. The Gorham Cave is more than 100 feet (30 meters) deep. _____

13. Neanderthals (humanlike creatures who lived 100,000 years ago) (once inhabited the cave). _____

14. Speleologists (scientists who study caves) have been fascinated with it since its discovery in 1907. _____

Great Getaways

Part 2

Add hyphens or parentheses where they belong.

15. In the 1980s Gibraltarians had high hopes of economic growth; they built a 150 million dollar office complex.

16. Many of the rooms in the 16 story hotel built during that time remain empty much of the year.

17. Gibraltar's best known attraction is still the Rock.

18. Despite its rich and unique history, Gibraltar has a less than certain future.

19. Some freedom loving residents wish for independence from Great Britain.

20. Others are Anglophiles people who love Britain and English things who want to continue to live under British rule.

Part 3

A dash is a punctuation mark used to signal a pause. A dash is longer than a hyphen. Think about how dashes are used in the sentences in the left-hand column. Then draw a line from each sentence to the rule it matches.

I'd like to visit Gorham Cave, but I—

Use a dash to stress a word or words at the end of a sentence.

The hike back up the Rock—all the guide books warn visitors about this—is exhausting.

Use dashes to set off a phrase or independent clause that interrupts an otherwise complete sentence.

I fear one thing more than anything else—heights.

Use a dash to mark an interrupted or unfinished sentence.

On the lines below, write your own example for each rule about the use of dashes.

21. _____

_____

_____

22. _____

_____

_____

23. _____

_____

_____

Name _____

Great Getaways

Read and Discover

Brigid asked, "Is Australia a continent or an island?"
Arthur explained that it is both.

Underline the sentence that shows a speaker's exact words. Circle the marks that begin and end this quotation. Circle the first letter of the quotation.

A **direct quotation** is a speaker's exact words. Use **quotation marks** at the beginning and end of a direct quotation. Use a comma to separate the speaker's exact words from the rest of the sentence. Begin a direct quotation with a capital letter. Add end punctuation (period, question mark, exclamation point, or comma in place of a period) before the last quotation mark. An **indirect quotation** is a retelling of a speaker's words. Do not use quotation marks when the words *that* or *whether* come before a speaker's words.

See Handbook Sections 4, 6

Part 1

Write *I* after each indirect quotation and *D* after each direct quotation. Then add quotation marks, commas, and end marks to direct quotations. Draw three lines (≡) under lowercase letters that should be capitalized.

1. Australia is the smallest continent said Arthur. _____

2. Ms. Wetzel added that Australia is the only continent that is also a country. _____

3. look at Australia on the map she said. _____

4. She asked why do you think Australia is called *the land down under*? _____

5. It's in the Southern Hemisphere Ramón replied. _____

6. Ms. Wetzel explained that many unique creatures live in Australia. _____

7. Wallabies, wombats, and bandicoots are three you may have heard of she said. _____

8. Andre asked what's a wallaby _____

9. Ramón explained that a wallaby is a marsupial similar to a kangaroo. _____

10. He added the wombat is also a marsupial, but you might mistake it for a bear cub. _____

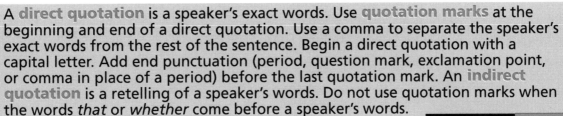

The platypus has a bill like a duck and fur like a beaver.

11. A bandicoot looks something like a rat he continued. _____

12. Ms. Wetzel said that the Australian emu is one of the world's largest birds. _____

13. I read that the platypus is a mammal that lays eggs Randall said. _____

14. This ability makes the platypus unique among mammals Ms. Wetzel replied. _____

15. Randall asked whether any living animals are related to the platypus. _____

16. The platypus is a *monotreme*, a primitive mammal, said Ms. Wetzel, and so is the echidna, a spiny anteater that lives in Australia, Tasmania, and New Guinea. _____

Part 2

Rewrite each indirect quotation as a direct quotation. Rewrite each direct quotation as an indirect quotation. (There is more than one right way to do this.) Be sure to use punctuation marks correctly.

17. Ramón asked whether Australia was once used as a penal colony. _____
_____

18. Ms. Wetzel explained that for almost a century, large numbers of British convicts were sent to Australia to serve their prison sentences. _____
_____
_____

19. Randall asked what the Australian outback is like. _____
_____

20. Arthur said, "It's dry and mostly flat." _____

21. "Kids who live in the outback sometimes attend school by radio," he explained. _____
_____

22. Brigid asked, "Who decided that Australia should be considered a continent?" _____
_____

23. Ms. Wetzel suggested that she do some research and find out. _____
_____

Part 3

Each clue describes an Australian animal. Write the answers in the puzzle. Use information in Part 1 or an encyclopedia if you need help.

Across
4. Small marsupial that resembles a rat
7. Large bird similar to an ostrich
8. Small marsupial similar to a kangaroo

Down
1. Mammal that hatches its young from eggs
2. Spiny anteater
3. Furry tree-dwelling marsupial
5. Wild dog (rhymes with *bingo*)
6. Marsupial that resembles a bear cub

Name _____

Great Getaways

Read and Discover

Coney Island Beach Chalet
Coney Island, New York 11235
August 15, 1998

Dear Carmen,

    Today my cousins took me to the Boardwalk at Coney Island. Wow! There must have been fifty thousand people there! I rode the roller coaster, which is large and really scary. Aren't you proud of me? This used to be a real island, but the land was filled in to form a peninsula. Now Coney Island is part of Brooklyn, New York. I think it's a really neat place!

Your friend,
Rosie

There are five different parts of this letter. Two have already been circled. Circle the other three.

A **friendly letter** has five parts. The **heading** gives the writer's address and the date. The **greeting** includes the name of the person who will receive the letter. It begins with a capital letter and ends with a comma. The **body** gives the message. The **closing** is a friendly way to say good-bye. It ends with a comma. The **signature** is the writer's name. A friendly letter may include informal language.

A **business letter** is a formal letter written to an employer or a business. It has the same parts as a friendly letter, but it also includes the complete address of the person to whom the letter will be sent. Use a colon after the greeting in a business letter.

See Handbook Sections 2, 34, 35

Part 1

Use the boldfaced words in the rule box above to label the five parts of this friendly letter.

                                                  425 Winters Street

1. _____ Augusta, Georgia 30903

                                                  August 25, 1998

Dear Rosie, _____ 2.

    Our camping trip in Minnesota was really fun. We hiked thirty miles in two days. Have you ever hiked that far? I saw a moose and went trout fishing. I have plenty of great pictures to show you.

3. _____

        4. _____ Your friend,

        5. _____ Carmen

Part 2

Rewrite this business letter correctly on the lines below. (Hint: The sender's address and the date go on the right. The business's, or receiver's, address goes on the left.)

Brooklyn Gazette 4005 Fifth Avenue New York, New York 10002 Dear Sir or Madam September 18, 1998 Please send me the September issue of your magazine. I am enclosing four dollars to cover the cost of the issue and the mailing expense. Sincerely Arthur Aiken 6323 Rose Street Detroit, Michigan 48231

_____

_____

_____

_____

_____

_____

_____

_____

_____

_____

_____

_____

_____

_____

Part 3

Think of a place you would like to visit. (This could be an island, but it doesn't have to be.) Find the address of the chamber of commerce for that place or the address of a travel agent. On another sheet of paper write a business letter to the chamber or the travel agent asking for information about the place you would like to visit. You may want to ask about travel options and costs, places to stay, sights to see, and special events. Be sure to use correct business letter form.

Name _____

Great Getaways

Look at each model sentence diagram below. Then diagram the numbered sentences on another sheet of paper. Look back at the lessons on diagraming sentences if you need help, or see Handbook Section 39.

Diagraming Subjects, Verbs, Adjectives, Articles, and Direct Objects (pages 29–30)

A distant rumble filled the air.

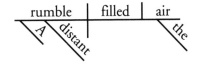

1. The mountain belched black smoke.
2. Frightened residents left the area.
3. The eruption surprised scientists.

Diagraming Compound Subjects, Compound Predicates, and Compound Sentences (pages 59–60)

Goats and sheep pawed the ground and bleated.

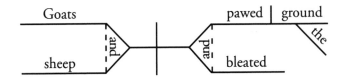

4. The mountain trembled and made loud noises.
5. An explosion rocked the village, and a strong odor filled the air.
6. Sulfur and other gases were released.

Diagraming Understood *You*, Possessive Pronouns, Demonstrative Pronouns, and Indefinite Pronouns (pages 89–90)

Cover your eyes!

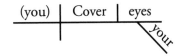

7. The villagers gathered their belongings.
8. Someone grabbed a flashlight.
9. That was good thinking!
10. Leave the village!

Diagraming Linking Verbs, Predicate Nouns, Predicate Adjectives, and Adverbs (pages 119–120)

Molten lava moves slowly.

The villagers were very courageous.

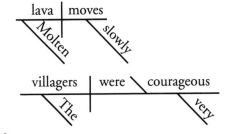

11. One woman quickly gathered the children.
12. The children were frightened, but most were quite brave.
13. A volcanic eruption is an awesome sight.

Diagraming Prepositional Phrases, Indirect Objects, and *There* (pages 149–150)

There was one man with a small infant.

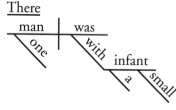

A woman handed her older son a camera.

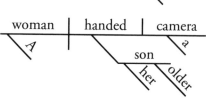

14. The boy put the camera in his pocket.
15. There was a family in a small truck.
16. They offered their neighbors a ride.
17. The driver drove quickly toward the highway.

Diagraming Subject and Object Pronouns, Adjective Clauses, and Adverb Clauses (pages 179-180)

Although some villagers feared the worst, everyone reached the safety of the distant hills.

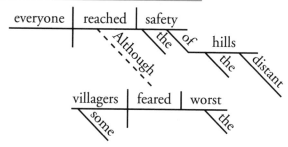

The emergency procedures that they practiced worked perfectly.

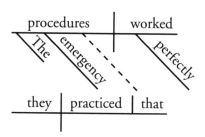

18. Because a sudden rainstorm drenched the area, fires from the lava were quickly extinguished.
19. Ash that spewed from the mountain covered everything.
20. It blanketed trees and houses.

Name _____

Great  Getaways

Writing Sentences

Rewrite each sentence so it makes sense. Make each one easier to understand by using correct punctuation and capitalization.

1. Nantucket is an island off the coast of Massachusetts: with an area of fifty seven square miles.

   _____

   _____

2. She told me that "it's a Native American word meaning *faraway island*." _____

   _____

3. Now I'm reading a book called nightbirds on Nantucket, by J Aiken; I'll lend it to you as soon as

   I get home. _____

   _____

4. Visiting my aunt my uncle (and my cousins) in Nantucket, and I'm having a great time. _____

   _____

   _____

5. I thought the island's name sounded interesting, I asked my aunt what does *Nantucket* mean? _____

   _____

   _____

A friendly letter has a heading, greeting, body, closing, and signature. A well-written letter has a friendly tone, includes specific information, uses description to create pictures in the mind of its reader, and asks the reader questions to give him or her ideas for writing a letter in return. As you read the model letter below, notice the use of specific details and questions to the reader.

> 24 Coral Drive
> Key Largo, Florida 33037
> July 7, 1999

Dear Lin,

   I can't believe it's already been a whole month since school let out! I've been having a good summer. For a few weeks I babysat the neighbors' three kids. It was hard work! I had fun taking them to the swimming pool, though. I even helped the youngest one learn how to swim.

   Now I'm visiting my grandparents in Key Largo. It's one of the Florida Keys, a chain of little islands off the southern tip of Florida. Key Largo is famous because an old Humphrey Bogart movie called <u>Key Largo</u> was filmed there.

   The best part of my vacation so far has been the glass-bottom boat ride we took over John Pennekamp Coral Reef State Park. Through the bottom of the boat we could see beautiful tropical fish and lots of scuba divers. I can see why Key Largo is called the Diving Capital of the World! I really want to take some scuba lessons while I'm here.

   I hope your summer is going well. How do you like your job as a camp counselor? Please write back and tell me all about it!

> Your friend,
> Lakeesha

Great Getaways

Writing a Paragraph

The sentences you revised on page 211 can be used as the body of a friendly letter. Decide what order the sentences should be in. Write them on the lines below. Then add a heading, greeting, closing, and signature.

_____

_____

_____

_____

_____

_____

_____

_____

_____

_____

Imagine that you have just spent five days on an island you've always wanted to visit. Write a friendly letter to a friend back home. Include facts, descriptions, and questions. Use the model on page 211 as your guide.

_____

_____

_____

_____

_____

_____

_____

_____

_____

Reread your letter. Use this checklist to make sure your letter is complete and follows the friendly letter form.

❑ Does my letter have all five parts?

❑ Have I punctuated the greeting and closing correctly?

❑ Have I included specific information?

❑ Have I used abbreviations correctly?

❑ Have I capitalized proper nouns?

❑ Have I asked questions my reader will want to answer in a return letter?

❑ Have I used commas and semicolons correctly?

Name _____

Great Getaways

Proofreading Others' Writing

Read this passage about the island of Tahiti. Use the proofreading marks below to show how each mistake should be fixed.

Proofreading Marks

Mark	Means	Example
ℐ	delete	Papayas, coconuts, and and bananas grow on Tahiti.
∧	add	Papayas, coconuts, bananas grow on Tahiti.
≡	make into a capital letter	papayas, coconuts, and bananas grow on Tahiti.
⊙	add a period	Papayas, coconuts, and bananas grow on Tahiti
⋏	add a comma	Papayas coconuts, and bananas grow on Tahiti.
sp	fix spelling	Papayas, cocconuts, and bananas grow on Tahiti.
/	make into a lowercase letter	Papayas, Coconuts, and bananas grow on Tahiti.

A Paradise Island

For 200 years, the lush tropical, island of Tahiti has been a dream destination for those who wish to return to a simpler life. Tahiti was first settled by polynesians who arrived by see from Asia. In 1767, a british explorer named samuel wallis visited the Island and claimed it for Great britain. Wallis was'nt the only european explorer to take notice of this South Pacific jewel. The following year a french navagator, Louis Antoine Bougainville, claimed the island for france. Today Tahiti is a French overseas territorie.

tahiti gained fame as a tropicle paradise in the late 1800s. The french painter paul gaugin made the island his home in 1891 he lived there for most of his later life. Gaugins' powerfull paintings illustrate the lush beauty of the island. Gaugin wrote about his life in Tahiti in the book Noa Noa which was published in 1897. At least three notable writers have also spent time in Tahiti James Michener herman melville and Robert louis Stevenson.

Tahiti is 402 square miles 1,041 square kilometers in size. The interior of the island is steep, rugged terrain covered by thick vegetation. Most of tahitis residents live near the coast or in papeete pah pee AY tee, it's largest city. Not surprisingly the islands' cheif industry is Tourism.

Proofreading Your Own Writing

You can use the list below to help you find and fix mistakes in your own writing. Write the titles of your own stories or reports in the blanks at the top of the chart. Then use the questions to check your work. Make a check mark (✓) in each box after you have checked that item.

Titles

Proofreading Checklist for Unit 7

Have I capitalized proper nouns and proper adjectives?				
Have I used commas correctly to punctuate items in a series and after introductory words?				
Have I used apostrophes correctly in possessives and contractions?				
Have I used colons and semicolons correctly?				
Have I used hyphens and parentheses correctly?				
Have I punctuated direct quotations correctly?				

Also Remember . . .

Does each sentence begin with a capital letter?				
Have I spelled each word correctly?				
Have I used the right end marks at the end of sentences?				

Your Own List

Use this space to write your own list of things to check in your writing.

Name _____

Great Getaways

Capitalization

Draw three lines (≡) under each letter that should be capitalized.

1. great britain is the largest european island.
2. On this island are the countries of england, scotland, and wales.
3. The full name of the british nation is the United kingdom of great Britain and northern Ireland.
4. the head of britain's monarchy is queen elizabeth II.

Initials, Abbreviations, and Titles

Draw three lines under each letter that should be capitalized. Add underlines, quotation marks, and periods where they are needed.

5. The game of golf may have been invented in scotland.
6. The most famous golf courses in the world are in st andrews, scotland.
7. I am reading a book titled golf for the enthusiastic beginner.
8. It was written by Dr p j gordon of Aberdeen, Scotland.
9. The movie Wuthering Heights takes place on the windy Scottish moors.
10. One of Scotland's best-known artists is w y Macgregor.
11. Robert burns is the national poet of Scotland; he wrote the poem O My Luv's Like a Red, Red Rose.

Apostrophes

Underline the correct word in each pair. Write *C* if the word is a contraction or *P* if the word is a possessive.

12. (Londons'/London's) most famous museum is the British Museum. _____
13. Some of the (worlds'/world's) most valuable artifacts are on display there. _____
14. I (didn't/did'nt) know that in Britain, soccer is called *football*. _____
15. (It's/Its) by far the most popular spectator sport in Britain. _____
16. Professional football in Britain is a (mens'/men's) sport, but both boys and girls there enjoy playing the game for fun. _____

Commas, Semicolons, and Colons

Add commas, semicolons, and colons where they are needed. (One item requires a colon.)

17. England Scotland Wales and Northern Ireland are all part of Great Britain.
18. The people of Northern Ireland are industrious and proud some wish for freedom from British rule, but others want to remain part of Great Britain.
19. Yes conflicts continue to occur in Northern Ireland.
20. Despite the violent actions of a few, there is hope for peace large numbers of people on both sides of the issue want the children of Northern Ireland to grow up in a more peaceful world.

Hyphens and Parentheses

Add hyphens and parentheses where they are needed.

21. The Scottish *lochs* lakes are world famous.

22. Loch Ness is the site of a real life mystery.

23. Dozens of people have claimed to have seen a dinosaur like creature swimming in the lake.

24. The monster is said to be as much as seventy five feet twenty three meters in length.

Quotations

Write *D* after each direct quotation and *I* after each indirect quotation. Add quotation marks and other marks where they are needed. Draw three lines (≡) under each letter that should be capitalized.

25. Have you ever visited Great Britain, Mr. Drake? asked Roger. _____

26. Mr. Drake answered yes I toured England and Northern Ireland. _____

27. Roger said that he would like to see the Scottish Highlands. _____

28. Andrea exclaimed I'd like to see the Loch Ness monster! _____

29. Roger said bring a camera with you. _____

Business Letter

Rewrite this business letter correctly on the blanks.

30. Dear Sir or Madam Eurotrek Travel Company 555 Montgomery Street San Francisco, California 94109 Please send me some travel brochures about Great Britain. Sincerely yours, Ronald Capelli 1435 Howard Street Santa Rosa, California 95436 October 14, 1998

_____

_____

_____

_____

_____

_____

_____

_____

_____

_____

Name _____

Great Getaways

COMMUNITY LEARNING OPPORTUNITIES

In Unit 7 of *G.U.M.*, students learned about **capitalization, punctuation, and other aspects of writing mechanics** and used what they learned to improve their writing. The content of these lessons focuses on the theme **Islands and Near-Islands**. As students completed the exercises, they learned about islands around the world and what makes each one distinctive. These pages offer a variety of activities that reinforce skills and concepts presented in the unit. They also provide opportunities for the student to make connections between the materials in the lessons and the community at large.

Friendly Skies

Have you ever wondered what it's like to work 30,000 feet above the ground? Invite a flight attendant who lives in your community to visit your class and describe his or her job. Before the visit, compile a list of questions to ask during the interview. You might want to find out about the training required to become a flight attendant, what responsibilities the job entails, or learn more about emergency procedures designed to keep airline passengers safe.

Passports

The United States requires its citizens to carry a passport when they are traveling to most international destinations. Find out about the process of obtaining a passport, the requirements for receiving a passport, the differences among the three kinds of passports issued in the United States, and the reasons why passports are required for international travel. Also find out which nations American citizens can visit without a passport and which require a visa. Use what you learn to create a passport guide for potential travelers.

Careers on the Go

Find out more about careers related to travel and the tourist industry. You may want to explore one of these careers:

- travel agent
- cruise ship captain or navigator
- airline pilot
- wilderness guide
- hotel manager
- air tower control operator

Try to arrange an interview with a person in your community who is in the profession that interests you. Find out what the job is like and about the qualifications and training required. If possible, arrange to accompany that person on a tour of his or her workplace.

Hometown Attractions

Think about and list the things you think make your community an enjoyable place to visit. Then produce a brochure that advertises your community to potential visitors and helps them get the most out of a trip to your area. If you need any additional information to complete your brochure, contact the local tourist information center or the chamber of commerce.

Big Plans

Create an itinerary for a trip to any island in the world. You can obtain travel information about the island in travel books, at an embassy or consulate, at a travel agency, or on the Internet. When making your travel plans, consider these issues:

- when you will go on the trip and what the weather will be like during that season
- how you will get to your destination and the cost of the airfare or boat ticket
- where you will stay and the cost of lodging
- how much money you will need for expenses and in what form you will bring it
- what travel documents (such as a passport or visa) you will need
- what inoculations (if any) you will need to remain healthy in a distant part of the world
- what you will pack

Use the planner below to help you organize the information you find.

Island Trip Planner

Destination: _____

Numbers to call for information:

_____

_____

Travel documents needed:

_____

_____

Transportation/travel dates:

Departure: _____

Arrival: _____

Departure: _____

Arrival: _____

Cost of transportation:

_____

_____

Inoculations needed:

_____

_____

Expected weather:

_____

_____

Lodging/dates needed:

_____

_____

_____

_____

Cost of lodging:

_____

_____

Additional costs:

_____

What to pack:

_____   _____   _____   _____

_____   _____   _____   _____

Name _____

Great Getaways

Lesson 1 Circle the complete subject in each sentence. Underline the complete predicate.

1. I am taking guitar lessons.

2. My lessons are on Thursdays.

3. Some of the exercises are difficult.

4. I practice really hard.

5. My teacher doesn't know any new songs.

6. His favorite songs are from the 1960s.

7. Alternative music is my favorite.

8. I took my teacher a tape of my favorite song.

9. He figured out the chords.

10. Most of the chords were actually very simple.

11. I learned them with no trouble.

12. My love for the song made practicing fun.

13. We played it together last week.

14. My teacher liked the song a lot.

15. Our lessons are teaching him about today's music.

Lesson 2 Circle the simple subject in each sentence. If the subject is understood *you*, write *you* on the line. Underline the simple predicate.

1. Hummus is a Middle Eastern dish. _____

2. My sister gave me the recipe. _____

3. Pour a can of garbanzo beans into a blender. _____

4. Some people call garbanzo beans chick peas. _____

5. Squeeze one whole lemon over the beans. _____

6. I use even more lemon sometimes. _____

7. Add crushed garlic, olive oil, salt, and tahini. _____

8. Tahini is sesame seed paste. _____

9. The action of the blender squashes the beans. _____

10. Hummus on pita bread makes a great sandwich. _____

11. Slice the bread into two half-circles. _____

12. Open the pita pocket carefully with your hand. _____

13. Pita bread breaks sometimes. _____

14. Put hummus, lettuce, tomato, and anything else into the pocket. _____

15. Many people simply dip the pita in the hummus. _____

Name

Lesson 3 Each sentence has a compound subject or a compound predicate. Circle the two or three simple subjects that make up each compound subject. Underline the two verbs that make up each compound predicate.

1. Marisa and Rachel play on a soccer team together.
2. Kelly, Raph, and I watched one of their games.
3. Rachel ran down the field and trapped the ball.
4. The goalie and a defensive player ran towards her.
5. Rachel saw Marisa and kicked the ball to her.
6. Marisa took a shot and scored a goal.
7. Raph and Kelly cheered.
8. I put two fingers in my mouth and whistled.
9. We shouted and clapped for a long time.
10. Marisa, Rachel, and I went out for pizza after the game.
11. Rachel and I wanted pizza with mushrooms and pepperoni.
12. Marisa didn't want mushrooms and suggested olives instead.
13. I went to the counter and ordered a large pizza.
14. Mushrooms and pepperoni were on one half of the pizza.
15. The other half was for Marisa and had olives on it.

Lesson 4 Circle each direct object in the sentences below.

1. An artist painted a mural in my neighborhood.
2. I watched her every afternoon.
3. First she sketched a plan.
4. She drew dancers at a carnival.
5. The artist chose bright colors at the paint store.
6. Then she mixed the colors together into new shades.
7. She built a scaffold next to the wall.
8. The scaffold raised her to the level of the mural.
9. The artist painted masks and feathers on the dancers.
10. One dancer in the mural carries a huge, colorful umbrella.
11. Another juggles flaming torches.
12. Some of the dancers resemble people in my neighborhood.
13. I recognized the face of my math teacher on the juggler.
14. One acrobat actually resembles me!
15. Everyone likes the new mural.

Name _____

Lesson 5 Circle the indirect object in each sentence below.

1. Charlie's uncle gave Charlie a ticket to a comic book convention.

2. Charlie's aunt gave them a ride to the convention center.

3. Inside, dealers offered collectors rare comic books.

4. Some collectors were paying dealers large sums for the best comics.

5. Charlie showed a dealer his prize old comic.

6. On the cover, a villain was giving a superhero a blast of supersonic cold rays.

7. The dealer offered Charlie a trade for another rare comic.

8. Charlie and his uncle gave the trade careful consideration.

9. They made the dealer an offer for two comics.

10. On the convention stage, a famous illustrator told the audience stories about his career.

11. The illustrator's friends had often given him ideas for comic book heroes.

12. An archaeologist friend had given him the inspiration for Dino-Woman.

13. She had told the illustrator many fascinating tales about dinosaurs.

14. The illustrator's talents had won him many awards.

15. Afterwards, the illustrator drew Charlie a picture and then signed it.

Lesson 6 Write *PN* if the boldfaced term is a predicate noun. Write *PA* if the boldfaced term is a predicate adjective. Circle the linking verb in each sentence.

1. The rafflesia is a **flower**. _____

2. Its home is the **rain forest**. _____

3. These blossoms are **huge**. _____

4. Some rafflesias are three feet **wide**. _____

5. They look **beautiful**. _____

6. The thick, heavy petals are dark **red**. _____

7. Rafflesias smell **terrible,** however. _____

8. The flower's scent is the **smell** of rotten meat. _____

9. But this scent smells **wonderful** to flies. _____

10. Flies are the main **pollinators** of this rare plant. _____

11. Rafflesias have become **endangered**. _____

12. Rain forest logging and slash-and-burn agriculture are the main **threats** to the

    flower's survival. _____

13. The rafflesia is still so little **understood**. _____

14. Scientists are **hopeful** about future studies of this plant. _____

15. Its extinction would be a **tragedy**. _____

Lesson 7 Underline each prepositional phrase. Circle the preposition that begins each phrase. Draw a box around the object of the preposition. There may be more than one prepositional phrase in each sentence.

1. In July my camp went on a rafting trip.

2. Our bus drove through the woods and stopped at a river.

3. We carried rubber rafts from the bus to the water.

4. Soon we were floating down the river.

5. Our paddles dipped into the water.

6. Across the river a bird fished with its beak.

7. After a calm stretch, we paddled through some rapids.

8. Foamy waves splashed over us.

9. We held tightly to the raft.

10. My friend Peg was swept into the water.

11. For a minute, we could only see her hat bobbing on the waves.

12. Then we saw Peg drifting down the rapids.

13. She floated on her back and kept her feet above the water.

14. We did exactly what we'd learned in safety class, and soon Peg was in the boat again.

15. Before nightfall, we climbed onto the bus and returned to camp.

Lesson 8 Underline each adjectival prepositional phrase. Circle the noun it tells about. Some sentences have more than one adjectival prepositional phrase.

1. Noel's summer job earns her money for CDs.

2. She washes the windows of her neighbors' houses.

3. First she gets a bucket of warm water.

4. Then she carefully adds one capful of ammonia.

5. The fumes from the ammonia sometimes make Noel's eyes water.

6. Noel next uses a wet cloth.

7. Then a quick wipe with a squeegee removes the streaks.

8. The sound of the squeegee makes Noel giggle.

9. A window without streaks is a beautiful sight.

10. The windows in Noel's neighborhood sparkle.

11. Noel's job gave me an idea for my own summer job.

12. I have started mowing the lawns in front of my neighbor's houses.

13. The smell of the grass is wonderful.

14. A cap with a big brim keeps away the glare of the sun.

15. My weekdays in the mowing business leave my Saturdays free.

Name _____

Lesson 9 Underline each adverbial prepositional phrase. Circle the verb or verb phrase it modifies. There may be more than one prepositional phrase in a sentence.

1. I like making origami figures in my spare time.

2. This craft originated in Japan.

3. Origami paper is folded into elaborate shapes.

4. On Tuesday I made an origami frog.

5. I folded some green paper in half.

6. Then I folded the right side over the left.

7. For twenty minutes I carefully made more and more folds.

8. In the end, I had a little green paper frog.

9. If you push on its back, the frog hops across the table.

10. I have placed many origami figures around my room.

11. A boat, a giraffe, a spider, and three fish, all made from paper, sit on my shelf.

12. With a hanger and ten origami cranes I made a mobile.

13. It hangs over my desk.

14. My friends received origami stars for the Fourth of July.

15. In my opinion, origami is a terrific hobby.

Lesson 10 Underline the appositive phrase in each sentence.

1. *Miacis,* a prehistoric weasel-like animal, was the ancestor of cats.

2. Ancient Egyptians, the first people to domesticate cats, considered the animal sacred.

3. Cats, excellent hunters of mice and rats, kept houses free of vermin.

4. In Medieval Europe, cats, supposedly "evil" animals, were killed in large numbers.

5. The resulting increase in rat populations helped spread the Black Death, a plague carried by the rats' fleas.

6. The Egyptian Mau, an ancient cat breed, has a striped and spotted coat and green eyes.

7. The Manx, a breed that originated on the Isle of Man in the Irish Sea, usually has no tail.

8. The Japanese bobtail, another breed with an unusually short tail, is considered good luck in Japan.

9. The Siamese is a breed with a *colorpoint* coat, a coat with contrasting patches of color on the face, ears, tail, and feet.

10. A *tabby* coat, one with patterns of dark stripes, is often found on American shorthair cats.

11. The Scottish fold, a breed with ears that fold down, originated in Scotland.

12. The largest breed, the Maine coon cat, resembles a raccoon.

13. *Crossbreds,* cats with characteristics from more than one breed, are often healthier than purebred cats.

14. Animal shelters, which are found in most communities, are excellent places to find a cat.

15. The cats at a shelter, crossbreds as well as cats of different breeds, are grateful to find a good home.

Extra Practice

Lesson 11 Add the correct punctuation mark to each sentence. Then label each sentence *declarative, interrogative, imperative,* or *exclamatory.*

1. Do you want to see my new pet _____

2. What kind of animal is it _____

3. It's a common garter snake _____

4. Wow, it's so thin and fast-moving _____

5. May I hold it for a while _____

6. Support it gently with both hands _____

7. Hey, it's wrapping around my arm _____

8. Don't worry about being bitten _____

9. What is its usual diet _____

10. I feed it earthworms and insects _____

11. Would you like to see it eat _____

12. Yes, I'd love to _____

13. Bring me that jar of grasshoppers _____

14. Yeesh, it strikes so quickly _____

15. Now it will lie quietly and digest its food for a while _____

Lesson 12 Write *S* next to each simple sentence and *CD* next to each compound sentence. Circle the comma and conjunction or the semicolon in each compound sentence.

1. Some people hate airline food, but I like it. _____

2. Those salty peanuts always taste delicious. _____

3. I enjoy opening the little packets of cheese and crackers. _____

4. You can have lasagna, or you can try the chicken. _____

5. Airline carrots are the most perfectly sliced vegetables in the world. _____

6. The silverware arrives in a sealed plastic bag; how clean and shiny it is! _____

7. The food sits invitingly in its neat compartments. _____

8. There is often entertainment; you can watch a movie during dinner. _____

9. Some people ask in advance for special vegetarian meals. _____

10. I've heard those meals are very good, but I have never tried them myself. _____

11. The air can become very dry on an airplane. _____

12. I often bring water with me, or I ask the attendant for some. _____

13. Chewing gum can help your ears on an airplane flight. _____

14. I always chew gum during the landing, and my ears don't hurt or "pop" from the pressure differences. _____

15. Airline travel is always an adventure. _____

Lesson 13 Draw one line under each independent clause and two lines under each dependent clause. Circle the subordinating conjunction that begins each dependent clause.

1. Because Tim enjoys acting, he auditioned for the school play.

2. Although he wanted the part of the hero, he was cast as the bandit.

3. If he hadn't had a cold for his audition, he would have gotten a bigger part.

4. He had trouble with his lines at the audition because his nose was stuffed up.

5. He was still happy with this part because the bandit is a colorful character.

6. As the curtain rose, the bandit was pacing back and forth on the stage.

7. He was planning revenge because the hero had laughed at his science experiments.

8. Although the hero called him crazy, he was making fantastic discoveries about time travel.

9. He would have the last laugh when he committed the perfect crime!

10. The audience booed when he announced his evil scheme.

11. While the hero innocently ate dinner, Tim tied knots in his shoelaces.

12. The hero was saved because his sister warned him.

13. Although they were all nervous, the cast performed well on opening night.

14. When they took their bows, the audience gave them a standing ovation.

15. Tim will be a professional actor someday, if everything goes according to his plan.

Lesson 14 Write *CX* next to each complex sentence and *CD* next to each compound sentence.

1. Although diatoms are invisible to the naked eye, they may be the most important sea creatures. _____

2. Diatoms are microscopic one-celled plants; most drift in the top layer of the ocean. _____

3. Diatoms live in the top layer because sunlight penetrates the water there. _____

4. Although most diatoms drift with the currents, some can move independently. _____

5. Diatoms have glasslike silica shells, and they come in shapes similar to saucers, flowers, propellers, buttons, and beads. _____

6. Because the shapes are so beautiful, hobbyists have collected diatom shells since the 1700s. _____

7. Collectors must use one tiny hair for a tool as they place diatoms on microscope slides. _____

8. Diatoms may be small, but their huge populations feed countless marine animals. _____

9. Diatoms have been called the "grass of the sea" because they are food for huge schools of krill. _____

10. These schools of krill feed small fish; they are the base of the marine food chain. _____

11. Small fish aren't the only ones that eat krill; some of the biggest sea creatures like krill as well. _____

12. As a baleen whale swims through a school of krill, it filters them out of the water. _____

13. The whale shark is the largest fish in the world, but it uses a similar method for eating krill. _____

14. If diatoms were to die out, all other life in the sea would probably die as well. _____

15. We land creatures depend on diatoms, too, because they produce much of our oxygen. _____

Extra Practice

Lesson 15 Underline the adjective clause in each sentence. Circle the noun it describes. Draw a box around the relative pronoun that begins the clause.

1. Last week I tried sea kayaking, which is an exciting sport.

2. Sea kayaks are large, stable boats that are hard to tip over.

3. The kayak paddle, which has two blades, allows kayakers to steer through the water.

4. Our instructor, who is an expert kayaker, showed us the best paddling methods.

5. We sat in the kayaks on the beach and waited for a wave, which pulled us out into the bay.

6. My friend Matt, who came along with me, paddled fast.

7. We encountered marine animals that we had never seen up close before.

8. We passed an otter whose stomach was draped in kelp.

9. Matt saw a whiskered, large-eyed seal, which swam behind his kayak.

10. Kayakers may encounter seals that seem curious about humans.

11. Were we the ones who were being watched?

12. The government has passed laws that protect marine mammals.

13. The instructor who led our trip kept a wide space between our kayaks and the seals and otters.

14. People who get too close to seals or otters may face fines and other penalties.

15. Sea kayaking is a sport that I would like to try again sometime.

Lesson 16 Underline the adverb clause in each sentence. Draw a box around the subordinating conjunction that begins the clause.

1. Because oceans are so broad and so deep, they have always been mysterious.

2. People imagined gigantic sea monsters before they were able to explore the ocean's depths.

3. Scylla and Charybdis, two sea monsters of Greek myth, supposedly lived where the sea passed through a narrow channel.

4. Whenever Charybdis sucked water into her huge mouth, a perilous whirlpool formed.

5. Although Charybdis was dangerous, sailors feared Scylla even more.

6. As a boat passed between the two monsters, Scylla used her twelve tentacles to grab a meal of sailors.

7. One of the exciting parts of Homer's *Odyssey* comes when Ulysses encounters Scylla and Charybdis.

8. Ulysses steers his ship through the middle of the passage because he knows the dangers on both sides.

9. Although Ulysses tries his best, Scylla drags his boat towards her with her tentacles.

10. As everyone shrieks in horror, Scylla devours six sailors.

11. Ulysses somehow steers the boat past the monsters before any more of his crew are lost.

12. Wherever sailors took to the sea, people told tales of monsters.

13. When a Scottish sea serpent died, its coiled body became the island of Iceland, according to a legend.

14. After oceanographers were able to study deep-sea life, they discovered truths behind some legends.

15. Some real "sea monsters" like the giant squid are even stranger than the imaginary creatures were.

Name _____

Lesson 17 Underline the infinitive phrase in each sentence.

1. In art class I learned how to make a clay pot.

2. The clay must be soft enough to mold easily.

3. To make the clay soft, potters knead it with their hands.

4. This also helps to remove any air bubbles from the clay.

5. Now the potter is ready to shape the pot.

6. Some potters use their fingers to pinch the pot into shape.

7. Others coil strips of clay to form the pot's sides.

8. The coil method is an ancient way to make pottery.

9. Potters use *slip,* a mixture of clay and water, to join the coils together.

10. To smooth the surface of a coil pot, the potter rubs it gently.

11. My favorite way to make a pot is the potter's wheel.

12. As the lump of clay spins on the wheel, the potter uses his or her hands to press it into shape.

13. Potters are able to create a wide range of shapes and sizes on the wheel.

14. The heat of a kiln helps to harden the finished pot.

15. Many potters use brilliant glazes to color their pots.

Lesson 18 Underline the participial phrase in each sentence. Circle the participle.

1. Wrestling with each other, lion cubs learn important skills.

2. These skills, acquired in play, will make the lions effective hunters as adults.

3. My kitten moves forward silently, stalking a ball of string.

4. Pretending the ball of string is a mouse, she bats it with her paw and then pounces on it.

5. I often play with my kitten, swinging a toy on a string.

6. Attracted by the sudden movements, she attacks the toy.

7. Other kinds of young animals also play games, developing different types of skills.

8. Fetching balls or sticks, dogs play happily with humans.

9. Growling at each other, puppies learn protective skills.

10. Young goats play in the mountains, jumping from rock to rock.

11. Dolphins play together in the water, leaping in pairs through the foamy wake.

12. Young chimpanzees, known for their high intelligence, chase one another for fun.

13. Playing just for the fun of it, children and young animals prepare for adulthood.

14. Human children also learn through play, imitating older children and adults.

15. Social skills learned in play stay with a person throughout life.

Name _____

Lesson 19 Underline each gerund phrase. Draw a box around the gerund.

1. Becoming a triathlete is my dream.

2. A triathlon involves competing in three different events.

3. Triathletes compete without even taking a rest between events!

4. Swimming almost a mile is the first event of most triathlons.

5. Bicycling 25 miles comes next.

6. The hardest part, though, may be running six miles at the end.

7. Finishing a triathlon successfully is considered the ultimate athletic challenge.

8. Each week I spend some time on training for the triathlon.

9. I really enjoy riding my bike to and from school.

10. Running long distance is my best event in track.

11. I am not as good at swimming laps, however.

12. I plan to work on swimming long distances at the pool this summer.

13. A friend will help me by timing my laps.

14. The real trick will be putting all three events together.

15. Training for three or four years should prepare me for the competition.

Lesson 20 Label each item *F* (fragment), *RO* (run-on), *CS* (comma splice), or *RA* (ramble-on).

1. The saguaro is often called the giant cactus it grows up to sixty feet tall. _____

2. Up to ten tons in weight. _____

3. The saguaro's trunk is shaped like a thick column, a few branches point upward. _____

4. When I saw a saguaro cactus I thought that in my opinion the branches looked like the arms of a human person who was waving hello to somebody the person knew. _____

5. Found in Arizona, southern California, and parts of Mexico. _____

6. Because the region receives very little rain. _____

7. The saguaro soaks up rain, grooves in its trunk expand to hold the water. _____

8. When the rainstorms finally come. _____

9. The saguaro's grooves expand and contract like an accordion, which is a musical instrument that has grooves that expand and contract in much the same way. _____

10. The saguaro has white, funnel-shaped flowers they bloom on summer nights. _____

11. State flower of Arizona. _____

12. Bats drink the flowers' nectar, pollen is spread from flower to flower on the bats' wings. _____

13. Pollinated cacti produce reddish-purple fruit black seeds spill out when the fruit splits open. _____

14. The saguaro is an essential part of the ecosystem its fruit provides food for many desert animals. _____

15. People eat the fruit raw, they also use it to make jam and syrup. _____

Lesson 21 Underline each proper noun. Circle each common noun.

1. Liechtenstein is a very small country.

2. It is about the size of Washington, D.C.

3. This country lies in the Alps, which are among the highest mountains in Europe.

4. Trains pass through Liechtenstein as they travel between Austria and Switzerland.

5. German is the official language of Liechtenstein.

6. This tiny country is ruled by a prince.

7. Vaduz is the capital of Liechtenstein, and it is also the location of the royal castle.

8. Surrounded by forested mountains, Liechtenstein lies on the banks of the Rhine River.

9. The region was once controlled by Charlemagne, king of the Franks.

10. It later became a part of the Holy Roman Empire.

11. In 1712 Johann-Adam Liechtenstein became ruler of what would become Liechtenstein.

12. Liechtenstein has been independent since 1719, except for a short time when Napoleon conquered it.

13. Tourists from around the world visit this picturesque country.

14. Collectors prize stamps from Liechtenstein.

15. The stamps are decorated with paintings by famous artists such as Rembrandt and Rubens.

Lesson 22 Write each noun in parentheses in its correct plural form.

1. Two (day) ago my (parent), my brother, and I moved to a new town. _____

2. I heard the (echo) of the movers' (voice) in our empty, new house. _____

3. Everything was packed in (box) and (crate). _____

4. My brother and I sat on the (step) and talked about our new (school). _____

5. My brother was scared to meet the (child) in his new second-grade class. _____

6. I wasn't looking forward to starting (class), either. _____

7. Mom said, "Don't dwell on your (worry). Set up your new (room)." _____

8. I unpacked my (book) and placed them on (shelf) in my room. _____

9. As I was changing my (shoe), I heard (noise) in the hall. _____

10. I opened my door and saw two (puppy) wagging their (tail). _____

11. I decided that not all the (surprise) in this new town would be bad. _____

12. One puppy was black with white (patch) on his paws, and the other was brown with black (fleck).

_____

13. We ran out into the garden, where the little dogs leaped like (fox) and howled like (wolf).

_____

14. Then they ran off to chase (butterfly) and hide under (bush). _____

15. My brother and I wrote about our new (pet) in our (diary). _____

Name _____

Extra Practice

Lesson 23 Write the possessive form of each noun in parentheses. Circle each plural possessive noun you write.

1. My (day) work begins with a ride on the bus. _____

2. The bus hurries through the (city) traffic. _____

3. The (wheels) rumbling is a relaxing sound. _____

4. (Passengers) minds wander as they ride. _____

5. Some find entertainment in a (book) pages. _____

6. I wonder if it is any (author) dream to be read on all the buses in the country. _____

7. You can learn a lot from (riders) conversations. _____

8. The sound of (children) giggling often fills the bus. _____

9. I enjoy looking out the (bus) windows. _____

10. That's the best way to get a feel for a (city) character. _____

11. (Shops) windows filled with interesting things can be seen all along the route. _____

12. You can watch different (pedestrians) walking rhythms. _____

13. The (leaves) shadows flicker on the sidewalk. _____

14. The (bus) engine wheezes as it climbs steep hills. _____

15. At the (ride) end, the doors swing open onto a new neighborhood. _____

Lesson 24 Circle each personal pronoun. Write *1* if it is a first person pronoun, *2* if it is second person, or *3* if it is third person.

1. I played handball with Marc yesterday. _____

2. Is he a good player? _____

3. You are just as good. _____

4. Juan beat him in three games last week. _____

5. They played at the park. _____

6. Marc beat me, though. _____

7. We played twice yesterday. _____

8. Did you play a good game? _____

9. I was moving fast. _____

10. You should play Marc. _____

11. Have you played against Maria? _____

12. She is surprisingly quick. _____

13. Juan lost to her in an intense game. _____

14. Marc said the two of them are the best players in the neighborhood. _____

15. Maybe Juan and Maria will play doubles against us sometime. _____

Name _____

Lesson 25 Circle each compound personal pronoun.

1. Shawn and I made ourselves a pizza for lunch.

2. Many people like pizza, but most never bake pizzas themselves.

3. I myself was surprised to see how easy it is.

4. Shawn dressed himself in an apron before starting to mix and knead the dough.

5. I gave myself the task of chopping up the vegetable toppings.

6. As we waited, the rising dough puffed itself into a big ball.

7. Shawn twirled the ball of dough in the air above himself to flatten it out.

8. We arranged toppings on the surface of the pizza, placing one mushroom by itself in the center.

9. The pizza was just the way we like it because we made it ourselves.

10. You should try it yourself sometime.

11. It's not very hard, but there is some work involved: pizzas don't make themselves.

12. Clear yourself a big area for kneading dough and slicing toppings.

13. A friend of mine got herself a special stone to cook pizzas on.

14. I myself don't think that's necessary.

15. Just find yourself a cookie sheet large and sturdy enough to hold the crust.

Lesson 26 Circle each possessive pronoun.

1. My dog is bigger than Lia's dog.

2. Hers is a tiny, yappy dog.

3. I don't like it as much as I like yours.

4. Mine is huge.

5. Most other dogs are afraid of my dog.

6. But he just wants to be their friend.

7. His tail thumps on the ground.

8. Soon the other dogs are wagging theirs.

9. Our neighborhood has lots of dogs in it.

10. Your dog is the nicest.

11. Lia's dog may be small, but have you seen her cat?

12. "Kitty" is bigger than both of my cats put together.

13. His fur puffs out in all directions.

14. That cat's enormous tail has stripes all down its length.

15. Some cats' meows sound strangely human, but his sound more like a lion's roar.

Name

Extra Practice

Lesson 27 Circle each relative pronoun and underline the noun it refers to. Draw a box around each interrogative pronoun.

1. What is a bobcat?

2. It is a wildcat that lives in North America.

3. The bobcat gets its name from its tail, which is short, or "bobbed."

4. You can also recognize bobcats by the long hairs on the sides of the face, which resemble sideburns.

5. Who has seen a bobcat?

6. These animals, which are shy and active mainly at night, are hard to observe.

7. What is a bobcat's habitat?

8. Bobcats live in areas that are wooded, swampy, or mountainous.

9. Mountain climbers who venture into the back country occasionally encounter bobcats.

10. For their dens, bobcats prefer small caves and hollow trees, which provide shelter and security.

11. Practically any animal that is not a predator can become a meal for a bobcat.

12. Which do bobcats hunt in the wild?

13. Rabbits, birds, mice, rats, and squirrels are some of the animals that make up a bobcat's diet.

14. Who must keep an eye out for bobcats on the prowl?

15. Farmers who keep chickens must protect their flocks from bobcats.

Lesson 28 Circle each indefinite pronoun.

1. Everyone in our family thinks that spaghetti is the best food on earth.

2. My dad knows everything there is to know about cooking spaghetti.

3. Nothing could taste better.

4. Most of us prefer spaghetti with marinara sauce.

5. My sister is the only one who likes carbonara sauce better.

6. Both are really delicious.

7. Would you prefer a spaghetti dish with meatballs or one with sun-dried tomatoes?

8. Either would make me happy.

9. Few enjoy spaghetti as much as I do.

10. No one could possibly be any hungrier than I am right now.

11. Won't someone bring me a plateful of spaghetti?

12. Everybody come to the table; it's dinnertime!

13. I can't think of anything I'd rather do.

14. Somebody pass the Parmesan cheese, please.

15. There's none left, so you'll have to eat your spaghetti plain.

Name _____

Lesson 29 Circle each adjective that *describes* or tells *what kind*. Underline each adjective that tells *how many*. Draw a box around each article (*a, an, the*).

1. An ancient oak leans over the bank of the lake.
2. Its numerous roots dip into the placid water.
3. A rope is tied to a high branch.
4. I have swung on it on many warm afternoons.
5. You should stand on the grassy bank and grab the thick rope.
6. Swing out over the deep, clear water.
7. Then let go and plunge in with a thunderous splash.
8. You may descend to a depth of ten feet.
9. Everything looks green under the glassy surface.
10. The cold water may make you feel breathless.
11. A few seconds of vigorous swimming will make you warm.
12. If you swim to shallow water, you can do impressive handstands.
13. You might even see a white egret fishing with its long beak in the slender reeds.
14. Then you can swim to shore and scramble up the slippery bank.
15. After a brief rest, you can catch the rope and swing again.

Lesson 30 Circle each demonstrative adjective. Underline each demonstrative pronoun.

1. This store sells loose beads for making jewelry.
2. I made this the last time I came here.
3. That is an interesting bracelet; how did you make it?
4. I strung these beads on wire and made loops to form flower petals.
5. What are those beads in the center of each flower?
6. Those are seeds with holes drilled through them.
7. These beads in the big jar are made out of old buttons.
8. Those beads over there are made of plastic.
9. This is a cowry shell.
10. People once used these shells as money.
11. Look at those colorful beads in the basket.
12. Craftspeople molded those out of multicolored glass.
13. That is my favorite one.
14. This wooden bead is carved in the shape of a turtle.
15. These would make a beautiful bead necklace.

Lesson 31 Underline each action verb. Circle each linking verb.

1. Plants make sugar with the sun's energy.

2. A water molecule is a combination of hydrogen and oxygen.

3. Plants obtain water from the soil.

4. Their leaves absorb carbon dioxide from the air.

5. Plants appear green because of the substance *chlorophyll*.

6. With energy from sunlight, a plant's chlorophyll splits water molecules into hydrogen and oxygen.

7. A combination of this hydrogen and carbon dioxide forms sugar.

8. Fruit tastes sweet because of this sugar.

9. *Photosynthesis* is the name of this process.

10. Oxygen is a waste product of photosynthesis.

11. Animals breathe this oxygen.

12. Plants are an important food source for animals.

13. Inside animals, plant sugars and oxygen become energy.

14. Animals exhale carbon dioxide for the plants.

15. Plants and animals depend on each other for survival.

Lesson 32 Underline each transitive verb and draw a box around its direct object. Draw a circle around each intransitive verb.

1. Like all the planets in our solar system, the earth orbits the sun.

2. It completes one rotation each year.

3. The earth's position in relation to the sun causes the seasons.

4. The earth's axis tilts during its orbit.

5. In North America's winter, the North Pole points away from the sun.

6. Rain and snow fall frequently in the Northern Hemisphere.

7. The winter solstice marks the shortest day of the year in the Northern Hemisphere.

8. It occurs on December 21 or 22.

9. This day marks the first day of summer in the Southern Hemisphere.

10. For the next three months, the Southern Hemisphere experiences its summer season.

11. The equator divides the earth's Northern and Southern hemispheres.

12. The vernal equinox, the start of spring, occurs in March.

13. The autumnal equinox happens in September.

14. During the equinoxes, the sun shines directly on the equator.

15. At these times, the length of the day equals the length of the night.

Lesson 33 Write *A* if the verb in the sentence is in the active voice. Write *P* if the verb in the sentence is in the passive voice.

1. Seafood is eaten by people all over the world. ___
2. Squid is called *calamari* by Italian chefs. ___
3. They often fry calamari in batter. ___
4. *Sashimi,* sliced raw fish, is offered as an appetizer in Japanese restaurants. ___
5. In the Japanese dish *sushi,* rice and raw fish are carefully wrapped in seaweed by master chefs. ___
6. Japanese chefs broil eels for another popular seafood dish. ___
7. Many people enjoy raw oysters on the half shell. ___
8. Sturgeon are caught by fishers in the Caspian Sea. ___
9. Restaurants serve the eggs of these large fish as caviar. ___
10. Chicken, sausage, rice, and several kinds of seafood are mixed together by skillful chefs in the Spanish dish *paella.* ___
11. Soft-shell crabs have shed their hard exoskeletons. ___
12. In Maryland these crabs are eaten whole by hungry diners. ___
13. Lobsters from Maine are considered a delicacy by gourmets. ___
14. These crustaceans have tender, sweet, pinkish meat inside their tough red shells. ___
15. Lobster bibs are often worn by diners for this messy treat. ___

Lesson 34 Circle each present tense verb. Underline each past tense verb. Draw a box around each future tense verb.

1. The monsoon cycle controls rainfall in parts of Asia, Africa, and Australia.
2. Temperature differences between sea air and inland air cause the monsoon.
3. Dry winds blow from the northeast in winter.
4. By midsummer, southwest winds will bring torrential rain to the parched land.
5. In July 1861, 366 inches of monsoon rain fell on Cherrapunji, India.
6. A violent cyclone devastated Bangladesh during the 1991 monsoon season.
7. More than 125,000 people died in that storm.
8. The rains bring new life along with destruction, however.
9. Heavy monsoon rains are essential for healthy crops.
10. A long delay in the 1982 monsoon rains caused terrible drought in Australia.
11. Every summer, people watch the weather reports anxiously for news of the monsoon.
12. Right now, no one accurately predicts the time or strength of the monsoon very far in advance.
13. Accurate predictions will come eventually, though.
14. In 1978 scientists began MONEX, a wide survey of the monsoon.
15. With more intensive study, we will understand this cycle better.

Name _____

Lesson 35 Circle the boldfaced verbs in present perfect tense. Underline the boldfaced verbs in past perfect tense. Draw a box around the boldfaced verbs in future perfect tense.

1. I **had liked** rubber bands since I was in kindergarten, but I **had never collected** them before last year.

2. My interest **has grown** even greater since then.

3. Every day, once I **have finished** my homework, I look for rubber bands to add to my collection.

4. As soon as I **had collected** twenty rubber bands, I began forming a rubber band ball.

5. The ball **has grown** much larger since then.

6. I **have added** rubber bands of all sizes and colors.

7. Once I had to knock my rubber band ball out of a tree; it **had bounced** up after I threw it at the sidewalk.

8. I began my collection several months ago; by March I **will have kept** it for one year.

9. My sister told me the biggest rubber band ball weighs 850 pounds; she **had seen** a picture of it in a book.

10. By the time I graduate from high school, my rubber band ball **will have grown** even larger than that one.

11. I **have researched** some other rubber band records recently.

12. Surely you **have heard** about the longest rubber band in the world.

13. Students who **had tied** thousands of rubber bands together found that the chain measured more than 19 miles in length.

14. I **have thought** about starting a rubber band chain myself.

15. I will not rest until I **have broken** a rubber band record!

Lesson 36 Circle each boldfaced verb in a progressive tense. Cross out each boldfaced verb that is not in a progressive tense.

1. I **am having** a bad day.

2. It **was raining** when I woke up.

3. My sister **had eaten** the last of my favorite cereal.

4. I still **have** not **forgiven** her for it.

5. Outside, a big gust of wind blew just as I **was opening** my umbrella.

6. Soon it **had turned** inside out; it was ruined.

7. I guess this weekend I **will be buying** a new umbrella.

8. As I got to the bus stop, the bus **was driving** away.

9. Since I **had missed** the bus, I had to walk to school.

10. I got very wet while I **was walking**.

11. I **have been** on time every day this semester, but today I was late.

12. Just as I walked in, my teacher **was distributing** a pop quiz.

13. Now, however, my day **is getting** a little better.

14. My teacher announced that next week we **will be going** to the aquarium.

15. I **have decided** to put this terrible morning behind me.

Lesson 37 Circle each adverb. Then tell whether the adverb explains *how, when, where,* or *to what extent.*

1. The dancers leaped high into the air. _____

2. They moved gracefully. _____

3. They balanced daintily on their toes to delicate music. _____

4. Then the music changed to a loud, dramatic piece. _____

5. The company stomped thunderously with their heels. _____

6. They seemed to dance effortlessly. _____

7. It must be extremely difficult to learn and practice complicated dance steps. _____

8. One dancer performed a solo beautifully. _____

9. He tripped on some scenery there. _____

10. He fell clumsily to the floor. _____

11. He painfully twisted his ankle. _____

12. Surgery was not necessary. _____

13. The ankle was only sprained. _____

14. Afterwards, he appeared for a curtain call. _____

15. Everyone clapped loudly for the dedicated dancer. _____

Lesson 38 Underline each prepositional phrase. Circle the preposition and draw a box around its object. There may be more than one prepositional phrase in a sentence.

1. The strangler fig grows in the rainforest.

2. Birds and bats drop its seeds over tall trees.

3. In the leafy canopy, a fig seed sprouts.

4. Long vines grow from that seed.

5. These strong vines encircle the trunk of a host tree.

6. The fig plant then drops roots to the forest floor.

7. After a while, the host tree dies and rots away.

8. The strong lacework of vines stands on its own.

9. You can climb inside the hollow strangler fig.

10. The interior of the hollow trunk towers above your head.

11. You could imagine you are in a deep well.

12. Then you grab onto the sturdy vines and climb through the hollow center.

13. The spaces between the vines resemble small windows.

14. You can see amazing sights from that vantage point.

15. The rainforest floor lies beneath you.

Name _____

Extra Practice

Lesson 39 Underline each coordinating conjunction. Circle each subordinating conjunction.

1. Before my brother started playing the bagpipe, I had never heard the instrument.

2. The bagpipe is an ancient instrument, but no one knows its origins.

3. Scottish bagpipes are made of a leather bag and five pipes.

4. When a musician blows into the *blowpipe,* the bag inflates.

5. The musician presses the bag, and air flows out of the pipes.

6. Each of the three *drone* pipes makes one continuous note, but the musician plays tunes by covering holes on the *chanter* pipe.

7. Although Scottish bagpipes can only produce nine notes, many bagpipe tunes are challenging.

8. Since my brother started playing, he has learned ten tunes.

9. Because bagpipes are expensive, my brother started with a practice instrument called a *chanter.*

10. The chanter is basically a blowpipe and a chanter pipe combined.

11. When my brother had learned to play the chanter well, he bought a real bagpipe.

12. If you've ever heard a bagpipe, you know it sounds very different from most other instruments.

13. Its sounds make me think of a person humming, the ocean roaring, or a duck quacking.

14. I like my brother's music, but I wish his bagpipes weren't so loud.

15. He practices outside, because he would drive everyone in the house crazy otherwise.

Lesson 40 Circle each conjunction. If a sentence contains correlative conjunctions, write *CC* on the line.

1. My sister and I are identical twins. _____

2. We not only look alike but also sound alike. _____

3. Both our friends and our parents can tell us apart, however. _____

4. Neither my sister nor I like to wear the same clothes. _____

5. We may look alike, but our personalities are different. _____

6. After school, my sister is usually either playing sports or practicing ballet. _____

7. I prefer reading and acting in plays. _____

8. Still, my twin is not only my sister but also a good friend. _____

9. Both she and I enjoy hiking in the wilderness. _____

10. We often take hikes or just short walks together. _____

11. We joke around and talk about whatever is on our minds. _____

12. We share a sense of humor; often either she is playing a practical joke or I am telling a funny story. _____

13. Once we switched clothes and pretended to be each other. _____

14. Some of our friends were fooled at first, but after talking to us for a while they figured out the trick. _____

15. Neither our teachers nor our parents were fooled. _____

Name _____

Extra Practice

Lesson 41 Fill in the blanks with *your* or *you're*. Remember to capitalize a word that begins a sentence.

1. What is _____ favorite sport?

2. Lucia told me that _____ a fan of gymnastics.

3. Is becoming an Olympic gymnast _____ dream?

4. If _____ planning to become a gymnast, be prepared to work very hard.

5. You will have to spend part of every day at _____ gym.

6. _____ coach will teach you many new skills.

7. She will also help you build _____ strength.

8. _____ going to need to eat lots of healthful foods to build up muscles.

9. Soon _____ going to be doing flips and handstands.

10. _____ safety is extremely important; a "spotter" will make sure you don't hurt yourself on difficult moves.

11. When _____ ready, you can enter competitions.

12. You'll need to put together all _____ new skills into a smooth routine.

13. _____ probably going to be nervous.

14. Still, try to keep _____ mind on the routine.

15. If you always do _____ best, you will be satisfied with whatever you accomplish.

Lesson 42 Fill in the blanks with *their, they're,* or *there*. Remember to capitalize a word that begins a sentence.

1. _____ are many European legends about elves.

2. _____ imaginary creatures who are said to have magic powers.

3. Elves are said to tell people where _____ are rich veins of gold.

4. In some stories elves use _____ powers to help people.

5. For example, elves might help lost travelers find _____ way.

6. In other stories, though, _____ mean and unpleasant.

7. Some stories tell about elves who kidnap humans and take them to _____ secret land.

8. When the humans return, _____ old and gray.

9. A storyteller may point out a round hill and say, "Elves live under _____!"

10. _____ also said to live on magical islands.

11. Time passes very slowly _____, so elves seem never to reach old age.

12. When elves ask humans for _____ help and the humans provide that help, the elves usually repay the humans handsomely.

13. Many authors have included elves in _____ stories.

14. You may have heard of Legolas, Elrond, or Galadriel; _____ all elves in books by J.R.R. Tolkien.

15. You can read more about elves in the book over _____ by the clock.

Lesson 43 Circle the correct word in parentheses.

1. (It's/Its) amazing how many different kinds of fish there are.

2. What is the largest fish in the world? (It's/Its) the whale shark, which can weigh more than 15 tons.

3. (It's/Its) diet is primarily made up of tiny aquatic organisms.

4. I was relieved to learn that (it's/its) harmless to people.

5. The black swallower can eat fish twice (it's/its) size.

6. It does this by unhinging (it's/its) jaw in the same way a boa constrictor does.

7. The flying hatchet fish can use (it's/its) pectoral fins as wings.

8. (It's/Its) actually able to take off from the water's surface and fly for up to ten feet.

9. The porcupine fish uses (it's/its) prickly spines for protection.

10. (It's/Its) also able to fill itself with water to appear larger than it actually is.

11. If someone asks you what fish has four eyes, tell her (it's/its) the anableps.

12. (It's/Its) eyes are divided in two, so it can swim just below the surface and see above and below the water.

13. A cave fish is adapted to life in total darkness; (it's/its) eyes may be small and sightless, or nonexistent.

14. An archerfish catches (it's/its) prey by spitting water through the air.

15. (It's/Its) an expert at catching small insects it knocks into the water.

Lesson 44 Circle the correct word in parentheses.

1. (Whose/Who's) interested in puppets?

2. I first became interested through a friend (whose/who's) mother is a puppeteer.

3. I know another puppeteer (whose/who's) going to teach me his craft.

4. He says that anyone (whose/who's) as interested as I am is sure to do well.

5. I made a puppet (whose/who's) head is a sock.

6. The puppet looks like the Cheshire Cat, (whose/who's) my favorite character.

7. I have a friend (whose/who's) working on a puppet of her own.

8. It's a paper bag puppet (whose/who's) hair is made of shredded newspaper.

9. We can't decide (whose/who's) puppet is funnier.

10. My hero is Jim Henson, (whose/who's) the creator of the Muppets.

11. I've been reading about different kinds of puppets in a book (whose/who's) author is a famous puppeteer.

12. Marionettes are puppets (whose/who's) movements are controlled by strings or wires.

13. (Whose/Who's) familiar with the Japanese form of puppetry known as *Bunraku*?

14. A friend of mine (whose/who's) seen Bunraku told me that the puppeteers dress all in black but don't hide out of sight.

15. The most popular entertainers in Indonesia are puppets (whose/who's) shadows are projected onto screens.

Name _____

Lesson 45 Fill in each blank with *to, too,* or *two* to complete each sentence correctly.

1. Yesterday I went _____ the African art museum.

2. I took the special tour on battles, which began at _____ o'clock.

3. The tour took _____ hours, but the time passed very quickly.

4. I learned about historic African weapons and armor and battle customs, _____.

5. Many Central African throwing knives had _____ points, one on each side.

6. The throwing method was similar _____ that of throwing a boomerang.

7. Although some knives were only used in battle, others had ceremonial functions, _____.

8. Some African cavalrymen rode _____ battle wearing quilted cloth armor.

9. Their horses wore this kind of armor, _____.

10. Fulani cavalrymen wore quilted battle coats, but they also protected their bodies from shoulder _____ waist with heavy iron armor.

11. A Fulani warrior who fell off his horse in battle could not remount because the armor was _____ heavy.

12. Often a soldier carried a sword and _____ spears into battle.

13. Most of the soldiers used shields, _____.

14. Beautiful silverwork often attached a lion's mane or tail _____ an Ethiopian warrior's shield.

15. The Maasai and the Kikuyu peoples often held a duel between their _____ best warriors before a battle.

Lesson 46 Fill in each blank with *than* or *then* to complete each sentence correctly.

1. Earthquakes happen almost every day in some part of California; now and _____ one of them is strong enough for people to feel.

2. I think small earthquakes are more exciting _____ frightening.

3. Some earthquakes begin more _____ 400 miles below ground.

4. First the earth's crust starts moving deep below the surface; _____ energy waves go through the ground.

5. *Compressional,* or primary, waves travel faster _____ *shear,* or secondary, waves.

6. This is why compressional waves arrive first, and _____ shear waves arrive.

7. Both of these waves travel faster deep inside the earth's crust _____ they do near the surface.

8. If the ground continues to shake for a long time, buildings may shake apart and _____ collapse.

9. If you're inside and feel an earthquake begin, take shelter right _____ under a desk or table.

10. Wait until you are sure the quake is over; only _____ should you come out.

11. When it comes to earthquakes, nothing is more important _____ being prepared.

12. Schools and businesses practice emergency procedures; _____ everyone knows what to do in a disaster.

13. Often more damage is caused by the by-products of earthquakes _____ by the earthquakes themselves.

14. An undersea earthquake may cause a tsunami, which may _____ roll toward land and do terrible damage.

15. Sometimes, fires started by ruptured gas lines cause more damage _____ the earthquake.

Extra Practice

Lesson 47 Write *X* after each sentence that uses negatives incorrectly. Write *C* after each sentence that is written correctly.

1. I haven't never had a pet before, but my father says I can get one for my birthday. _____

2. I can't decide what kind of pet I want. _____

3. My dad doesn't want no cat in the house because he's allergic to them. _____

4. Tropical fish are beautiful, but they don't do nothing but swim. _____

5. You can't take them nowhere, neither. _____

6. A friend of mine has a gerbil, and it never stops running on its exercise wheel. _____

7. My dad doesn't like the idea of having a rat in the house. _____

8. Snakes are cool, but I wouldn't want to feed them no live mice. _____

9. Insects aren't really pets, in my opinion. _____

10. An ant farm doesn't count, and neither does a beehive. _____

11. Parrots are pretty, but my dad wouldn't never let me have such a noisy pet. _____

12. Besides, birds aren't very cuddly, and you can't really play with them. _____

13. I can't think of nothing wrong with dogs. _____

14. My dad doesn't have any problems with dogs either. _____

15. It won't be long before we have a new puppy in the family. _____

Lesson 48 Cross out each incorrect usage of *go, went, like,* and *all.* (If the word *was* is part of the incorrect expression, cross that out also.) Write correct words to replace the crossed out words if a replacement is needed.

1. Jamal was all, "My friend Tatiana is going to enter a math competition." _____

2. Then he goes, "She is one of the smartest people I know." _____

3. He was, like, so insistent that she would win, like, no matter who else entered the contest. _____

4. Marjorie was like, "What will happen if she does win?" _____

5. Jamal said if she, like, *did* win locally, she'd go against students from, like, all over the state. _____

6. Then he went, "All the winners of the state contest will form a team to compete with others from around the country." _____

7. So Marjorie goes, "Do you think she'll get that far?" _____

8. Jamal was like, "She was on the winning team last year, and I think she can do it again." _____

9. Marjorie was all, "Tatiana sounds like a very smart person. I'd like to meet her sometime." _____

10. Jamal said that he would, like, introduce us after school. _____

11. Then we, like, ran into Tatiana. _____

12. She went, "Oh, hi, how are you?" _____

13. At first I thought she was kind of, like, snobby. _____

14. Then she goes, "I heard you guys are really good in math." _____

15. She, like, asked us to join her team for the competition! _____

242

Name _____

G.U.M.

Lesson 49 Circle the correct word in parentheses.

1. From where we (sit/set), we can see the pyramids of ancient Egypt on the west bank of the Nile River.

2. The mummified bodies of pharaohs once (lay/laid) in them.

3. Realistic statues showing a pharaoh (sitting/setting) on his throne were believed to help the pharaoh's spirit recognize the pyramid as its home.

4. Statues' eyes were often (sit/set) with quartz crystal to make them as lifelike as possible.

5. Some experts believe that the pyramids were built by farm laborers during the part of each year when Nile floodwaters (lay/laid) on the fields.

6. A major step in building the pyramids was to build ramps and (lie/lay) planks on them to reduce friction.

7. Then workers slid enormous blocks of limestone up the ramps and (sat/set) them in layers.

8. Archaeologists have calculated that the workers had to (sit/set) one block every two and a half minutes.

9. Finally, workers (lay/laid) a smooth coating of smaller stones over the top.

10. Once these smaller stones were (sat/set) in place, the pyramid looked like solid stone from a distance.

11. Archaeologists have made interesting discoveries about the lives of the workers who (lay/laid) the stones.

12. The remains of a bakery and of a workers' graveyard still (lie/lay) near the pyramids.

13. Some workers were (lay/laid) to rest under miniature pyramids made of mud bricks.

14. Ancient robbers looted the pharaohs' pyramids for the treasures that (lay/laid) inside them.

15. After about 1700 B.C., Egyptians (lay/laid) their pharaohs in secret tombs to hide them from robbers.

Lesson 50 Circle the correct word in parentheses.

1. I (thought/thinked) I saw a dog in the alley.

2. It turned and (shaked/shook) its tail at me.

3. I (threw/throwed) a rubber ball to it.

4. The next day I (bringed/brought) it some food.

5. Someone had (built/builded) a small shelter for it.

6. Unfortunately, the wind had (blew/blown) some of the boards apart.

7. I was glad I had (wore/worn) a scarf.

8. The alley was (lit/litten) by a rosy sunset.

9. As it (grew/grown) darker, I worried that I wouldn't see the dog again.

10. My heart (sang/singed) when I saw the dog come around the corner.

11. It (ate/eated) the food eagerly.

12. Then I (gone/went) home slowly.

13. At my door I turned and saw that the dog had (ran/run) after me, wagging its tail.

14. My parents (said/sayed) we could keep the dog if no one reported it as missing.

15. We (drived/drove) to the vet to make sure the dog was healthy and to get it its shots.

Name _____

Lesson 51 Circle each boldfaced word that is a subject pronoun. Underline each boldfaced word that is an object pronoun.

1. **You** won't believe what **we** got from Mildred.

2. **She** gave **us** a fruitcake.

3. **We** thanked **her** politely.

4. **It** was as hard as a rock.

5. Floyd told **me** that **he** likes fruitcake.

6. I sent the cake to **him**.

7. **He** could not eat **it**.

8. His cousins like sweets; **he** gave it to **them**.

9. **They** don't want **it** either.

10. Maybe **they** will send it to **you**.

11. I have thought of a gift that **we** all want.

12. **It** is useful to all of **us**.

13. I will give **you** a hint.

14. **You** record music on **it**.

15. **You** guessed **it**: blank cassette tapes.

Lesson 52 Circle the correct pronoun in each pair. Write *S* if you chose a subject pronoun and *O* if you chose an object pronoun.

1. Brock and (I/me) met MacDougal at the scene of the crime. _____

2. (He/Him) and Findley were dusting for fingerprints. _____

3. I asked them to give Brock and (I/me) the lowdown. _____

4. They said Lizzie had given the Tenth Precinct and (we/us) the slip. _____

5. As Brock and (I/me) interviewed Mrs. Patel, the owner of the jewelry store, her son Billy came in. _____

6. (He/Him) and Mrs. Patel got into an argument about whether Mrs. Patel had locked the door. _____

7. (She/Her) and Billy were the last to leave the store before the robbery. _____

8. They told Brock and (I/me) that everything had seemed normal that night. _____

9. I told Brock and (they/them) that Lizzie and her accomplices always strike when you least expect it. _____

10. I knew it would be hard to catch Lizzie and (they/them). _____

11. Brock and (I/me) were determined to give it our best shot. _____

12. There's an old score to settle between Lizzie and (I/me). _____

13. (She and I/Her and me) worked together once, before she turned to the wrong side of the law. _____

14. I knew Lizzie couldn't resist the lasagna served at the restaurant where (she and I/her and me) used to get lunch on our break. _____

15. We staked out the restaurant, and, sure enough, the lasagna and (I/me) captured the master thief. _____

Lesson 53 Circle the antecedent or antecedents of each boldfaced pronoun.

1. Rachelle and her mother and brother drove across the United States when **they** moved from Philadelphia to Los Angeles.

2. Rachelle kept a diary of everything **she** saw along the way.

3. In her diary Rachelle wrote about the Sears Tower in Chicago; **it** is the tallest building in the world.

4. Rachelle's mother pointed out the Mississippi River to **her,** and Rachelle wrote about that, too.

5. When the trip got boring, Rachelle played the license plate game to pass the time; **she** kept track of each new state's license plate she saw.

6. The car broke down somewhere near Denver, but a mechanic fixed **it.**

7. The mechanic was friendly, and Rachelle wrote about **him** in her diary.

8. Rachelle wrote about the Rocky Mountains when her mother drove through **them.**

9. In Utah, Rachelle's brother asked to visit Zion National Park; **he** had read that the park is beautiful.

10. Rachelle, her mother, and her brother parked the car so **they** could go hiking in the colorful canyons.

11. In some places the canyon walls were so close together Rachelle could touch **them** both at the same time.

12. Back in the car, Rachelle wrote about Zion; she said **it** was the most amazing place she had ever visited.

13. As Rachelle's mother navigated the streets of Las Vegas, **she** pointed out all the flashing neon signs.

14. Rachelle wrote in her diary that the lights looked like stars to **her.**

15. Finally, the family arrived at the Pacific Ocean, and **they** went for a swim.

Lesson 54 Circle the pronoun in parentheses to complete each sentence correctly.

1. (Who/Whom) is playing first base?

2. The player (who/whom) the league named MVP for last year is the first baseman.

3. (Who/Whom) or what is an "MVP"?

4. MVP stands for Most Valuable Player, a player without (who/whom) the team would be lost.

5. I have a cousin (who/whom) admires that player very much.

6. (Who/Whom) is that over there?

7. To (who/whom) are you referring?

8. I am referring to the person (who/whom) is sitting in the front row of the bleachers.

9. I still can't tell to (who/whom) you are pointing.

10. I mean that woman (who/whom) is eating a hot dog.

11. Oh, she is someone of (who/whom) you may have heard.

12. She's the one (who/whom) starred in that movie.

13. Do you mean the movie with the director (who/whom) won an Academy Award?

14. That's a person (who/whom) I would like to meet!

15. Let's find someone (who/whom) will introduce us.

Name

Lesson 55 Circle the simple subject in each sentence. Then underline the correct form of each verb in parentheses.

1. A new set of watercolors (is/are) what I want for my birthday.

2. Tubes of paint (works/work) best for my style of painting.

3. Mineral-based pigments (gives/give) the paints their colors.

4. Paints made with the pigment cadmium (looks/look) red.

5. Cobalt, another pigment, (turns/turn) paints blue.

6. Compounds of chrome and lead (produces/produce) brilliant pigments.

7. The many colors of chrome (includes/include) red, yellow, orange, and bright green.

8. The health risks of lead (necessitates/necessitate) handling these pigments with great care.

9. A mixture of iron oxide, clay, and sand (creates/create) ocher, a yellowish-brown pigment.

10. A material called *gum arabic* (holds/hold) water colors together.

11. Blobs of paint (dot/dots) my mixing palette.

12. A skillful artist always (mixes/mix) shades carefully.

13. Drops of water (lightens/lighten) a color; I add the drops slowly.

14. Long, quick strokes with a big brush (creates/create) a thin *wash* of color.

15. Layers of transparent color (overlaps/overlap) to make a new shade.

Lesson 56 Look at the compound subject in each sentence. Circle the conjunction. Then underline the correct verb.

1. My friends and my brother (likes/like) eating in the cafeteria.

2. Either Mr. Novak or Mrs. MacGee usually (serves/serve) us the entree.

3. The window table or the corner table (is/are) a good place to sit.

4. Fresh-baked bread or muffins often (appears/appear) on Mondays.

5. Jaia and Piper (likes/like) muffins a lot.

6. A vegetarian entree and a sugar-free dessert (is/are) always available.

7. On Tuesdays, hamburgers or vegetable lasagna (is/are) the featured entree.

8. Gerome and Garth always (chooses/choose) hamburgers.

9. Sometimes Gerome or Garth (lets/let) me have a few french fries.

10. Either baked ziti or fried chicken (is/are) served on Wednesdays.

11. Thursdays are my favorite because fajitas and black bean chili (is/are) on the menu that day.

12. Neither the fried chicken nor the hamburgers (tastes/taste) as good as the black bean chili.

13. Neither cake nor pie (is/are) ever served for dessert on Fridays.

14. Jaia and I usually (orders/order) bread pudding that day.

15. Today, a baked potato and a salad from the salad bar (sounds/sound) good to me.

Lesson 57 Circle the simple subject in each clause. Then underline the correct form of each verb in parentheses.

1. "Megatoaster" (is/are) the name of our band.

2. Dimitri and Damon (is/are) in the group with me.

3. The group (sounds/sound) really good now.

4. We always (plays/play) our own original music.

5. "Walls and Windows" (is/are) a new song I've just written.

6. The band (plays/play) at school dances and talent shows.

7. Everyone (dances/dance) when we play.

8. "Pomegranate Seeds" (is/are) our most popular song.

9. The whole crowd (cheers/cheer) when we start playing it.

10. At that moment, everything (seems/seem) great.

11. My family (does/do) not come to hear us very often.

12. No one (says/say) the music is too loud, but all of them cover their ears when we play.

13. Earplugs (helps/help) protect our eardrums from the noise.

14. Nothing (stops/stop) us in the middle of a song.

15. Our sound equipment sometimes (blows/blow) fuses, but we keep playing.

Lesson 58 Underline the verbal phrase that begins each sentence. If the phrase is a dangling modifier, write *dangling* on the line. If the phrase is used correctly, circle the word it modifies and write *C* on the line.

1. Learning to knit, sweaters can be made. _____

2. Wanting to try a new hobby, Maxine learned to knit. _____

3. Never having knitted before, a simple pattern was chosen. _____

4. Looping yarn around long needles, the project seemed easy. _____

5. Glancing briefly at the instructions, Maxine began knitting very quickly. _____

6. Knitting the front of the sweater, mistakes were made. _____

7. Covered with holes and lumps in the stitches, the sweater was not wearable. _____

8. Unraveling it stitch by stitch, disappointment was inevitable. _____

9. Determined to learn, it was time to make a new start. _____

10. Studying the instructions carefully, Maxine realized where she had gone wrong. _____

11. Knitting carefully this time, the sweater grew slowly but steadily. _____

12. Spaced evenly and neatly, the rows of stitches looked better. _____

13. Taking her time, Maxine created a beautiful sweater. _____

14. Made with her own two hands, she was very content. _____

15. Having knit one sweater successfully, she is ready to begin another. _____

Lesson 59 Think about how many things are being compared in each sentence. Then underline the correct form of the adjective or adverb in parentheses.

1. Jamal runs (faster/fastest) than I do.

2. But Aya is the (faster/fastest) runner on the track team.

3. She runs even (better/best) than our coach.

4. Last month I started practicing (harder/hardest) than I ever had before.

5. I ate the (healthier/healthiest) foods I could find.

6. I spent (longer/longest) than usual warming up each day before races.

7. Yesterday was the (bigger/biggest) race of the season.

8. It was scheduled (earlier/earliest) than I had expected.

9. Still, I felt (more ready/most ready) than I feel before most races.

10. I also felt the (more nervous/most nervous) I had ever felt in my life.

11. I pushed myself (more determinedly/most determinedly) than anyone else in the race.

12. I almost ended up with a (better/best) finishing time than Aya.

13. Even though I didn't win, I was the (prouder/proudest) one there.

14. She's still the (swifter/swiftest) runner of all.

15. But now no one will think of me as the (slower/slowest) on the team.

Lesson 60 Underline the correct helping verb in each sentence.

1. If you like mazes, you (have/might) be interested in learning about the Labyrinth of Minos.

2. This legendary building (did/may) have been the first maze.

3. The legend of the Labyrinth (has/should) been told for over two thousand years.

4. According to the Greek myth, King Minos (was/had) asked Daedalus to build the Labyrinth.

5. A bull-headed monster called the Minotaur (should/was) imprisoned inside.

6. Greeks of ancient Athens (would/may) sacrifice seven young men and women each year to the Minotaur.

7. The Greek hero Theseus felt that the sacrifices to the Minotaur (have/must) be stopped.

8. He said he (is/would) be one of the seven to enter the Labyrinth.

9. King Minos's daughter gave Theseus a ball of twine so that he (was/could) mark his path through the confusing passages of the Labyrinth.

10. After Theseus (had/should) killed the Minotaur, he escaped with King Minos's daughter.

11. The Labyrinth of legend (can/might) have been based on a real place.

12. Archaeologists (did/may) have found the original Labyrinth at the ancient palace of Knossos in Crete.

13. No Minotaur lived in the real Labyrinth, but, according to wall paintings young athletes (did/is) jump over bulls there.

14. Today visitors (had/can) tour the rebuilt palace at Knossos.

15. That tour (would/is) be fascinating to take.

Lesson 61 Draw three lines (≡) under each lowercase letter that should be capitalized. Draw a line (/) through each capital letter that should be lowercase.

1. The country of fiji is in the South pacific.

2. more than 300 Islands and 500 reefs make up this tropical Nation.

3. viti levu, or Big Fiji, is the Largest island.

4. Smaller islands include Kandavu and vanua levu.

5. thousands of years ago, people migrated to fiji from indonesia.

6. Nearly 2,000 years ago, a group of polynesians settled there.

7. A dutch navigator named abel tasman was the first european explorer to visit the islands.

8. In 1774 captain james cook visited a southern Island called vatoa.

9. In the decades that followed, many european traders and Missionaries settled in Fiji.

10. Thousands of workers from india were brought to fiji to work on sugar plantations.

11. A few escaped convicts from australia also made fiji their home.

12. Many of today's Fijians are of indian, polynesian, Chinese, micronesian, and european descent.

13. Fiji has been an independent Nation since 1970.

14. The official language of fiji is english, but many island residents speak fijian or hindi.

15. Fiji's capital and largest City is suva, which lies along the southern coast of viti levu.

Lesson 62 Rewrite each item below. Use initials and abbreviations where you can.

1. Doctor Martha Jane Brown _____

2. Mister Miguel Garcia _____

3. Stanyan Street _____

4. Mount Shasta _____

5. Riverland Avenue _____

6. Mistress Madeline Trimble _____

7. Castle Corporation _____

8. General Robert Edward Lee _____

9. Monterey Boulevard _____

10. Mister Gino Raffetto _____

11. Bonnview Road _____

12. Doctor Peter Murray _____

13. Cellular Network, Incorporated _____

14. Cassock Drive _____

15. Mister Robert Elwood Jones _____

Lesson 63 Draw three lines (≡) under the letters that should be capitalized. Underline or add quotation marks where they are needed in titles.

1. My family rented the movie south pacific, and we found it very entertaining.

2. Now I am writing an adventure story titled lost in the south Pacific.

3. I found information about the region in the book journeys in paradise.

4. I also found information in a video titled island escapes.

5. I read a book called in search of the coral reef.

6. My favorite short story in the book was shark escape.

7. I also enjoyed the story marlin adventure.

8. My sister wrote a beautiful poem called Reef dream.

9. She also wrote a silly song titled the stingray's revenge.

10. Her poem was printed in a literary magazine called fresh voices.

11. If you visit the South Pacific, you should read the book basic canoeing tips.

12. Bring a copy of the cookbook Tropical island delights.

13. You should also rent the video documentary how to avoid electric eels.

14. I saw a short film titled exotic wildlife of Borneo.

15. It was based on the book wild creatures of Borneo.

Lesson 64 Underline the correct word in parentheses. If the word is a possessive, write *possessive*. If the word is a contraction, write the two words it was made from.

1. In 1994 a group of adventurers traveled the length of (Canada's/Canadas') largest island, Baffin Island. _____

2. Baffin Island is the (world's/worlds') fifth largest island. _____

3. The majority of the (island's/islands') land mass lies above the Arctic Circle. _____

4. Most of Baffin Island (is'nt/isn't) accessible by car. _____

5. The (men's/mens') journey required the use of skis, kayaks, and sleds. _____

6. The (explorer's/explorers') goal was to travel 1,800 miles in six months. _____

7. They knew such a journey (couldn't/could'nt) be done during winter. _____

8. They started in March, when (winter's/winters') icy grip had eased. _____

9. The travelers (weren't/were'nt) able to escape the cold weather entirely, however; they encountered temperatures of more than 40 degrees below zero. _____

10. On the (journey's/journeys') first leg, they skied more than 1,000 miles. _____

11. Maps (didn't/did'nt) prepare them for the reality of the rugged terrain. _____

12. The (mens'/men's) sleds weighed 200 pounds apiece, making travel slow and difficult. _____

13. Next the explorers paddled 600 miles in kayaks, but their journey (wasn't/was'nt) over. _____

14. They hiked the final 230 miles to Baffin (Island's/Islands') southern tip. _____

15. The (adventurer's/adventurers') entire journey took 192 days. _____

Lesson 65 Add commas where they belong. Use the delete mark (⟨) on commas that don't belong. Remember that a comma is not needed to separate two items, but it is needed to separate two adjectives of the same kind.

1. The three Aran Islands, are called Inishmore Inishmaan and Innishneer.

2. They lie, six miles off the coast, of Ireland.

3. The islands are isolated windswept and barren.

4. The islands had no running water electricity or telephones until 1970.

5. Then the islands gained rapid, popularity as a tourist destination.

6. Despite the damp windy weather, people from Europe and America began choosing the Aran Islands as a destination.

7. Visitors were fascinated by the Iron Age structures ancient monasteries and quaint villages.

8. Soon restaurants tour buses and inns became part of life in the Aran Islands.

9. Tourists visit the islands today to hear the Gaelic language spoken and to get a sense of traditional, Irish culture.

10. Permanent residents love the islands' ruggedness solitude and beauty.

11. Most islanders either farm, or fish for a living.

12. Lobster crab and mackerel are harvested from the icy Atlantic.

13. The limestone cliffs are studded with small well-kept villages.

14. Aran Islanders keep traditions alive through music, and dancing.

15. The lively melodic music played by islanders is popular with natives and tourists alike.

Lesson 66 Add the missing comma to each sentence. Then decide why the comma is needed. Write *I* for introductory word, *C* for compound sentence, and *D* for direct address.

1. "Maya please show us your pictures of Puget Sound," we asked. _____

2. "I'd like to but I have so many!" Maya replied. _____

3. "Well let's see all of them," Mike said. _____

4. Maya cleared a space on the table and then she took out her photographs. _____

5. She spread out the photographs and we crowded around. _____

6. "Wow this is you!" Sabrina said to Maya as she pointed to one photograph. _____

7. "Yes this picture shows me on our kayaking trip," Maya said. _____

8. "Maya weren't you scared out there in the open ocean?" Mike asked. _____

9. "Well we weren't exactly in the open sea," Maya responded. _____

10. "Puget Sound is protected by islands and a peninsula and the water is usually quite calm." _____

11. "I was nervous at first but I followed the leader's instructions," she continued. _____

12. "A seal swam up to my kayak and it looked right at me!" Maya said. _____

13. "Well weren't you at least a little frightened?" Mike asked. _____

14. "No the seal was just curious," Maya replied. _____

15. "Seals often approach kayakers and kayakers usually feel lucky to see them," she continued. _____

Name _____

Lesson 67 Write a semicolon or a colon to separate the independent clauses in each sentence. Three sentences require a colon.

1. Sicily is the Mediterranean's largest island it lies off Italy's southern tip.

2. The Greeks first settled Sicily 2,800 years ago they built temples and theaters.

3. Many peoples have claimed Sicily as their own Romans, Arabs, and Normans are among them.

4. Each culture left its mark Sicilian architecture reveals many influences.

5. Tourists may visit Norman castles and cathedrals they can also explore Greek ruins.

6. Sicily is prone to earthquakes and volcanic activity Mt. Etna, in northeastern Sicily, is Europe's tallest volcano.

7. Sicily's warm Mediterranean climate makes it possible for farmers to raise a variety of crops pistachios, lemons, melons, and oranges are just a few of those.

8. Family is an important part of Italian culture family members gather at mealtime.

9. Farmers produce much of the island's foods fresh pasta, olives, and sheep's cheese are among the delicacies.

10. Many traditional values and customs persist in Sicily some modern residents resist the old ways.

Write a colon where it should be in each item.

11. We brought home five souvenirs a leather purse, three T-shirts, and a book of postcards.

12. The plane will arrive from Sicily at 1 45 P.M.

13. Martinez, Iris A. *Italy's Volcanic Island.* Rome Dante Brothers, 1998.

14. The guide told us a good nickname for Sicily "One Island, Many Cultures."

15. **Michel** The view of the harbor is spectacular!

    Maria I wish we could see Rome from here.

Lesson 68 Add parentheses and hyphens to these sentences where they are needed.

1. The island of New Guinea, which is in the Indian Ocean north of Australia, is the second largest island in the world.

2. In 1963 Indonesia claimed the island's western half and named it *Irian Jaya* victorious hot land.

3. After twenty five years of Indonesian rule, much of Irian Jaya remains unchanged.

4. Out of the way villages are insulated from the modern world by dense forests and rugged mountains.

5. The mountains of Irian Jaya rise to a height of 16,000 feet 4,877 meters.

6. The tropical highlands are home to many native groups collectively called Papuans PAP yuh wuhns.

7. The Asmat, a fierce mountain dwelling people, are one of many native groups who face a huge dilemma.

8. Their age old traditions are being challenged by the temptations and demands of the modern age.

9. Many Papuans still live as hunters or as *sustenance farmers* farmers who grow only enough for their families.

10. Until recently, many had never seen an honest to goodness modern vehicle.

11. Ready to wear clothing is a rarity in rural New Guinea.

12. For most people a visit to New Guinea would be an exotic vacation, a once in a lifetime experience.

13. For many workers, though, a trip to New Guinea is a journey made in search of a steady job at better than average wages.

14. New Guinea's mineral wealth copper, gold, petroleum has attracted both international corporations and fly by night operators.

15. Mineral resources create jobs and wealth, but they often spell the end for long established ways of life.

Lesson 69 Write *I* after each indirect quotation and *D* after each direct quotation. Then add quotation marks and other punctuation to the direct quotations. Draw three lines (≡) under each lowercase letter that should be capitalized.

1. Rick said that he visited San Francisco with his family. _____

2. Rick did you visit Alcatraz Island on your trip Jared asked. _____

3. Rick said yes, my family took a tour of Alcatraz. _____

4. Jared asked whether the island was still a federal prison. _____

5. Rick replied no, it hasn't been used as a prison since 1963. _____

6. Now it is part of the Golden Gate National Recreation Area, he continued. _____

7. Rick explained that the name *Alcatraz* comes from a Spanish word meaning "pelican." _____

8. More than a mile of cold, rough water separates Alcatraz from San Francisco Rick said. _____

9. Some of America's most dangerous criminals were held at Alcatraz he added. _____

10. Jared asked who lives on the island now? _____

11. Rick said that the island is inhabited mostly by birds. _____

12. He told us that the birds have become a real problem. _____

13. Jared asked if the tour was spooky. _____

14. It was a little spooky, but it was also fascinating Rick replied. _____

15. Jared said when I visit San Francisco, I'm going to take the first ferry in the morning out to Alcatraz. _____

Lesson 70 Rewrite this business letter in correct letter form.
Western Sporting Goods 143 Arkansas Way Nacogdoches, Texas 75961 Dear Sir or Madam I am interested in purchasing some camping equipment. Will you please send me a copy of your latest catalog? Sincerely yours Benjamin Ross 1434 Laughlin Road Derry, New Hampshire 03038 October 24,1999

_____

_____

_____

_____

_____

_____

_____

_____

_____

_____

_____

_____

Name _____

G.U.M.

Decide which word is the simple subject of each sentence. Fill in the circle that matches your answer.

1. Modern inventors register their ideas with the United States Patent Office.

   (a) ideas   (b) inventors   (c) understood *you*   (d) register

2. Many inventions in the patent record were never successful.

   (a) inventions   (b) patent   (c) record   (d) understood *you*

3. Imagine yourself in a pair of metal shoes.

   (a) shoes   (b) understood *you*   (c) Imagine   (d) yourself

Choose the answer that describes the underlined part of each sentence. Fill in the circle next to your answer.

4. <u>Thousands of other inventions</u> have been equally impractical.

   (a) complete subject   (b) complete predicate

5. <u>Someone</u> invented an unusual foot warmer.

   (a) simple predicate   (b) complete subject

6. This foot-warmer <u>runs on breath power</u>.

   (a) simple predicate   (b) complete predicate

7. The wearer <u>breathes</u> into a funnel.

   (a) simple predicate   (b) simple subject

8. Tubes <u>carry the warm breath to the wearer's cold feet</u>.

   (a) complete subject   (b) complete predicate

9. <u>Housework</u> and <u>play</u> were combined in the Clean Swing.

   (a) compound subject   (b) compound predicate

10. The motion of the swing <u>turns</u> a crank and <u>runs</u> a washing machine.

    (a) compound subject   (b) compound predicate

11. With this invention, a person <u>swings</u> and <u>washes</u> clothes at the same time.

    (a) compound subject   (b) compound predicate

12. The Wood-Awake alarm clock is another odd <u>invention</u>.

    (a) direct object   (b) predicate noun

13. Its inventor was probably a heavy <u>sleeper</u>.

    (a) predicate noun   (b) predicate adjective

14. The owner hangs this <u>clock</u> over the bed.

    (a) direct object   (b) indirect object

15. Each morning, the clock gives its <u>owner</u> a big surprise.

    (a) direct object   (b) indirect object

Name _____

16. It drops wooden <u>blocks</u> on its owner's head.

    (a) direct object   (b) indirect object

17. This clock could awaken <u>anyone</u>!

    (a) predicate noun   (b) direct object

18. It might give its <u>owner</u> a headache, however.

    (a) direct object   (b) indirect object

19. Not surprisingly, the device has never been <u>popular</u>.

    (a) predicate adjective   (b) predicate noun

20. Which underlined phrase is an appositive phrase?
Another invention, <u>the carry-all hat</u>, also risks giving its owner <u>a headache</u>.
                              a   b   (a) (b)

21. Which is a prepositional phrase?
Makeup <u>and other small items</u> fit <u>inside this box-shaped hat</u>.
                  a   b   (a) (b)

22. Which is a prepositional phrase?
A strap <u>around the chin</u> secures <u>the hat</u> tightly.
              a   b   (a) (b)

23. Which is a prepositional phrase?
It was once the custom <u>for men</u> to tip <u>their hats</u>.
                a   b   (a) (b)

24. Which is an appositive phrase?
The Tipsy Derby, <u>an even stranger hat</u>, lifts up and <u>tips itself mechanically</u>.
                        a   b   (a) (b)

25. Which is an adjectival prepositional phrase?
The inventor <u>of the self-cleaning house</u> must have hated housework <u>for years</u>!
                  a   b   (a) (b)

26. Which is an adverbial prepositional phrase?
Each room <u>in the self-cleaning house</u> had a soap-and-water tank <u>on the ceiling</u>.
                a   b   (a) (b)

27. Which is an adjectival prepositional phrase?
Jets <u>on the tank</u> would squirt soapy water <u>onto the walls and the floor</u>.
              a   b   (a) (b)

28. Which is an adverbial prepositional phrase?
The dirt <u>in the room</u> would be washed away <u>by the soapy waterfall</u>.
              a   b   (a) (b)

29. Which is an adjectival prepositional phrase?
<u>After the shower</u>, a hot-air blower <u>on the wall</u> would dry the room.
          a   b   (a) (b)

30. Which is an adverbial prepositional phrase?
<u>In the future</u>, perhaps a new, improved version <u>of the self-cleaning house</u> will be invented.
          a   b   (a) (b)

31. Which is an adjectival prepositional phrase?
Anyone <u>with this invention</u> will probably need waterproof furniture <u>in every room</u>!
          a   b   (a) (b)

Fill in the circle next to the choice that correctly describes each sentence.

1. Listen to these facts about undersea exploration.
   (a) declarative   (b) interrogative   (c) imperative   (d) exclamatory

2. Ancient Greek skin divers held their breath underwater.
   (a) declarative   (b) interrogative   (c) imperative   (d) exclamatory

3. Did you know that expert skin divers can hold their breath for two minutes?
   (a) declarative   (b) interrogative   (c) imperative   (d) exclamatory

4. Wow, that's a long time!
   (a) declarative   (b) interrogative   (c) imperative   (d) exclamatory

5. People used diving bells from ancient times until the early 1900s.
   (a) simple sentence   (b) compound sentence   (c) complex sentence

6. These hulls were bell-shaped, and their undersides were open.
   (a) simple sentence   (b) compound sentence   (c) complex sentence

7. Because the air inside the bell pressed down, water did not enter the bell.
   (a) simple sentence   (b) compound sentence   (c) complex sentence

8. Diving bells were useful, but divers could not descend very deep in them.
   (a) simple sentence   (b) compound sentence   (c) complex sentence

9. When the *bathysphere* was developed in 1930, deep-sea exploration became possible.
   (a) simple sentence   (b) compound sentence   (c) complex sentence

10. This vehicle consisted of a hollow ball on a cable.
    (a) simple sentence   (b) compound sentence   (c) complex sentence

11. Although the bathysphere was a breakthrough, scientists would later develop much more efficient exploration devices.
    (a) simple sentence   (b) compound sentence   (c) complex sentence

12. Some oceanographers live underwater for short periods of time, research stations have been built on the sea floor.
    (a) fragment   (b) run-on   (c) comma splice   (d) ramble-on

13. Leaving the station each day for exploration.
    (a) fragment   (b) run-on   (c) comma splice   (d) ramble-on

14. One man spent almost 70 days in a submerged chamber in Florida he was studying the effects on humans of life underwater.
    (a) fragment   (b) run-on   (c) comma splice   (d) ramble-on

15. In my opinion, I think living underwater would be difficult because there would be nothing but water around, and you would be living in the middle of it all the time, with no fresh air to breathe.
    (a) fragment   (b) run-on   (c) comma splice   (d) ramble-on

Name

Fill in the circle next to the choice that correctly describes each underlined phrase.

16. Locating the wreck of the *Titanic* took treasure hunter Mel Fisher 13 years.

    (a) infinitive phrase   (b) gerund phrase

17. After the initial discovery was made, Fisher decided to send Dudley Foster, Ralph Hollis, and Robert Ballard on a series of dives to the site of the wreck inside *Alvin*.

    (a) gerund phrase   (b) infinitive phrase

18. Riding inside the tough little submersible, Fisher's crew could explore the wreck carefully.

    (a) infinitive phrase   (b) participial phrase

19. Although submersibles allow oceanographers to visit the depths, they are expensive to launch.

    (a) dependent clause   (b) independent clause

20. If modern oceanographers want to gather data, they no longer have to dive themselves.

    (a) dependent clause   (b) independent clause

21. There are now machines that will dive for them.

    (a) dependent clause   (b) independent clause

22. The term for these machines is *ROV,* which stands for "Remotely Operated Vehicle."

    (a) adjective clause   (b) adverb clause

23. An ROV records information and videotapes the ocean's depths while oceanographers control it from a ship on the surface.

    (a) adjective clause   (b) adverb clause

24. ROVs that have mechanical arms collect samples.

    (a) adjective clause   (b) adverb clause

25. Although ROVs are extremely effective, scientists are working to develop even more advanced robotic devices.

    (a) independent clause   (b) adverb clause

26. Submersibles are designed to carry scientists to the ocean's farthest depths.

    (a) gerund phrase   (b) infinitive phrase

27. The submersible *Alvin* allowed scientists to visit deep-sea rifts.

    (a) infinitive phrase   (b) participial phrase

28. Seeing giant clams and tube worms in the Galápagos Rift must have been a thrill for researchers.

    (a) infinitive phrase   (b) gerund phrase

29. Sent to the bottom of the ocean by an iceberg, the *Titanic* lay undisturbed for more than 70 years.

    (a) participial phrase   (b) gerund phrase

Fill in the circle next to the plural form that will complete each sentence correctly.

1. One of the greatest _____ of all time, Ludwig von Beethoven began to go deaf at the age of thirty.

   (a) composers   (b) composeres

2. Soon he could hear only faint _____ of sound.

   (a) patches   (b) patchs

3. But he was able to compose brilliant _____ in his head.

   (a) symphonys   (b) symphonies

Choose the answer that correctly identifies the underlined item in each sentence. Fill in the circle next to your answer.

4. Elizabeth Blackwell was the first woman granted a medical degree in the United States.

   (a) common noun   (b) proper noun

5. Blackwell desperately wanted to be a doctor, but almost every medical school in the United States rejected her application because she was a woman.

   (a) common noun   (b) proper noun

6. Thinking her application was a joke, Geneva Medical College accepted Blackwell.

   (a) common noun   (b) proper noun

7. The students' scorn turned into respect as Blackwell succeeded in her studies.

   (a) singular possessive noun   (b) plural possessive noun

8. Blackwell's struggle was far from over when she received her medical degree in 1849.

   (a) singular possessive noun   (b) plural possessive noun

9. She found that no hospital would hire a woman doctor.

   (a) personal pronoun: first person   (b) personal pronoun: second person

   (c) personal pronoun: third person

10. Blackwell decided to open her own hospital, which would treat women's health problems.

   (a) singular possessive noun   (b) plural possessive noun

11. I have seen the building in New York where Blackwell founded her hospital.

   (a) personal pronoun: first person   (b) personal pronoun: second person

   (c) personal pronoun: third person

12. It is a small building; you would never guess that it was once a hospital.

   (a) personal pronoun: first person   (b) personal pronoun: second person

   (c) personal pronoun: third person

13. Blackwell also decided to open a medical school for women, since she had had so much trouble getting into medical school herself.

   (a) compound personal pronoun   (b) possessive pronoun   (c) indefinite pronoun

14. Blackwell is remembered because she dared to do what no one had done before.

   (a) relative pronoun   (b) interrogative pronoun   (c) indefinite pronoun

Name _____

15. Thor Heyerdahl, on the other hand, is remembered for doing <u>what</u> others may have done long ago.
    - (a) relative pronoun
    - (b) interrogative pronoun
    - (c) indefinite pronoun

16. <u>Who</u> was Thor Heyerdahl?
    - (a) relative pronoun
    - (b) interrogative pronoun
    - (c) indefinite pronoun

17. He was a researcher <u>who</u> studied the spread of ancient civilizations.
    - (a) relative pronoun
    - (b) interrogative pronoun
    - (c) indefinite pronoun

18. Heyerdahl was convinced that ancient Inca sailors could have traveled across the Pacific, and he decided to prove that <u>his</u> theory was sound.
    - (a) compound personal pronoun
    - (b) possessive pronoun
    - (c) indefinite pronoun

19. <u>What</u> did he do?
    - (a) relative pronoun
    - (b) interrogative pronoun
    - (c) indefinite pronoun

20. Heyerdahl built <u>himself</u> a balsa wood raft, which he called the *Kon Tiki*.
    - (a) compound personal pronoun
    - (b) possessive pronoun
    - (c) relative pronoun

21. <u>Few</u> would have dared sail across the Pacific Ocean on such a small and primitive craft, but Heyerdahl and five others set out from Peru in 1947.
    - (a) relative pronoun
    - (b) interrogative pronoun
    - (c) indefinite pronoun

22. <u>Their</u> journey was long and hard.
    - (a) compound personal pronoun
    - (b) possessive pronoun
    - (c) relative pronoun

23. But Heyerdahl achieved <u>his</u> goal: the *Kon Tiki* landed safely on an island 4,300 miles from Peru.
    - (a) possessive pronoun
    - (b) relative pronoun
    - (c) indefinite pronoun

24. <u>Nobody</u> knows for sure whether the ancient voyages Heyerdahl imagined occurred, but we know they were possible.
    - (a) compound personal pronoun
    - (b) interrogative pronoun
    - (c) indefinite pronoun

25. Ellen Craft faced <u>a</u> challenge of a very different kind.
    - (a) adjective telling *what kind*
    - (b) adjective telling *how many*
    - (c) article

26. Born into slavery in nineteenth-century Georgia, she and her husband planned a <u>dangerous</u> escape to freedom.
    - (a) adjective telling *what kind*
    - (b) adjective telling *how many*
    - (c) article

27. <u>This</u> was their strategy: Craft disguised herself as a white man and posed as her husband's owner.
    - (a) demonstrative pronoun
    - (b) demonstrative adjective

28. During their 1,000-mile journey, there were <u>many</u> moments when Craft's identity was almost discovered.
    - (a) adjective telling *what kind*
    - (b) adjective telling *how many*
    - (c) article

29. But despite <u>these</u> close calls, Craft never lost her courage.
    - (a) demonstrative pronoun
    - (b) demonstrative adjective

30. <u>That</u> is the reason she and her husband made it to safety.
    - (a) demonstrative pronoun
    - (b) demonstrative adjective

Identify the verb in each sentence. Fill in the circle that matches your answer.

1. Comets **follow** oval-shaped **paths around** the sun.
           a   b   c   (a) (b) (c)

2. A few **comets are frequent** visitors to our sky.   (a) (b) (c)
           a   b   c

3. Halley's Comet **is visible** to people on Earth **every** 76 years or so.   (a) (b) (c)
                  a   b   c

4. Other comets **require more** than 400,000 years for the **completion** of a single orbit.   (a) (b) (c)
                  a   b   c

Decide which word describes the boldfaced verb. Fill in the circle next to your answer.

5. Comets **are** actually huge balls of dirty ice.
   (a) action   (b) linking

6. A comet **may develop** a tail during its approach to the sun.
   (a) action   (b) linking

7. Some of the ice in its nucleus **evaporates**.
   (a) action   (b) linking

8. Evaporation **releases** many dust particles and gas molecules.
   (a) action   (b) linking

9. Many of these particles and molecules **remain** near the nucleus.
   (a) transitive   (b) intransitive

10. The pressure of the sun's light **pushes** particles and molecules away from the nucleus in a long stream, or tail.
    (a) transitive   (b) intransitive

11. In 1997 the Hale-Bopp Comet **was seen** by millions of people in North America.
    (a) active voice   (b) passive voice

12. That comet **shone** brightly for several weeks that spring.
    (a) active voice   (b) passive voice

Choose the correct verb or verb phrase to complete each sentence. Fill in the circle next to your answer.

13. Yesterday I ____ a bottle of iced tea.
    (a) buy   (b) bought   (c) have bought   (d) will have bought

14. I ____ this kind of tea many times before.
    (a) am buying   (b) will have bought   (c) have bought   (d) was buying

15. In the past I ____ empty tea bottles into the trash, but this time I wanted to make sure my bottle would be recycled.
    (a) had thrown   (b) throw   (c) will throw   (d) was throwing

16. Right now it ____ on my desk with a flower in it.
    (a) has sat   (b) sat   (c) will sit   (d) is sitting

17. Next Tuesday I ____ the bottle in a bin for the recycling truck.
    (a) will put   (b) will have put   (c) put   (d) had put

18. I always ___ the bottles from the paper.

  (a) am separating   (b) separate   (c) was separating   (d) will have separated

19. After the truck driver finishes her route, she ___ the bottle to a recycling plant.

  (a) has taken   (b) took   (c) had taken   (d) will take

20. By the end of the week, a furnace ___ my bottle into liquid glass.

  (a) is melting   (b) melted   (c) will have melted   (d) melts

21. Soon someone else ___ from a new glass bottle made from the one I placed in my recycling bin.

  (a) drank   (b) drinks   (c) is drinking   (d) will be drinking

Decide which boldfaced word is an adverb. Fill in the circle that matches your answer.

22. Recyclers sort garbage **carefully** to sell as **reusable material**.   (a) (b) (c)
                a   b   c

23. **Often** these materials are **made** into a completely **new** product.   (a) (b) (c)
      a   b   c

24. **The** use of **recycled** materials can be **very** economical.   (a) (b) (c)
      a   b   c

Decide which boldfaced word is a preposition. Fill in the circle that matches your answer.

25. Comfortable shoes **have** been produced **from** used grocery bags **and** coffee filters.   (a) (b) (c)
                 a   b   c

26. Plastic soft drink bottles **can** be made **into** carpets **and** pillow stuffing.   (a) (b) (c)
               a   b   c

27. Perhaps **someday** you will live **in** a house made of old cans **and** tires.   (a) (b) (c)
          a   b   c

Decide which boldfaced word is a conjunction. Fill in the circle that matches the answer.

28. The United States **now** recycles 65% of aluminum cans, **but** only 2% **of** plastic.   (a) (b) (c)
          a   b   c

29. Aluminum cans **are** recycled **because** that is less **expensive** than mining aluminum.   (a) (b) (c)
            a   b   c

30. **Although** recycling has grown, each American **still** wastes 3.6 pounds **per** day.   (a) (b) (c)
      a   b   c

Decide whether each boldfaced word or phrase is a coordinating conjunction, a subordinating conjunction, or a correlative conjunction. Fill in the circle next to your answer.

31. Environmentalists work to make recycling **not only** right, **but also** cheaper than throwing trash away.

  (a) coordinating conjunction   (b) subordinating conjunction   (c) correlative conjunction

32. The U. S. produces 200 million tons of garbage per year, **and** that makes it the world's biggest trash producer.

  (a) coordinating conjunction   (b) subordinating conjunction   (c) correlative conjunction

33. We must **both** reduce the amount of trash we create **and** recycle more of that trash.

  (a) coordinating conjunction   (b) subordinating conjunction   (c) correlative conjunction

34. **If** we do these things, we will have more resources available for the future.

  (a) coordinating conjunction   (b) subordinating conjunction   (c) correlative conjunction

G.U.M.

Decide which word completes each sentence correctly. Fill in the circle next to your answer.

1. ___ common all over the world to hold agricultural festivals.

    (a) Its   (b) It's

2. People ___ land gets very little rain often conduct rain dances or similar rituals.

    (a) who's   (b) whose

3. Rice farmers in Japan plant pine, chestnut, or bamboo trees in ___ fields for good luck.

    (a) there   (b) their   (c) they're

4. They plant rice seeds in February and ___ hold festivals when they transplant seedlings in June or July.

    (a) then   (b) than

5. The rhythmic way the farmers move can seem more like dancing ___ planting.

    (a) then   (b) than

6. Every year the Cuchumatan people of Guatemala go ___ a cliff where, according to tradition, frost lives.

    (a) to   (b) too   (c) two

7. Once they get ___, they lower one person over the cliff.

    (a) there   (b) their   (c) they're

8. ___ counting on him to seal the rock with cement so the frost won't ruin the corn plants.

    (a) There   (b) Their   (c) They're

9. ___ deities, Wuro and Dwo, are important in the farming traditions of the Bobo people of Burkina Faso.

    (a) To   (b) Too   (c) Two

10. According to legend, Wuro gave the world ___ balance of earth, rain, and sun, but people ruined
    the balance by farming.

    (a) its   (b) it's

11. Dwo is the deity ___ helping people restore the natural order.

    (a) who's   (b) whose

12. Each year the Bobo people ask Dwo for his help in keeping away evil and restoring order and
    in bringing the rains, ___.

    (a) to   (b) too   (c) two

13. If you study ethnology or anthropology, ___ going to learn about agricultural festivals around the world.

    (a) your   (b) you're

14. Does ___ community hold an agricultural festival?

    (a) your   (b) you're

Decide whether each sentence uses negatives correctly. Fill in the circle next to your answer.

15. Some people don't want no garlic in none of their food.

    (a) correct   (b) incorrect

Name _____

16. Those people shouldn't never visit the Gilroy Garlic Festival in Gilroy, California.

    (a) correct   (b) incorrect

17. If you haven't eaten a big bowl of garlic ice cream, you're not a real garlic lover.

    (a) correct   (b) incorrect

Decide whether each sentence uses go, like, went, *or* all *correctly. Fill in the circle next to your answer.*

18. Madeleine went, "Did you know Turkey has a holiday called Children's Day?"

    (a) correct   (b) incorrect

19. "On that day, children go to the national and local government offices and take them over," she continued.

    (a) correct   (b) incorrect

20. Fuad was all, "I would pass a law guaranteeing free ice cream forever!"

    (a) correct   (b) incorrect

21. Then Madeleine was like, "On Children's Day, children get free ice cream, movies, and transportation all day!"

    (a) correct   (b) incorrect

22. Madeleine said that she hopes she can visit Turkey on that holiday before she is, like, too old to join in the fun.

    (a) correct   (b) incorrect

Decide which word completes each sentence correctly. Fill in the circle next to your answer.

23. Last Thanksgiving I ___ felt pads down on the dining room table and then spread out a green tablecloth.

    (a) lay   (b) laid

24. My brother ___ plates and glasses at each place.

    (a) sat   (b) set

25. When the turkey was ready, everyone ___ around the table.

    (a) sat   (b) set

26. Later I ___ on a soft rug in front of the fire and talked with my cousins.

    (a) lay   (b) laid

Decide which form of the verb completes each sentence correctly. Fill in the circle next to your answer.

27. Last year my relatives in Nice, France, ___ flowers for the Carnival celebration.

    (a) grown   (b) grew   (c) growed

28. They ___ the flowers to the parade.

    (a) brang   (b) brung   (c) brought

29. The ground ___ as the large floats thundered past.

    (a) shaken   (b) shaked   (c) shook

30. The best one had been ___ almost entirely out of flowers.

    (a) built   (b) build   (c) builded

31. When the signal was given, everyone ___ flowers at one another.

    (a) threw   (b) throwed   (c) thrown

Choose the correct pronoun to replace each boldfaced word or phrase. Fill in the circle next to your answer.

1. Alexandra's grandmother told Pilar and **Alexandra** a story about Baba Yaga.

   (a) she   (b) them   (c) her   (d) I

2. Pilar told the story to Shanna and **Jeremy**.

   (a) he   (b) him   (c) his   (d) them

3. Baba Yaga is a popular character in **Russian folktales**.

   (a) them   (b) it   (c) they   (d) her

4. **This old woman** lives in a house that walks on huge chicken legs.

   (a) Her   (b) They   (c) It   (d) She

5. **Baba Yaga** rides around in a magical stone bowl.

   (a) They   (b) She   (c) Her   (d) Them

6. Alexandra and **Pilar** decided to do research on Baba Yaga tales at the library.

   (a) her   (b) I   (c) she   (d) it

Decide which phrase the boldfaced word replaces in each sentence. Fill in the circle next to your answer.

7. In some tales Baba Yaga tries to capture Russian children, because she likes to eat **them**.

   (a) Russian children   (b) Pilar and Alexandra   (c) Baba Yaga   (d) some tales

8. In one story, a girl escapes from Baba Yaga by dropping a magic comb; **it** turns into an impenetrable forest.

   (a) a girl   (b) one story   (c) a magic comb   (d) an impenetrable forest

9. Baba Yaga is not always a wicked character; in one story **she** helps a prince find his love.

   (a) a princess   (b) Baba Yaga   (c) a wicked character   (d) his love

Choose the word or phrase that completes each sentence correctly. Fill in the circle next to your answer.

10. One of folklore's greatest trickster characters ___ the Monkey King.

    (a) is   (b) are

11. Stories about the Monkey King ___ entertained people in China for centuries.

    (a) has   (b) have

12. He is a mischievous immortal ___ protects a monk on an important pilgrimage to India.

    (a) who   (b) whom

13. When the story begins, the Monkey King has been imprisoned under a mountain by the other immortals ___ he has annoyed with his mischief.

    (a) who   (b) whom

14. The wandering monk passes by the mountain prison of the Monkey King, ___ asks the monk to set him free.

    (a) who   (b) whom

15. The magic powers of the Monkey King ___ the monk a great deal on his journey.

    (a) helps   (b) help

Name _____

16. The Monkey King has a magic needle that he keeps tucked behind his ear; he can make it grow ___ than a log, to become a powerful weapon.

(a) larger   (b) largest

17. Sandy and Pigsy ___ two monsters who turn good and join the Monkey King and the monk.

(a) is   (b) are

18. Neither Sandy nor Pigsy ___ as effective as the Monkey King at defending the monk from the demons who live in the mountains.

(a) is   (b) are

19. The Monkey King thinks Sandy and Pigsy ___ help out more.

(a) should   (b) have

20. He exposes Pigsy's cowardice, and the shamefaced Pigsy begins to act ___ than before.

(a) more bravely   (b) most bravely

21. Eventually the travelers must cross the ___ mountain of all, which is defended by thousands of demons.

(a) higher   (b) highest

22. The Monkey King realizes that he ___ disguise himself as a demon and spy on the enemy to find out their weaknesses.

(a) is   (b) must

23. He discovers that one of the head demons ___ suck enemies into his stomach in an instant.

(a) has   (b) can

24. The Monkey King, ___ is a brilliant strategist, lets the demon swallow him whole and then threatens to eat the demon from the inside out.

(a) who   (b) whom

25. The entire demon army ___ away because of the Monkey King's ingenious tricks.

(a) runs   (b) run

26. No one ___ more clever than the Monkey King.

(a) is   (b) are

27. *Folktales from Many Lands* ___ the book in which I found this story.

(a) is   (b) are

Decide whether the boldfaced phrase is a dangling modifier or is used correctly. Fill in the circle next to your answer.

28. **Using a clever disguise,** the demons never suspect they are being tricked.

(a) dangling modifier   (b) correct

29. **Tricking powerful enemies,** protection is given to the monk.

(a) dangling modifier   (b) correct

30. **Containing ancient folktales,** *The Pilgrimage to the West* is a classic work of Chinese literature.

(a) dangling modifier   (b) correct

Decide which boldfaced word needs to be capitalized. Fill in the circle with the letter that matches it.

1. My **uncle** sailed across the **pacific** Ocean.　　ⓐ ⓑ
　　 a　　　　　　　　　b

2. **he** made the voyage in **summer**.　　ⓐ ⓑ
　　a　　　　　　　　b

3. He reached the **island** of **maui** in August.　　ⓐ ⓑ
　　　　　　　　　a　　　b

4. He became a fan of **hawaiian** music and bought a **ukulele**.　　ⓐ ⓑ
　　　　　　　　　a　　　　　　　　　　　b

Choose the correct way to rewrite the boldfaced part of each sentence. Fill in the circle next to your answer.

5. **Mistress Mary Ellen Riley** is an expert sailor.
　　ⓐ Mrs. M. E Riley　　ⓑ Mss. M. E. Riley　　ⓒ Mrs. M. E. Riley

6. She lives on **Edmonton Boulevard**.
　　ⓐ Edmon. Blvd.　　ⓑ Edmonton Blvd.　　ⓒ Edmonton blvd.

7. She works for **Pacific Winds Corporation**.
　　ⓐ Pacific Winds Corp.　　ⓑ Pacific W. Cor'tion　　ⓒ Pac Winds Cor

8. She wrote a book titled **Following the trade winds**.
　　ⓐ Following The Trade Winds　　ⓑ "Following the Trade Winds"　　ⓒ Following the Trade Winds

9. I read her short story **escape from the volcano**.
　　ⓐ "Escape from the Volcano"　　ⓑ Escape From The Volcano　　ⓒ Escape from the Volcano

10. Mrs. Riley **has not** answered my letter.
　　ⓐ hasn't　　ⓑ hasnt'　　ⓒ has'nt

11. **The enthusiasm of her fans** is amazing.
　　ⓐ Her fans' enthusiasm　　ⓑ Her fan's enthusiasm　　ⓒ Her fans enthusiasm

12. Every day **the mailbox of Mrs. Riley** is stuffed with fan mail.
　　ⓐ Mrs. Riley's mailbox　　ⓑ Mrs. Rileys' mailbox　　ⓒ Mrs. Rileys mailbox

13. I **have not** read Mrs. Riley's latest book.
　　ⓐ havent'　　ⓑ have'nt　　ⓒ haven't

14. It **is not** in the library yet.
　　ⓐ isn't　　ⓑ is'nt　　ⓒ isnt'

Decide where the comma belongs in each sentence. Fill in the circle with the matching letter.

15. Rex saw manta rays, sharks and dolphins in Hawaii.　　ⓐ ⓑ
　　　　　　　　　　　　　a　b

16. "Rex did you see any giant sea turtles?" asked Pete.　　ⓐ ⓑ
　　　　a　　　　　　　b

17. "Yes I saw one swimming in the ocean," Rex replied.　　ⓐ ⓑ
　　　a　　　　　b

Name _____

18. "I swam up to it but it swam away," he said.   (a) (b)
          a b

19. "Those big gentle animals are quite shy," said Pete.   (a) (b)
          a   b

Decide where the semicolon or colon is needed in each sentence. Fill in the circle next to your answer.

20. Centuries ago; volcanoes erupted in the Pacific; these became the Hawaiian islands.   (a) (b)
          a   b

21. The islands are still volcanic; eruptions occur often; on the Big Island.   (a) (b)
                        a   b

22. Volcanoes can cause great damage: entire communities have been destroyed by: lava.   (a) (b)
                  a   b

23. Hawaii is not yet complete: volcanoes and ocean waves continually reshape: the islands.   (a) (b)
          a   b

Decide whether each sentence is missing quotation marks or is correct as written. Fill in the circle next to your answer.

24. Anna asked Have you ever seen an extinct volcano?

    (a) needs quotation marks   (b) correct as written

25. Bill said that he had visited the Haleakala Crater in Hawaii.

    (a) needs quotation marks   (b) correct as written

Decide what kind of punctuation each sentence needs. Fill in the circle next to your answer.

26. The Haleakala Crater is 21 miles 34 kilometers in circumference.

    (a) needs parentheses   (b) needs a hyphen

27. Haleakala *house of the sun* is on the island of Maui.

    (a) needs parentheses   (b) needs a hyphen

28. Haleakala has been a national park for more than thirty five years.

    (a) needs parentheses   (b) needs a hyphen

29. The volcano *imploded* crashed inward to form a huge crater.

    (a) needs parentheses   (b) needs a hyphen

Find the part of the letter below that is the answer to each question. Fill in the circle next to your answer.

30. Which part of the letter is the greeting?   (a) (b) (c) (d) (e)

31. Which part of the letter is the body?   (a) (b) (c) (d) (e)

32. Which part of the letter is the closing?   (a) (b) (c) (d) (e)

(a) Haleakala National Park
    Pukalani, Maui, Hawaii 96788
    February 9, 1998

Dear Mark, (b)

(c) The Haleakala Crater is awesome! The colors inside the crater are beautiful.

(d) Your friend,

(e) Liam

Language Handbook Table of Contents

Mechanics

Sentence Structure and Parts of Speech

(Continued on page 270)

Name _____

(Continued from page 269)

Usage

Writing a Letter

Guidelines for Listening and Speaking

(you) | Diagram | sentences

Mechanics

Section 1 Capitalization

- **Capitalize the first word in a sentence.**
  The kangaroo rat is an amazing animal.

- **Capitalize all *proper nouns*, including people's names and the names of particular places.**
  Gregory Gordon   Washington Monument

- **Capitalize titles of respect.**
  Mr. Alvarez   Dr. Chin   Ms. Murphy

- **Capitalize family titles used just before people's names and titles of respect that are part of names.**
  Uncle Frank   Aunt Mary   Governor Adamson

- **Capitalize initials of names.**
  Thomas Paul Gerard (T.P. Gerard)

- **Capitalize place names.**
  France   Utah   China   Baltimore

- **Capitalize *proper adjectives*, adjectives that are made from proper nouns.**
  Chinese   Icelandic   French   Latin American

- **Capitalize the months of the year and the days of the week.**
  February   April   Monday   Tuesday

- **Capitalize important words in the names of organizations.**
  American Lung Association   Veterans of Foreign Wars

- **Capitalize important words in the names of holidays.**
  Veterans Day   Fourth of July

- **Capitalize the first word in the greeting or closing of a letter.**
  Dear Edmundo,   Yours truly,

- **Capitalize the word *I*.**
  Frances and I watched the movie together.

- **Capitalize the first, last, and most important words in a title. Be sure to capitalize all verbs, including *is* and *was*.**
  Island of the Blue Dolphins   *Always Is a Strange Place to Be*

- **Capitalize the first word in a direct quotation.**
  Aunt Rose said, "Please pass the clam dip."

Section 2 Abbreviations and Initials

Abbreviations are shortened forms of words. Many abbreviations begin with a capital letter and end with a period.

- **You can abbreviate words used in addresses when you write.**
  Street (**St.**)   Avenue (**Ave.**)   Route (**Rte.**)   Boulevard (**Blvd.**)   Road (**Rd.**)   Drive (**Dr.**)

- **You can abbreviate the names of states when you address envelopes.**
  Note: State names are abbreviated as two capital letters, with no periods.

Alabama (AL)	Idaho (ID)	Missouri (MO)	Pennsylvania (PA)
Alaska (AK)	Illinois (IL)	Montana (MT)	Rhode Island (RI)
Arizona (AZ)	Indiana (IN)	Nebraska (NE)	South Carolina (SC)
Arkansas (AR)	Iowa (IA)	Nevada (NV)	South Dakota (SD)
California (CA)	Kansas (KS)	New Hampshire (NH)	Tennessee (TN)
Colorado (CO)	Kentucky (KY)	New Jersey (NJ)	Texas (TX)
Connecticut (CT)	Louisiana (LA)	New Mexico (NM)	Utah (UT)
Delaware (DE)	Maine (ME)	New York (NY)	Vermont (VT)
District of	Maryland (MD)	North Carolina (NC)	Virginia (VA)
Columbia (DC)	Massachusetts (MA)	North Dakota (ND)	Washington (WA)
Florida (FL)	Michigan (MI)	Ohio (OH)	West Virginia (WV)
Georgia (GA)	Minnesota (MN)	Oklahoma (OK)	Wisconsin (WI)
Hawaii (HI)	Mississippi (MS)	Oregon (OR)	Wyoming (WY)

- You can abbreviate titles of address and titles of respect when you write.
  Mister (**Mr.** Brian Davis)   Mistress (**Miss** or **Mrs.** Maria Rosario)   General (**Gen.** Robert E. Lee)
  Doctor (**Dr.** Emily Chu)   Junior (Everett Castle, **Jr.**)   Saint (**St.** Andrew)
  Note: *Ms.* is a title of address used for women. It is not an abbreviation, but it requires a period
  (**Ms.** Anita Brown).

- You can abbreviate certain words in the names of businesses when you write.
  Computers, Incorporated (Computers, **Inc.**)   Zylar Corporation (Zylar **Corp.**)

- You can abbreviate days of the week when you take notes.

Sunday (**Sun.**)	Wednesday (**Wed.**)	Friday (**Fri.**)
Monday (**Mon.**)	Thursday (**Thurs.**)	Saturday (**Sat.**)
Tuesday (**Tues.**)		

- You can abbreviate months of the year when you take notes.

January (**Jan.**)	April (**Apr.**)	October (**Oct.**)
February (**Feb.**)	August (**Aug.**)	November (**Nov.**)
March (**Mar.**)	September (**Sept.**)	December (**Dec.**)

  (May, June, and July do not have abbreviated forms.)

- You can abbreviate directions when you take notes.
  North (**N**)   East (**E**)   South (**S**)   West (**W**)

An *initial* is the first letter of a name. An initial is written as a capital letter and a period. Sometimes initials are used in the names of countries or other places.

Michael Paul Sanders (**M.P.** Sanders)   United States of America (**U.S.A.**)
Washington, District of Columbia (Washington, **D.C.**)

Section 3 Titles

- Underline titles of books, newspapers, TV series, movies, and magazines.
  <u>Island of the Blue Dolphins</u>   <u>Miami Herald</u>   <u>I Love Lucy</u>
  Note: These titles are written in italics in printed text.

- Use quotation marks around articles in magazines, short stories, chapters in books, songs, and poems.
  "This Land Is Your Land"   "The Gift"   "Eletelephony"

- Capitalize the first, last, and most important words in titles. Articles, short prepositions, and conjunctions are usually not capitalized. Be sure to capitalize all verbs, including forms of the verb *be* (*am, is, are, was, were, been*).
  A Knight in the Attic   *My Brother Sam Is Dead*

Section 4 Quotation Marks

- Put quotation marks (" ") around the titles of articles, short stories, book chapters, songs, and poems.
  My favorite short story is "Revenge of the Reptiles."

- Put quotation marks around a *direct quotation,* or a speaker's exact words.
  "Did you see that alligator?" Max asked.

- Do not put quotation marks around an *indirect quotation,* a person's words retold by another speaker. An indirect quotation is often signalled by *whether* or *that.*
  Max asked whether Rory had seen an alligator.

Writing a Conversation

- Put quotation marks around the speaker's words. Begin a direct quotation with a capital letter. Use a comma to separate the quotation from the rest of the sentence.
  Rory said, "There are no alligators in this area."

- When a direct quotation comes at the end of a sentence, put the end mark inside the last quotation mark.
  Max cried, "Look out!"

- When writing a conversation, begin a new paragraph with each change of speaker.
  Max panted, "I swear I saw a huge, scaly tail and a flat snout in the water!"
  "Relax," Rory said. "I told you there are no alligators around here."

Section 5 Spelling

Use these tips if you are not sure how to spell a word you want to write:

- Say the word aloud, and break it into syllables. Try spelling each syllable. Put the syllables together to spell the whole word.
- Write the word. Make sure there is a vowel in every syllable. If the word looks wrong to you, try spelling it other ways.
- Think of a related word. Parts of related words are often spelled the same.
  Decide is related to *decision*.

Correct spelling helps readers understand what you write. Use a dictionary when you need help.

Section 6 End Marks

Every sentence must end with a period, an exclamation point, or a question mark.

- Use a *period* at the end of a statement (declarative sentence) or a command (imperative sentence).
  Dad and I look alike. (*declarative*)   Step back very slowly. (*imperative*)
- Use an *exclamation point* at the end of a firm command (imperative sentence) or at the end of a sentence that shows great feeling or excitement (exclamatory sentence).
  Get away from the cliff! (*imperative*)   What an incredible sight! (*exclamatory*)
- Use a *question mark* at the end of an asking sentence (interrogative sentence).
  How many miles is it to Tucson? (*interrogative*)

Section 7 Apostrophes

An apostrophe (') is used to form the possessive of a noun or to join words in a contraction.

- Possessives show ownership. To make a singular noun possessive, add *'s*.
  The bike belongs to Carmen. It is Carmen's bike.
- To form a possessive from a plural noun that ends in *s*, add only an apostrophe.
  Those books belong to my sisters. They are my sisters' books.
- Some plural nouns do not end in *s*. To form possessives with these nouns, add *'s*.
  The children left their boots here. The children's boots are wet.
- Use an apostrophe to replace the dropped letters in a contraction.   it's (it *is*)   hasn't (has n**ot**)

Section 8 Commas, Semicolons, and Colons

Commas in Sentences

- Use a comma after an introductory word in a sentence.
  Yes, I'd love to go to the movies.   Actually, we had a great time.
- Use a comma to separate items in a series. A series is a list of three or more items. Put the last comma before *and* or *or*. A comma is not needed to separate two items.
  Shall we eat cheese, bread, or fruit?   Let's eat cheese and fruit.
- Use a comma to separate a noun of direct address from the rest of a sentence.
  Akila, will you please stand up?   We would like you to sing, Akila.
- Use a comma to separate a direct quotation from the rest of a sentence.
  Joe asked, "How long must I sit here?"   "You must sit there for one hour," Vic said.
- Use a comma with the conjunction *and, or,* or *but* when combining independent clauses in a compound sentence.   Lisa liked the reptiles best, but Lyle preferred the amphibians.
- Use a comma to separate a dependent clause at the beginning of a sentence from the rest of the sentence.   Because Lisa likes reptiles, she is considering a career as a herpetologist.
- Use a comma to separate a pair of adjectives that are of a similar kind. To decide whether to put a comma between adjectives, try reading the sentence with the word *and* inserted between the adjectives. If the word *and* sounds natural there, you should use a comma.
  Reptiles have dry, scaly skin. (*needs a comma*)
  Look at that big green lizard! (*does not need a comma*)

- Use commas to set off a nonrestrictive adjective clause. A nonrestrictive clause is one that adds information about the word it modifies but is not essential to the meaning of the sentence. Walt Jackson**, who sold me a turtle last year,** has a new pet gecko. (*The adjective clause just tells more about the noun it modifies. Because the information in the clause is not essential, the clause is nonrestrictive. Commas are needed.*)
The woman **who runs the pet store** offered me a job. (*The adjective clause tells which woman is being talked about. Because the information in the clause is essential, no commas are used.*)

Semicolons and Colons in Sentences

- You may use a semicolon in place of a comma and a conjunction when combining independent clauses. Lisa likes reptiles**;** Lyle prefers amphibians.
- A colon can be used when the second clause states a direct result of the first or explains the first. Lisa owns reptiles**:** she has two pet snakes.
- Use a colon to introduce a list or series. I like three kinds of cheese**:** cheddar, Swiss, and colby.
- Use a colon to introduce a quotation. Cory always follows this motto**:** "A penny saved is a penny earned."
- Use a colon after the speaker's name in a play. LOGAN**:** Where were you on the night of October 5th, when the gold bullion was stolen? BLAKE**:** I was attending the opening night of *Carmen* at the opera house.
- Use a colon to separate hours and minutes in an expression of time. 8**:**15 P.M. 11**:**45 A.M.
- Use a colon between the city of publication and the publisher in a bibliographical reference. O'Dell, Scott. *Cruise of the Arctic Star.* Boston**:** Houghton Mifflin, 1973.

Commas with Dates and Place Names

- Use a comma to separate the day from the date and the date from the year. We clinched the pennant on Saturday**,** September 5**,** 1998.
- Use a comma to separate the name of a city or town from the name of a state. I visited Memphis**,** Tennessee.

Commas and Colons in Letters

- Use a comma after the greeting and the closing of a friendly letter. Dear Reginald**,** Your friend**,** Deke
- Use a colon after the greeting of a business letter. Use a comma after the closing. Dear Ms. Brocklehurst**:** Sincerely**,**

Section 9 Hyphens and Parentheses

Hyphens in Sentences

- When you break a word at the end of a line, use a hyphen to separate the syllables. There is no single "perfect food." Milk, for example, contains most of the nutri**-**ents needed by the human body, but it lacks enough iron.
- Use hyphens to link the parts of some compound words. **son-in-law** **city-state**
- Use hyphens to link some pairs or groups of words that precede a noun and act as an adjective. a **family-style** meal a **horse-drawn** carriage an **up-to-date** schedule
- Use hyphens to link the parts of numbers between twenty-one and ninety-nine. eighty**-**two fifty**-**seven seventy**-**six thirty**-**five

Parentheses in Sentences

- Use parentheses to set off an explanation. I interviewed my uncle **(he raises goats for a living)** for my report on animal husbandry. Rolf and Dana's farm is 100 miles **(160 km)** outside of Chicago.
- Use parentheses to set off an example. Many types of cheese **(chèvre, for example)** are made with goats' milk.

Sentence Structure and Parts of Speech

Section 10 The Sentence

A *sentence* is a group of words that tells a complete thought. A sentence has two parts: a *subject* and a *predicate*.

- The subject tells *whom* or *what*.   <u>The swimmers</u> race.
- The predicate tells *what happened*.   The judges <u>watch carefully</u>.

There are four kinds of sentences: *declarative, interrogative, imperative,* and *exclamatory.*

- A *declarative sentence* makes a statement and ends with a period.
  Jake swam faster than anyone.
- An *interrogative sentence* asks a question and ends with a question mark.
  Did Sammy qualify for the finals?
- An *imperative sentence* gives a command and usually ends with a period; a firm command can end with an exclamation point.
  Keep your eyes on the finish line.   Watch out for that bee!
- An *exclamatory sentence* ends with an exclamation point.   Jake has won the race!

Section 11 Subjects

The *subject* of a sentence tells whom or what the sentence is about.

- A sentence can have one subject.   <u>Mary</u> wrote a book.
- A sentence can have a *compound subject,* two or more subjects that are joined by a conjunction (*and, or*) and that share the same predicate.
  <u>Alex and Mark</u> have already read the book.
- Imperative sentences have an unnamed *understood subject,* the person being spoken to. This subject is referred to as "understood *you.*"   Give me the book, please.

The *complete subject* includes all the words that name and tell about the subject.

      <u>Many students</u> have borrowed the book.

The *simple subject* is the most important noun or pronoun in the complete subject.

      Many <u>students</u> have borrowed the book.   <u>They</u> discussed the book yesterday.

Note: Sometimes the simple subject and the complete subject are the same.   <u>Ricardo</u> is writing a book.

Section 12 Predicates

The *predicate* of a sentence tells what happened. The *complete predicate* includes a verb and all the words that tell what happened.

- A complete predicate can include an action verb to tell what the subject of the sentence did.
  Mary <u>won an award</u>.
- A complete predicate can include a linking verb to tell more about the subject.
  Mary <u>is a talented writer</u>.

The *simple predicate* is the most important word or words in the complete predicate. The simple predicate is always a verb.

      Mary <u>won</u> an award for her performance.   She <u>will receive</u> a trophy next week.

- A *compound predicate* is two or more predicates that share the same subject. Compound predicates are often joined by the conjunction *and* or *or.*
  Ramon <u>sang</u> and <u>danced</u> in the play.   Mary <u>wrote</u> the play and <u>directed</u> it.

A *predicate noun* follows a linking verb and renames the subject.

      Mary is a <u>writer</u>.   Ramon is a <u>singer</u>.

A *predicate adjective* follows a linking verb and describes the subject.

      Mary is <u>talented</u>.   Ramon is <u>clever</u>.

Section 13 Simple, Compound, and Complex Sentences

A *simple sentence* tells one complete thought.

> Arthur has a rock collection.

A *compound sentence* is made up of two simple sentences (or *independent clauses*) whose ideas are related. The clauses can be joined by a comma and a conjunction (*and, or, but*).

> Arthur has a rock collection**, and** Mary collects shells.

The two independent clauses in a compound sentence can also be joined by a semicolon.

> Arthur collects rocks**;** Mary collects shells.

Two clauses in a compound sentence can be separated by a colon when the second clause is a direct result of the first clause.

> Arthur enjoys visiting new places**:** he can hunt for rocks to add to his collection.

A *complex sentence* is made up of one independent clause (or *simple sentence*) and at least one dependent clause. A *dependent clause* is a group of words that has a subject and a predicate, but it cannot stand on its own.

> **Dependent Clause:**   when Arthur visited Arizona
> **Independent Clause:**   He learned a lot about desert plants.
> **Complex Sentence:**   When Arthur visited Arizona, he learned a lot about desert plants.

A *compound-complex sentence* includes two or more independent clauses and at least one dependent clause.

> **Independent Clauses:**   Arizona is proud of its saguaro cactus.
>   The saguaro cactus can grow up to sixty feet tall.
> **Dependent Clause:**   which is also called the giant cactus
> **Compound-complex Sentence:** Arizona is proud of its saguaro cactus; the saguaro, which is also called the *giant cactus,* can grow up to sixty feet tall.

An *adjective clause* is a dependent clause that describes a noun or pronoun. An adjective clause always follows the word it describes and begins with a relative pronoun such as *who, whom, whose, which,* or *that.*

> My cousin Arthur, **who has a rock collection**, visited the Arizona desert. (*describes* Arthur)
> He studied the interesting rock formations **that rise above the desert floor**. (*describes* formations)

An *adverb clause* is a dependent clause that tells more about a verb, an adjective, or an adverb. Adverb clauses tell *where, when, why,* or *how much.* They often begin with a subordinating conjunction such as *after, since, where, than, although, because, if, as, as if, while, when,* or *whenever.*

> **Whenever Arthur came across an unfamiliar rock**, he took a photograph of it.
> (*tells* when *Arthur* took *a photograph*)
> Arthur didn't take any rocks away **because the desert environment is fragile**.
> (*tells* why *Arthur* didn't take *rocks away*)

Section 14 Fragments, Run-ons, Comma Splices, and Ramble-ons

A *fragment* is an incomplete sentence that does not tell a complete thought.

> Sumi and Ali. (*missing a predicate that tells what happened*)
> Went hiking in the woods. (*missing a subject that tells who*)

A *run-on sentence* is two complete sentences that are run together. To fix a run-on sentence, use a comma and a conjunction (*and, or, but*) to join the two sentences. (You may also join the sentences with a semicolon instead of with a comma and a conjunction.)

> **Incorrect:** Sumi went hiking Ali went swimming.
> **Correct:**   Sumi went hiking**, but** Ali went swimming.

A *comma splice* is two complete sentences that have a comma between them but are missing a conjunction (*and, or, but*). To fix a comma splice, add *and, or,* or *but* after the comma.

> **Incorrect:** Sumi went hiking yesterday, Ali went swimming.
> **Correct:**   Sumi went hiking yesterday, **and** Ali went swimming.

A *ramble-on sentence* is grammatically correct but contains extra words that don't add to its meaning.

Incorrect: Hiking through the wilderness to enjoy nature is my favorite outdoor sports activity, probably because it is so enjoyable and such good exercise, and because I enjoy observing wild animals in the wilderness in their natural environment.

Correct: Hiking through the wilderness to enjoy nature is my favorite outdoor sports activity. I enjoy observing wild animals in their natural environment.

Try not to string too many short sentences together when you write. Instead, combine sentences and take out unnecessary information.

Incorrect: I stared at him and he stared at me and I told him to go away and he wouldn't so then I called my big sister.

Correct: We stared at each other. I asked him to go away, but he wouldn't. Then I called my big sister.

Section 15 Nouns

A *common noun* names any person, place, thing, or idea.

Ira visited an auto **museum** with his **friends**. Ira has always had an **interest** in **cars**.
He likes that blue **convertible**.

A *proper noun* names a certain person, place, thing, or idea. Proper nouns begin with a capital letter. A proper noun that is made up of two or more words is considered one noun.

Ira wants to visit the **Sonoran Desert** in **Mexico** in **April 1999**.
He is reading a guidebook about the region entitled **The Undiscovered Desert**.

A *collective noun* names a group of people or things that act as one unit.

jury   family   committee   audience   crowd

Section 16 Adjectives

An *adjective* is a word that tells more about a noun or a pronoun.

- **Some adjectives tell what kind.**
  Jim observed the **huge** elephant. The **enormous** beast towered above him.

- **Some adjectives tell how many.**
  The elephant was **twelve** feet tall. It weighed **several** tons.

- A *predicate adjective* follows a linking verb and describes the subject.
  Jim was **careful** not to anger the elephant. He was **happy** when the trainer led it away.

- *A, an,* and *the* are special kinds of adjectives called *articles*. Use *a* and *an* to refer to any person, place, thing, or idea. Use *the* to refer to a specific person, place, thing, or idea. Use *a* before a singular noun that begins with a consonant sound. Use *an* before a singular noun that begins with a vowel sound.
  An elephant is heavier than **a** rhino. **The** elephant in this picture is six weeks old.

- A *demonstrative adjective* tells which one. *This, that, these,* and *those* can be used as demonstrative adjectives. Use *this* and *these* to talk about things that are nearby. Use *that* and *those* to talk about things that are farther away.
  This book is about rhinos.   **These** rhinos just came to the zoo.
  That rhino is enormous!   **Those** funny-looking creatures are wildebeests.
  Note: Never use *here* or *there* after the adjectives *this, that, these,* and *those*.

- A *proper adjective* is made from a proper noun. Capitalize proper adjectives.
  Italian cooking   **Democratic** convention   **Apache** legend

Section 17 Pronouns

A *pronoun* can replace a noun.

17a Personal Pronouns

Personal pronouns include *I, me, you, we, us, he, she, it, they,* and *them*. Personal pronouns can be used to stand for the person speaking, the person spoken to, or the person spoken about.

- *First person pronouns* refer to the speaker (*I, me*) or include the speaker (*we, us*).
  Let **me** know when **I** am next at bat.   It took **us** hours, but **we** managed to get to the stadium.

- *Second person pronouns* refer to the person or people being spoken to (*you*).
  Are **you** going to the game?   I asked Marisa to give the bases to **you**.
- *Third person pronouns* refer to the person, people, or thing(s) being spoken about (*he, him, she, her, it, they, them*).
  They played well.   Pass the ball to **him**.   Kick **it** to **her**.
- The third person pronoun *he* (with *him* and *his*) was once accepted as a universal pronoun that could refer to anyone, male or female, if a generalization about people was being made. Now most writers try to avoid the use of universal *he*.

  One solution to this pronoun problem is to make the pronoun and the word it refers to plural.
  When a chef cooks, **he** displays creativity. becomes: When chefs cook, **they** display creativity.
  Each player should bring **his** own racket. becomes: Players should bring **their** own rackets.

  Another solution is to replace *he* with *he or she*, or replace *his* with *his or her*.
  Each player should bring **his** own racket. becomes: Each player should bring **his or her** own racket.

17b Subject and Object Pronouns

A *subject pronoun* takes the place of the subject of a sentence. Subject pronouns are said to be in the *subjective case*. Subject pronouns include *I, he, she, we,* and *they*.

    Incorrect: Rita is an excellent soccer player. **Rita she** made the team.
    Correct: Rita plays goalie. **She** never lets the other team score.

An *object pronoun* replaces a noun that is the object of a verb or a preposition. Object pronouns are said to be in the *objective case*. Object pronouns include *me, him, her, us,* and *them*.

    Rita's team played the Bobcats. Rita's team beat **them**.

The pronouns *it* and *you* can be either subjects or objects.

    It was a close game. (*subject pronoun*)   The Bobcats almost won **it**. (*object pronoun*)

- Use a subject pronoun as part of a compound subject. Use an object pronoun as part of a compound object. To test whether a pronoun is correct, say the sentence **without** the other part of a compound subject or object.
  Incorrect: Rita told Ellen and **I** it was a close game. (Rita told **I** it was a close game.)
  Correct: Rita told Ellen and **me** it was a close game. (Rita told **me** it was a close game.)
- When the pronouns *I* and *me* are used in a compound with a noun or another pronoun, *I* or *me* always comes second in a pair or last in a series of three or more.
  Incorrect: The coach gave the Most Improved Players awards to **me and Carlos**.
  Correct: The coach gave the Most Improved Players awards to **Carlos and me**.

17c Pronoun Antecedents

An *antecedent* is the word or phrase a pronoun refers to. The antecedent always includes a noun.

    The **Bobcats** are excellent players. They won every game last season.

- A pronoun must agree with its antecedent. An antecedent and a pronoun agree when they have the same *number* (singular or plural) and *gender* (male or female).
  Nick's mother cheered. **She** was very excited.

17d Possessive Pronouns

Possessive pronouns show ownership.

- The possessive pronouns *my, your, his, her, its, their,* and *our* replace possessive nouns.
  Those skates belong to **my** brother Jorge.
  Those are **his** kneepads, too. (*the pronoun* his *replaces the possessive noun* Jorge's)
- The possessive pronouns *mine, ours, yours, hers, his, its,* and *theirs* replace both a possessive noun and the noun that is possessed.
  Alisha's kneepads are blue. **Mine** are red and **hers** are blue.
  (*The possessive pronoun* hers *replaces both the possessive noun* Alisha's *and* kneepads.)
- *Whose* is the possessive form of the relative pronoun *who*. It is also used as the possessive form of the relative pronoun *which*.
  The skaters **whose** parents cannot pick them up at 6 P.M. must wait inside the office.
  (Whose *indicates that the parents belong to the skaters.*)

17e Compound Personal Pronouns

A *compound personal pronoun* contains the word *self* or *selves*. Compound personal pronouns include *myself, herself, himself, itself, yourself, ourselves,* and *themselves.*

- **They often show that the action of a sentence is reflecting back to the subject.**
  My brother bought <u>himself</u> a new puck.   We cheered for <u>ourselves</u>.
- **Compound personal pronouns can also be used to show emphasis.**
  She made the winning goal <u>herself</u>.   I <u>myself</u> thought it was a terrific game.

17f Indefinite Pronouns

Indefinite pronouns refer to persons or things that are not identified as individuals. These pronouns include *all, anybody, both, anything, few, most, no one, either, nothing, everyone, one, several, none, everybody, nobody, someone, everything, something, anyone,* and *somebody.*

<u>Somebody</u> lost the ball.   We can't play <u>anything</u> until we find it.

17g Relative Pronouns

When the pronouns *who, whom, whose, which,* and *that* are used to introduce an adjective clause, they are called *relative pronouns.* A relative pronoun always follows the noun it refers to.

The player <u>who brought the volleyball</u> can serve first.
I joined the team <u>that chose me.</u>
This net, <u>which I found in my closet,</u> will be perfect for our volleyball game.

Note: For more information on using *who, whom, which,* and *that,* see Section 32, Problem Words.

17h Interrogative Pronouns

When the pronouns *who, whom, which,* and *what* are used to begin a question, they are called *interrogative pronouns.*

<u>Who</u> has brought the volleyball?   <u>What</u> is a wicket used for?
<u>Which</u> net is used for volleyball?   To <u>whom</u> did you hit the ball?

17i Demonstrative Pronouns

This, that, these, and *those* can be used as *demonstrative pronouns.*

- **Use *this* and *these* to talk about one or more things that are nearby.**
  <u>This</u> is a soft rug.   <u>These</u> are sweeter than those over there.
- **Use *that* and *those* to talk about one or more things that are far away.**
  <u>That</u> is where I sat yesterday.   <u>Those</u> are new chairs.

Section 18 Verbs

18a Action and Linking Verbs

An *action verb* shows action.

Scientists <u>study</u> the natural world.   They <u>learn</u> how the laws of nature work.

A *linking verb* does not show action. It connects the subject of a sentence to a word or words in the predicate that tell about the subject. Linking verbs include *am, is, are, was, been,* and *were. Seem, appear,* and *become* can be used as linking verbs, too.

Explorers <u>are</u> brave.   That route <u>seems</u> long and dangerous.

Some verbs, such as *appear, look, smell, feel, grow,* and *taste,* can be either action verbs or linking verbs, depending on how they are used. You can test whether a verb is a linking verb by substituting a form of the verb *be* (*am, is, are, was,* or *were*) in its place. If the form of *be* makes sense, the verb is a linking verb.

I <u>looked</u> at the bear. (*"I <u>was</u> at the bear" does not make sense:* looked *is an action verb.*)
The bear <u>looked</u> hungry. (*"The bear <u>was</u> hungry" makes sense:* looked *is a linking verb.*)

18b Transitive and Intransitive Verbs

A *transitive verb* is an action verb that transfers its action to a direct object.

The polar bear <u>watched</u> a seal's air hole in the ice.   The polar bear <u>caught</u> the seal.

An *intransitive verb* does not have a direct object. An intransitive verb shows action that the subject does alone.

The bear **waited** patiently.   Suddenly the bear **struck**.

Many verbs can be either transitive or intransitive, depending on whether or not there is a direct object.

The bear **ate** the seal. (*Seal* is the direct object: *ate* is a transitive verb.)
The bear **ate** hungrily. (*Hungrily* is an adverb, and there is no direct object: *ate* is an intransitive verb.)

18c Main Verbs and Auxiliary Verbs

A *main verb* is the most important verb in a sentence. An *auxiliary verb,* or helping verb, comes before the main verb to help it show action. Auxiliary verbs such as *had, are,* and *will* indicate the tense of the main verb. Others, such as *could, might,* and *may,* show how likely it is that something will happen.

Scientists **are studying** glaciers.   The studies **may help** us learn more about Earth.

18d The Principal Parts of a Verb

Each verb has three *principal parts:* its *present form,* its *past form,* and its *past participle form.*

- Most verbs add *-ed* to the present form to create both the past form and the past participle form. These verbs are called *regular verbs.*
- *Irregular verbs* form their past and past participle forms in other ways. The chart below shows the principal parts of several common irregular verbs.

Present	Past	Past Participle
arise	arose	arisen
(be) is	was	been
blow	blew	blown
bring	brought	brought
build	built	built
cut	cut	cut
drive	drove	driven
eat	ate	eaten
fall	fell	fallen
fly	flew	flown
give	gave	given
go	went	gone
grow	grew	grown
have	had	had
hear	heard	heard
hide	hid	hidden
hold	held	held
know	knew	known
lay	laid	laid
leave	left	left
lie	lay	lain
light	lit	lit
make	made	made
ring	rang	rung
run	ran	run
say	said	said
see	saw	seen
shake	shook	shaken
sing	sang	sung
swim	swam	swum
take	took	taken
tell	told	told
think	thought	thought
throw	threw	thrown
wear	wore	worn
write	wrote	written

- Almost all verbs add *-ing* to the present form to create the *present participle* form: *sing/singing; talk/talking.*

18e Verb Tense

Verb tense places an action in time.

- The *present tense* is used to show that something happens regularly or is true now.
  Squirrels <u>bury</u> nuts each fall.

  Add *s* to most verbs to show present tense when the subject is *he, she, it,* or a singular noun. Add *es* to verbs ending in *s, ch, sh, x,* or *z.* Do not add *s* or *es* if the subject is a plural noun or *I, you, we,* or *they.*

add *s*	add *es*	change *y* to *i*
speak/speak<u>s</u>	reach/reach<u>es</u>	carry/carr<u>ies</u>

- The *past tense* shows past action. Add *-ed* to most verbs to form the past tense. Verbs that do not add *-ed* are called *irregular verbs.*   reach/reach<u>ed</u>   speak/<u>spoke</u>

- The *future tense* shows future action. Use the verb *will* to form the future tense.
  Mom <u>will visit</u> Antarctica next year.   She <u>will photograph</u> penguins.

- The *present perfect tense* shows action that began in the past and may still be happening. To form the present perfect tense, add the helping verb *has* or *have* to the past participle of a verb.
  Mom <u>has studied</u> Antarctica for years.   Her articles <u>have appeared</u> in science journals.

- The *past perfect tense* shows action that was completed by a certain time in the past. To form the past perfect tense, add the helping verb *had* to the past participle of a verb.
  Before she visited Antarctica, Mom <u>had imagined</u> it as a wasteland.

- The *future perfect tense* shows action that will be complete by a certain time in the future. To form the future perfect tense, add the helping verbs *will have* to the past participle form of a verb.
  By the end of next year, Mom <u>will have published</u> a book on Antarctic wildlife.

- The *progressive tenses* show continuing action. To form the *present progressive* tense, add *am, is,* or *are* to the *present participle* of a verb (usually the present form + *-ing*). To form the *past progressive* tense, add *was* or *were* to the present participle. To form the *future progressive* tense, add *will be* to the present participle.
  Scientists <u>are learning</u> new facts about Antarctica every day. (*present progressive tense*)
  When Mom <u>was traveling</u> in Antarctica, she saw its beauty. (*past progressive tense*)
  Someday soon I <u>will be visiting</u> Antarctica with Mom. (*future progressive tense*)

18f Subject and Verb Agreement

The subject and its verb must agree in number. Be sure that the verb agrees with its subject and not with the object of a preposition that comes before the verb.

An Antarctic explorer needs special equipment.
(*singular subject:* **An Antarctic explorer;** *singular verb* [*verb + s or es*]: **needs**)
Explorers in Antarctica carry climbing tools and survival gear.
(*plural subject:* **Explorers;** *plural verb* [*verb without s or es*]: **carry**)

A *compound subject* and its verb must agree.

- **Compound subjects joined by *and* are plural.**   Snow and ice <u>make</u> exploration difficult.

- If a compound subject is joined by *or,* the verb must agree with the last item in the subject.
  Either the helpers or the leader <u>checks</u> the weather report.

There are special rules for agreement with certain kinds of subjects.

- Titles of books, movies, magazines, newspapers, stories, and songs are always considered singular, even if they end in *s.*
  The Secret Life of Penguins is the title of Mom's book.
  "Ice and Darkness" is the name of a poem I wrote.

- A collective noun, such as *collection, group, team, country, kingdom, family, flock,* and *herd,* names more than one person or object acting as a group. These nouns are usually considered singular.
  My <u>family</u> lives in southern Australia.   A <u>flock</u> of seagulls is flying overhead.

- Most indefinite pronouns, including *everyone, nobody, nothing, everything, something,* and *anything,* are considered singular.
  <u>Somebody</u> has left the tent flap open.   Is <u>anything</u> missing?   <u>Everything</u> is fine.

- Some indefinite pronouns that clearly refer to more than one, such as *many, most, few,* and *both,* are considered plural.
  <u>Many</u> are interested in Antarctica, but <u>few</u> are able to make the journey there.

18g Active and Passive Voice

A verb is in *active voice* if its subject performs an action. A verb is in *passive voice* if its subject is acted upon by something else. Many sentences in the passive voice have a prepositional phrase that begins with the word *by* and follows the verb.

> Explorers **plan** trips months in advance. (*active voice*)
> Trips **are planned** by explorers months in advance. (*passive voice*)

The active voice can communicate action briefly and powerfully. In most cases, the active voice is stronger and clearer than the passive voice. Try to write most of your sentences in the active voice.

> **Strong active voice:** The penguin **snapped** up the fish.
> **Weak passive voice:** The fish was **snapped up** by the penguin.

Some writers believe that the passive voice should be used only when an action is done by an unknown or unimportant agent.

> The tent flap **was left** open. (*The agent who left the tent flap open is unknown.*)

Section 19 Adverbs

An *adverb* describes a verb, an adjective, or another adverb. Adverbs tell how, when, where, or to what extent.

- **Many adverbs end in** *-ly*. **Some adverbs do not end in** *-ly*. **These include** *now, then, very, too, often, always, again, sometimes, soon, later, first, far, now,* **and** *fast*.
  Andrew approached the snake cage **slowly**. He knew that snakes can move **fast**.

- **Some adverbs tell** *how*.
  She spoke **confidently**.   He **eagerly** bit into the sandwich.

- **Some adverbs tell** *when*.
  Then the bell rang.   School ended **yesterday**.   I eat pizza **only** on Friday.

- **Some adverbs tell** *where*.
  We went **inside**.   They built a house **there**.   Come **here**.

- **Some adverbs tell** *to what extent*.
  It is **very** quiet.   I am **almost** finished.

Section 20 Prepositions

A *preposition* shows a relationship between a word in a sentence and a noun or pronoun that follows the preposition. Prepositions tell when, where, what kind, how, or how much.

- Prepositions include the words *after, in front of, without, above, down, among, with, of, from, for, about, such as, throughout, into, onto, inside, in, at, under, over, on, through, to, across, around, by, beside, during, off,* and *before*.
  Jeff left the milk **on** the table.   He knew it belonged **in** the refrigerator.

- A *prepositional phrase* is a group of words that begins with a preposition and ends with its object. The object of a preposition is a noun or a pronoun. A prepositional phrase can be at the beginning, middle, or end of a sentence.
  Jeff's mom would be home **in five minutes**. **Within three minutes** he had put it away.

- Prepositional phrases that modify (or tell more about) nouns or pronouns are called *adjectival prepositional phrases*. An adjectival prepositional phrase usually comes after the noun or pronoun it modifies. Adjectival prepositional phrases often tell *which*.
  The milk **in the refrigerator** is spoiled. (*modifies the noun* milk *and tells* which milk)
  I can't stand the odor **of spoiled milk**! (*modifies the noun* odor *and tells* which odor)

- *Adverbial prepositional phrases* modify a verb, an adverb, or an adjective. Many adverbial prepositional phrases tell *when, where, how,* or *how long* something was done.
  Jeff usually drinks orange juice **before breakfast**. (*modifies the verb* drinks *and tells* when)
  He says his mom's fresh-squeezed orange juice is the best **in the world**.
  (*modifies the adjective* best *and tells* where)
  Late **in the evening** I heard a knock at my door. (*modifies the adverb* late *and tells* when)

Section 21 Direct Objects and Indirect Objects

A *direct object* is the noun or pronoun that receives the action of the verb. Direct objects follow action verbs. To find the direct object, say the verb and then "Whom?" or "What?"

> Jacques painted a **picture**. (Painted whom or what? Picture. *Picture* is the direct object.)

- A *compound direct object* occurs when more than one noun receives the action of the verb.
  He used a **brush** and oil **paints**. (*Brush* and *paints* comprise the compound direct object.)

A sentence with a direct object may also have an *indirect object*. An indirect object is a noun or pronoun and usually tells to whom something is given, told, or taught.

> Jacques gave his **mom** the painting.

Section 22 Conjunctions

The words *and*, *or*, and *but* are *coordinating conjunctions*.

- **Coordinating conjunctions may be used to join words within a sentence.**
  My favorite reptiles are snakes **and** lizards.   Najim doesn't like snakes **or** lizards.

- **A comma and a coordinating conjunction can be used to join two or more simple sentences. (The conjunction *and* does not need a comma if both sentences are short.)**
  I like snakes, **but** he says they're creepy.   We can get a snake, **or** we can get a lizard.

A *subordinating conjunction* relates one clause to another. Dependent clauses begin with a subordinating conjunction. Subordinating conjunctions include *because, so, if, although, when, where, as, while, though, than, as if, whenever, since, wherever, after, often, over,* and *before*.

> **Before** his mom left, Bo cleaned his room. He had a favor to ask, **so** he vacuumed, too.

Correlative conjunctions always appear in pairs. They connect words or groups of words and provide more emphasis than coordinating conjunctions. Some common correlative conjunctions are *both—and, either—or, neither—nor, not only—but (also),* and *whether—or*.

> She is **not only** a good singer **but also** an excellent athlete.
> **Neither** Raj **nor** Chris came to the concert.

Section 23 Interjections

An *interjection* expresses emotion and is not part of any independent or dependent clause.

> **Wow**! This bread is delicious.   **Mmmm**, this bread tastes good!

Section 24 Appositives

An *appositive* is a phrase that identifies a noun.

> My favorite snack, **cornbread with honey**, is easy to make.

- Most appositives are separated from the rest of a sentence by commas. These appositives just give more information about the nouns they describe.
  Tara, **my friend who figure skates**, is traveling to Dallas for a competition.

- Some appositives should not be set off by commas. If an appositive is vital to the meaning of the sentence, it should not be set off by commas.
  His book *The Basics of Automobile Maintenance* tells how to take care of a car.
  My sister **Katie** likes to read on the porch.

Section 25 Verbals

Sometimes a verb does not act as a predicate. *Verbals* are forms of verbs that play other roles in sentences.

- One type of verbal, a *participle,* acts as an adjective. A participle may be the present participle or the past participle form of a verb. (See Handbook Section 18d.)
  George heard the bell <u>ringing</u>. (*acts as an adjective describing the noun* bell)

  A *participial phrase* is made up of a participle and other words that complete its meaning.
  <u>Filled</u> with pride, Angela accepted her medal. (*acts as an adjective modifying the noun* Angela)
  Matt noticed a skunk <u>waddling</u> through the bushes. (*acts as an adjective modifying the noun* skunk)

- An *infinitive* is a phrase made up of *to* followed by the present form of a verb (*to defend*). Infinitives may act as adjectives, adverbs, or nouns. An *infinitive phrase* is made up of an infinitive and other words that complete its meaning.
  I like <u>to walk</u> in the woods. (*acts as a noun; the direct object of the verb* like)
  This is a good way <u>to appreciate</u> nature. (*acts as an adjective modifying the noun* way)
  I listen carefully <u>to hear</u> the sounds of woodland creatures. (*acts as an adverb modifying the verb* listen)

- A *gerund* is a verbal that acts as a noun. All gerunds are present participles. (See Handbook Section 18d.)
  My brother enjoys <u>swimming</u>. (*acts as a noun; the direct object of the verb* enjoys)

  A *gerund phrase* is made up of a gerund and the other words that complete its meaning.
  <u>Riding</u> the waves on a surfboard is his great ambition. (*acts as the subject of the sentence*)

Usage

Section 26 Negatives

A *negative word* means "no" or "not."

- The words *no, not, nothing, none, never, nowhere,* and *nobody* are negatives.
  The notebook was <u>nowhere</u> to be found.　　<u>Nobody</u> wanted to miss the party.

- Often negatives are in the form of contractions.
  Do <u>not</u> enter that room.　　<u>Don't</u> even go near the door.

- In most sentences it is not correct to use two negatives.

Incorrect	Correct
We <u>can't</u> see <u>nothing</u>.	We <u>can't</u> see anything.
We <u>haven't</u> got <u>no</u> solution.	We <u>haven't</u> got a solution.

- Some sentences express ideas that require the use of two negative words.
  <u>No</u> one will work for you for <u>nothing</u>. (*In other words, anyone who works will expect to be paid.*)
  I <u>couldn't</u> *not* say hello to her. (*In other words, the speaker had to say hello, even if the speaker might not have wanted to.*)

Section 27 Comparisons

- The *comparative form* of an adjective or an adverb compares two people, places, or things. The comparative form is often followed by "than." To compare two people, places, or things, add *-er* to short adjectives and adverbs.
  An elephant is <u>tall</u>. A **giraffe** is <u>taller</u> than an **elephant**. (Giraffe *is compared with* elephant.)
  A lion runs <u>fast</u>. A **cheetah** runs <u>faster</u> than **any other animal**. (Cheetah *is compared with* any other animal.)

- The *superlative form* of an adjective or an adverb compares three or more people, places, or things. The article *the* usually comes before the superlative form. To compare three or more items, add *-est* to short adjectives and adverbs.
  The giraffe is the <u>tallest</u> land animal.　　The cheetah is the <u>fastest</u> animal alive.

- When comparing two or more persons, places, or things using the ending *-er* or *-est*, never use the word *more*.

Incorrect	Correct
She is <u>more faster</u> than he is.	She is <u>faster</u> than he is.

- The word *more* is used with longer adjectives to compare two persons, places, or things. Use the word *most* to compare three or more persons, places, or things.
  Mario is <u>excited</u> about the field trip.
  Duane is <u>more excited</u> than Mario.
  Kiki is the <u>most excited</u> student of all.

- Sometimes the words *good* and *bad* are used to compare. These words change forms in comparisons.

  Mario is a <u>good</u> athlete.　　The basketball court is in <u>bad</u> shape.
  Kiki is a <u>better</u> athlete.　　The tennis court is in <u>worse</u> shape than the basketball court.

  Bill is the <u>best</u> athlete of all.　　The ice rink is in the <u>worst</u> shape of all.
  Note: Use *better* or *worse* to compare two things. Use *best* or *worst* to compare three or more things.

Section 28 Contractions

When two or more words are combined to form one word, one or more letters are dropped and replaced by an apostrophe. These words are called *contractions.* For example, when *he will* becomes the contraction *he'll,* the apostrophe replaces *wi*.

- Here are some other common contractions.

can't (cannot)	**haven't** (have not)	**she'd** (she would)
couldn't (could not)	**I'll** (I will)	**they've** (they have)
doesn't (does not)	**it's** (it is)	**we're** (we are)

Section 29 Plural Nouns

- A *singular noun* names one person, place, thing, or idea.

  girl   pond   arrow   freedom

- A *plural noun* names more than one person, place, thing, or idea. To make most singular nouns plural, add *s*.

  girl<u>s</u>   pond<u>s</u>   arrow<u>s</u>   freedom<u>s</u>

- For nouns ending in *sh, ch, x,* or *z,* add *es* to make the word plural.

  bush/bush<u>es</u>   box/box<u>es</u>
  lunch/lunch<u>es</u>   quiz/quiz<u>zes</u>

- For nouns ending in a consonant and *y,* change the *y* to *i* and add *es*.

  penny/penn<u>ies</u>   army/arm<u>ies</u>

- For some nouns that end in *f* or *fe,* replace *f* or *fe* with *ves* to make the noun plural.

  shelf/shel<u>ves</u>   wife/wi<u>ves</u>   (*Exceptions*: cliff/cliff<u>s</u>; reef/reef<u>s</u>; cafe/cafe<u>s</u>)

- Some words change spelling when the plural is formed.

  man/m<u>e</u>n   woman/wom<u>e</u>n   mouse/m<u>ice</u>   goose/g<u>ee</u>se

- Some words have the same singular and plural form.

  deer   sheep   rice   offspring   scissors

Section 30 Possessives

A *possessive* shows ownership.

- To make a singular noun possessive, add an apostrophe and *s*.

  John<u>'s</u> bat   the girl<u>'s</u> bike

- When a singular noun ends in *s,* add an apostrophe and *s*.

  Ross<u>'s</u> project   James<u>'s</u> glasses

- To make a plural noun that ends in *s* possessive, add an apostrophe.

  the soldiers<u>'</u> songs   the girls<u>'</u> bikes

- When a plural noun does not end in *s,* add an apostrophe and *s* to show possession.

  the men<u>'s</u> ideas   the children<u>'s</u> shoes

Section 31 Dangling Modifiers

A verbal phrase acting as an adjective must modify, or refer to, a specific word in the main part of a sentence. A *dangling modifier* is a phrase that does not refer to any particular word in the sentence.

Incorrect: <u>Walking down the street</u>, deep thoughts come to mind.
(Are deep thoughts walking down the street? No. This verbal phrase does not refer to any particular word in the main part of the sentence: it is a dangling modifier.)

Dangling modifiers make your writing unclear, so avoid them. When you begin a sentence with a verbal phrase such as "Walking down the street," make sure that the question "Who is walking down the street?" is answered clearly in the first part of the rest of the sentence.

Correct: <u>Walking down the street</u>, I often think deep thoughts.
(<u>Who</u> is walking down the street? I am. This verbal phrase clearly relates to the pronoun I.)

Section 32 Problem Words

These words are often misused in writing.

sit	*Sit* means "rest or stay in one place." Sit down and relax for a while.
sat	*Sat* is the past tense of *sit*. I sat in that chair yesterday.
set	*Set* is a verb meaning "put." Set the chair here.
lay	*Lay* means "to put something down somewhere." It takes a direct object. The past tense form of *lay* is *laid*, and the past participle form of *lay* is also *laid*. Each day I lay a tablecloth on the table. Yesterday I laid the yellow tablecloth. I had never laid that one on the table before.
lie	*Lie* means "to recline." It does not take a direct object. The past tense form of *lie* is *lay*, and the past participle form of *lie* is *lain*. Most mornings I lie half awake just before the alarm rings. Early this morning I lay with my eyes open, waiting for the alarm. I had lain there for a few minutes before I realized that it was Saturday.
may	*May* is used to ask permission or to express a possibility. May I have another hot dog? I may borrow that book someday.
can	*Can* shows that someone is able to do something. I can easily eat three hot dogs.
learn	*Learn* means "to get knowledge." Who will help you learn Spanish?
teach	*Teach* means "to give knowledge." Never use *learn* in place of *teach*. Incorrect: My sister will learn me to speak Spanish. Correct: My sister will teach me to speak Spanish.
is	Use *is* to tell about one person, place, or thing. Alabama is warm during the summer.
are	Use *are* to tell about more than one person, place, or thing. Also use *are* with the word *you*. Seattle and San Francisco are cool during the summer. You are welcome to visit me anytime.
doesn't	The contraction *doesn't* is used with the singular pronouns *he, she,* and *it*. He doesn't like sauerkraut. It doesn't agree with him.
don't	The contraction *don't* is used with the plural pronouns *we* and *they*. *Don't* is also used with *I* and *you*. They don't like Swiss cheese. I don't care for it, either.
I	Use the pronoun *I* as the subject of a sentence. When using *I* or *me* with another noun or pronoun, always name yourself last. I am going to basketball camp. Renée and I will ride together.
me	Use the pronoun *me* after action verbs. Renée will call me this evening. Also use *me* after a preposition, such as *to, at,* and *with*. Pass the ball to me. Come to the game with Renée and me.
good	*Good* is an adjective.
well	*Well* is an adverb. These words are often used incorrectly. Incorrect: Renée plays good. Correct: Renée is a good basketball player. She plays well.

287

G.U.M.

raise	*Raise* must be followed by a direct object. I **raise** the flag every morning.
rise	*Rise* does not need a direct object. I **rise** at dawn every morning.

like	*Like* means "similar to" or "have a fondness for." Do not use *is like* to indicate a pause or to mean "says." Incorrect: I enjoy, **like**, all kinds of water sports. He was **like**, "Swimming is fun." Correct: I **like** swimming and water polo. He said, "I **like** the water."
go	*Go* means "move from place to place." Don't use *go* or *went* to mean "says" or "said." Incorrect: She **went**, "The swim meet was yesterday." Correct: She said, "I **went** to the swim meet."
all	*All* means "the total of something." Avoid using *was all* to mean "said." Incorrect: He **was all**, "Everyone likes swimming." Correct: He said, "Everyone likes swimming."
you know	Use the phrase *you know* only when it helps a sentence make sense. Try not to use it in places where it does not belong. Incorrect: We can, **you know**, go canoeing. Correct: Did **you know** that my family has a canoe?

let	*Let* is a verb that means "allow." Please **let** me go to the mall with you.
leave	*Leave* is a verb that means "go away from" or "let stay." We will **leave** at noon. **Leave** your sweater here.

was	*Was* is a past tense form of *be*. Use *was* to tell about one person or thing. Hana **was** sad yesterday.
were	*Were* is also a past tense form of *be*. Use *were* to tell about more than one person or thing. Also use the word *were* with *you*. Hana and her friend **were** both unhappy. **Were** you home yesterday?

has	Use *has* to tell about one person or thing. Rory **has** a stamp collection.
have	Use *have* to tell about more than one. Also use *have* with the pronoun *I*. David and Lin **have** a rock collection. I **have** a bottle cap collection.

who	*Who* is in the subjective case and should be used as the subject of a clause. Use *who* to refer to people. The man **who** picked me up is my father.
whom	*Whom* is in the objective case and should be used as a direct or indirect object or as the object of a preposition. Use *whom* to refer to people. To **whom** am I speaking?
which	Use *which* to refer to things. His rear tire, **which** was flat, had to be repaired.
that	*That* can refer to people or things. Use *that* instead of *which* to begin a clause that is necessary to the meaning of the sentence. The picture **that** Stephen drew won first prize.

very	*Very* is an adverb. It means "extremely." I was **very** tired after the hike.
real	*Real* is an adjective. It means "actual." Never use *real* in place of *very*. Incorrect: The hike was **real** long. Correct: I used a **real** compass to find my way.

Homophones sound alike but have different spellings and meanings.

are	*Are* is a form of the verb *be*.	We **are** best friends.
our	*Our* is a possessive pronoun.	**Our** favorite color is green.
hour	An *hour* is sixty minutes.	Meet me in an **hour**.

its	*Its* is a possessive pronoun.	The horse shook **its** shaggy head.
it's	*It's* is a contraction of the words *it is*.	**It's** a beautiful day for a ride.

there — *There* is an adverb meaning "in that place." It can also be used as an introductory word.
Please put the books **there**.　　　**There** are three books on the table.

their — *Their* is a possessive pronoun. It shows something belongs to more than one person or thing.
Their tickets are in my pocket.

they're — *They're* is a contraction made from the words *they are*.
They're waiting for me inside.

two — *Two* is a number.　　　Apples and pears are **two** fruits I like.

to — *To* can be a preposition meaning "toward." *To* can also be used with a verb to form an infinitive.
I brought the pot **to** the stove. (*preposition*)　　I like **to** cook. (*infinitive*)

too — *Too* means "also."　　　I'd like some lunch, **too**.
Too can mean "more than enough."　　That's **too** much pepper!

your — *Your* is a possessive pronoun.
Where are **your** socks?

you're — *You're* is a contraction made from the words *you are*.
You're coming with us, aren't you?

whose — *Whose* is a possessive pronoun. It can refer to people or things.
Whose raincoat is this?　　　The raincoat **whose** buttons are blue is mine.

who's — *Who's* is a contraction made from the words *who* and *is* or *who* and *has*.
Who's at the front door?　　　**Who's** got the correct time?

than — *Than* is a subordinating conjunction used to make comparisons.
We waited for more **than** an hour.　　She is taller **than** you.

then — *Then* can be an adverb that tells about time. It can also mean "therefore."
Then I went home.
If you like mangoes, **then** you should try this mango ice cream.

principal — A *principal* is a person with authority.
The **principal** made the rule.

principle — A *principle* is a general rule or code of behavior.
He lived with a strong **principle** of honesty.

waist — The *waist* is the middle part of the body.
She wore a belt around her **waist**.

waste — To *waste* something is to use it in a careless way.
She would never **waste** something she could recycle.

aloud	*Aloud* means out loud or able to be heard.	He read the poem **aloud**.
allowed	*Allowed* is a form of the verb *allow*.	We were not **allowed** to swim after dark.

Writing a Letter

Section 34 Friendly Letters

A *friendly letter* is an informal letter written to a friend or a family member.

In a friendly letter, you might send a message, invite someone to a party, or thank someone for a gift. A friendly letter has five parts.

- The *heading* gives your address and the date.
- The *greeting* includes the name of the person you are writing to. It begins with a capital letter and ends with a comma.
- The *body* of the letter gives your message.
- The *closing* is a friendly or polite way to say good-bye. It ends with a comma.
- The *signature* is your name.

> 35 Rand Street
> Chicago, Illinois 60606
> July 15, 1998
>
> Dear Kim,
>
> Hi from the big city. I'm spending the summer learning to skateboard. My brother Raj is teaching me. He's a pro.
>
> I have one skateboard and hope to buy another one soon. If I can do that, we can practice together when you come to visit.
>
> Your friend,
> *Art*

Section 35 Business Letters

A *business letter* is a formal letter.

You would write a business letter to a company, an employer, a newspaper, or any person you do not know well. A business letter looks a lot like a friendly letter, but a business letter also includes the name and address of the business you are writing to. The *greeting* of a business letter begins with a capital letter and ends with a colon (:).

> 35 Rand Street
> Chicago, Illinois 60606
> July 15, 1998
>
> Swenson Skateboard Company
> 10026 Portage Road
> Lansing, Michigan 48091
>
> Dear Sir or Madam:
>
> Please send me your latest skateboard catalog. I am particularly interested in your newest models, the K-7 series.
> Thank you.
>
> Sincerely yours,
> *Arthur Quinn*
> Arthur Quinn

Section 36 Addressing Letters

The envelope below shows how to address a letter. A friendly letter and a business letter are addressed the same way.

> Arthur Quinn
> 35 Rand St.
> Chicago, IL 60606
>
>
>
> Kim Lee
> 1555 Montague Blvd.
> Memphis, TN 38106

Guidelines for Listening and Speaking

Section 37 Listening

These steps will help you be a good listener:

- **Listen carefully** when others are speaking.
- **Keep in mind your reason for listening.** Are you listening to learn about a topic? To be entertained? To get directions? Decide what you should get out of the listening experience.
- **Look directly at the speaker.** Doing this will help you concentrate on what he or she has to say.
- **Do not interrupt** the speaker or talk to others while the speaker is talking.
- **Ask questions** when the speaker is finished talking if there is anything you did not understand.

Section 38 Speaking

Being a good speaker takes practice. These guidelines can help you become an effective speaker:

Giving Oral Reports

- **Be prepared.** Know exactly what it is that you are going to talk about and how long you will speak. Have your notes in front of you.
- **Speak slowly** and **clearly.** Speak **loudly** enough so everyone can hear you.
- **Look** at your audience.

Taking Part in Discussions

- **Listen** to what others have to say.
- **Disagree politely.** Let others in the group know you respect their point of view.
- **Try not to interrupt** others. Everyone should have a chance to speak.

(you) | Diagram | sentences

Section 39 Diagraming Sentences

A sentence diagram is a map of a sentence. It shows how the parts of a sentence fit together and how the individual words in a sentence are related. Sentence diagrams can represent every part of speech and every type of sentence. The models below demonstrate how to create sentence diagrams, beginning with the simplest kinds of sentences.

- In a sentence consisting of a subject and an action verb, the subject and the verb are separated by a vertical line that bisects the horizontal line.

  Rain fell.   Rain | fell

- An adjective (or article) that modifies a noun or pronoun belongs on a slanted line below the word it modifies.

  A drenching rain fell.

  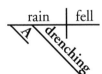

- An adverb that modifies a verb belongs on a slanted line below the verb it modifies.

  A drenching rain fell **steadily.**

- A direct object is placed on a horizontal line to the right of the verb. It is separated from the verb by a short vertical line that does not bisect the horizontal line.

  The downpour drenched the **land.**

  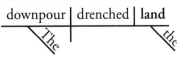

- An indirect object goes below the verb to show *who* or *what* receives something.

  It gave the **crops** a welcome soaking.

- Two separate horizontal lines show a compound predicate. The conjunction joins the verbs.

  Seedlings **uncurled** and **grew**.

- A compound subject is placed on two horizontal lines with a conjunction joining the subjects.

  Leaves and **flowers** glistened.

- A compound sentence is diagramed as two sentences with a conjunction joining them.

  The rain stopped and the sun appeared.

- A demonstrative pronoun takes the place of a noun. It belongs wherever the noun it replaces would go in the diagram.

  This prompted a collective cheer.

- A possessive pronoun belongs on a slanted line under the noun that is the possession.

  The children left **their** homes gleefully.

- An indefinite pronoun, a subject pronoun, or an object pronoun also belongs wherever the noun it replaces would go.

  Someone started a soccer game.

  I watched **it**.

- The understood *you* belongs where the subject of the sentence would go. It is written in parentheses.

  Remove your muddy shoes.

- A linking verb has the same position in a diagram that an action verb has, but the linking verb is separated from the predicate adjective or predicate noun by a diagonal line instead of by a vertical line.

  Your clothes **are** incredibly muddy.

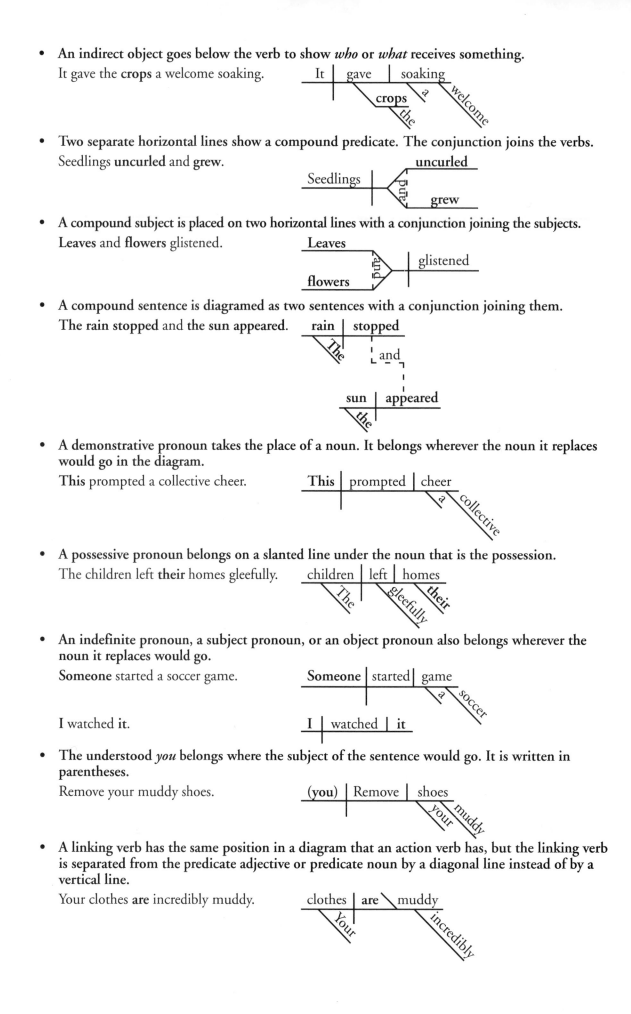

Soccer **is** a rough sport.

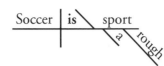

- **An adverbial prepositional phrase that modifies a verb is connected to that verb.**
  Leave your shoes **on the porch.**

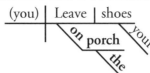

- **An adjectival prepositional phrase that modifies a noun is connected to that noun.**
  The mud **in the field** is quite deep.

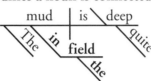

- **When *there* begins a sentence, it is placed on a separate line above the rest of the diagram.**
  There are fresh towels inside the house.

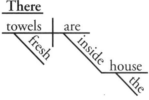

- **An adjective or an adverb is written on a slanted line and is connected to the word it modifies.**
  The **bright** green towel is mine.

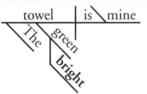

You must clean your shoes **very** carefully.

- **To diagram a sentence containing an adjective clause, first identify the independent clause and diagram it. Then place the dependent clause below the first diagram. Connect it to the first diagram with a slanted, dashed line that joins the clause to the noun it modifies. Write the subordinating conjunction on the dashed line.**
  The new shoes **that you bought** are very wet.

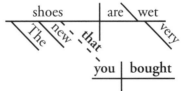

- **Diagram a sentence containing an adverb clause in a similar way, but connect the dependent clause to the independent clause with a slanted, dashed line connecting to the verb.**
  They looked nice **until you wore them in the mud.**

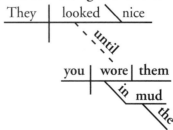

Topic Index

Language Index